“For most teachers of Scripture and pastors the probl
good resources for biblical study. Wi
issue is determining the best resourc
research this problem will be solved f

Sampey Professor of
Old Testament Interpretation
The Southern Baptist Theological Seminary

“It’s great to have a consensus commentary and reference survey that combines the judgments of many other surveys. I highly recommend it.”

—GEORGE W. KNIGHT III
Professor of New Testament
Greenville Presbyterian Theological Seminary

“In this excellent survey, Glynn has provided novice and expert alike with a very full listing of commentaries. He has solicited input from many qualified experts and on that basis has developed this extremely useful tool. All of us stand in his debt for having pulled together a listing of what surely represents the best of contemporary as well as classical scholarship.”

—EUGENE H. MERRILL
Distinguished Professor of Old Testament
Dallas Theological Seminary

“Preachers need books. Preachers need good books. Preachers need workable leads about which book to buy. Glynn has served the church well by producing this marvelous bibliographic reference. For students, preachers, and teachers, there is much here that can be found no place else in a similar form. This survey answers the question, Where will I get the best book for my bucks?”

—HADDON ROBINSON
Harold John Ockenga
Distinguished Professor of Preaching
Gordon-Conwell Theological Seminary

"Glynn's work is not just another listing of books, but a useful method by which the busy pastor can maintain currency on interpretative issues and methodology and theological students can begin to acquire a 'center of gravity' in sorting out all of the books and series available in different categories. His listings represent the most significant titles (both current and forthcoming) in biblical and theological scholarship. The author has a watchful eye on the publishing landscape, alerting his readers to the new features in an ever-changing terrain."

—DENNIS M. SWANSON
Seminary Librarian
The Master's Seminary

"My students approach me constantly with questions about library building and commentary recommendations. I am delighted to be able to direct them to Glynn's *Commentary and Reference Survey.* His assessment of student needs and quality of reference works are consistently on target. If you want to do Bible study, this is the help you need."

—JOHN WALTON
Professor of Old Testament and Hebrew
Wheaton Graduate School and College

Commentary & Reference Survey

Commentary & Reference Survey

A COMPREHENSIVE GUIDE TO BIBLICAL AND THEOLOGICAL RESOURCES

John Glynn

Foreword by Darrell L. Bock

Commentary and Reference Survey: A Comprehensive Guide to Biblical and Theological Resources

Ninth Edition

Published by Kregel Publications, a division of Kregel, Inc., P.O. Box 2607, Grand Rapids, MI 49501.

ISBN 0-8254-2736-3

Printed in the United States of America

03 04 05 06 07 / 5 4 3 2 1

Dedicated to the memory of my grandfather,
George S. Murray (1905–1997),
who filled all but the bookends of a century
and the better part of my life.

CONTENTS

FOREWORD

This survey is a genuine service to the student of the Bible. Often, I am asked what books are best for the serious study of Scripture, and many times I am forced to make the question more precise because of the varied elements that go into serious engagement of the Bible's message and background. Now I have a place to which I can send students that gives them both a clear array of choices and good guidance.

John Glynn started work on this survey as a labor of love years ago as a seminary student. He has run it by dozens of professors, and he has written publishers to stay current on what was coming next. It has gone through multiple editions and updates. It is as thorough a presentation of works on biblical studies as one could hope to find, a ready reference into the seeming maze of serious Bible study. But that maze, once understood, can be a source of rich reflection.

In Glynn's survey, he classifies works by theme and theological orientation. One can consider the various types of commentaries on any book or the themes that the book raises by consulting the "Special Studies" sections.

Like a map taking one on a great tour of a wonderful city, this survey orients the student about where to find the rich and varied discussion that is a part of biblical study. So pick up the map and begin the tour. In this book you have a faithful and helpful guide.

—Darrell L. Bock

ACKNOWLEDGMENTS

I would like to express my gratitude to Drs. Darrell Bock and Eugene Merrill of Dallas Theological Seminary for both the inspiration to seek after the best that scholarship had to offer and the significant time they spent going over the earliest drafts of my survey from 1993–1994. I can't begin to recount the number of times my faith has been reinforced by the knowledge that men of such meticulous learning believe in Jesus also.

I can't thank God enough for my editor, Jim Weaver, who not only saw past my lack of credentials and allowed this book to come to you in its present form but also offered countless suggestions that improved this work well beyond my own point of satisfaction. I have been truly blessed to have been the benefactor of a man who was so conversant with the literature and so able to dissect it.

I would also like specifically to thank Denver Seminary professor M. Daniel Carroll R.[1] for sending me a prerelease copy of his annotated bibliography on Amos and for the significant input provided by the Old Testament survey that he coauthored with Richard Hess (see bibliography for both).

Thanks also to the Hampton Keathleys III and IV of the Biblical Studies Foundation (www.bible.org) for carrying my survey in its prepublication list form for several years and to Haddon Robinson for mentioning my survey in his revision of *Biblical Preaching* and on Radio Bible Class.

1. R. stands for Rodas (the maiden name of his Guatemalan mother).

ABBREVIATIONS

Bible Versions

AMPLIFIED	*Amplified Bible*
ESV	*English Standard Version*
HCSB	*Holman Christian Standard Bible* (Broadman & Holman)
KJV	King James Version
NASB	New American Standard Bible (various publishers)
NIV	*New International Version* (Zondervan)
NLT	*New Living Translation* (Tyndale)
NRSV	*New Revised Standard Version* (various publishers)
RSV	Revised Standard Version
TNIV	*Today's New International Version* (Zondervan)

General Abbreviations

AB	Anchor Bible (Doubleday)
ABRL	Anchor Bible Reference Library
ABS	American Bible Society
ACCS	Ancient Christian Commentary on the Scripture (IVP)
AGNT	Timothy and Barbara Friberg. *Analytical Greek New Testament.* Baker, 1981.
ANE	Ancient Near East
ANTC	Abingdon New Testament Commentary
AOTC	Abingdon Old Testament Commentary
Apollos	Apollos Old Testament Commentary Series (IVP)

BAS	Biblical Archaeology Society
BBC	Blackwell Bible Commentary
BCBC	Believers Church Bible Commentary (Herald)
BDAG	Walter Bauer, Frederick Danker, William Arndt, and F. Wilbur Gingrich. *A Greek-English Lexicon of the New Testament and Other Early Christian Literature.* 3d ed. University of Chicago Press, 2000.
BDB	Brown, F., S. R. Driver, and C. A. Briggs. *A Hebrew and English Lexicon of the Old Testament.* Oxford, 1907.
BECNT	Baker Exegetical Commentary on the New Testament
BHL	*Biblia Hebraica Leningradensia*
BHS	*Biblia Hebraica Stuttgartensia*
BibSac	*Bibliotheca Sacra* (Dallas Theological Seminary)
BNTC	Black's New Testament Commentaries (formerly Harper's New Testament Commentaries [HNTC]) (Black/Harper/Hendrickson/Continuum)
BSC	Bible Study Commentary (Zondervan)
BST	The Bible Speaks Today (IVP)
CAH	Cambridge Ancient History
CBC	Cambridge Bible Commentary
CBD	Christian Book Distributors
CCNT	Crossroad Companions to the New Testament
DBC	Doubleday Bible Commentary
DJG	*Dictionary of Jesus and the Gospels* (IVP)
DLNTD	*Dictionary of the Latter New Testament and Its Developments* (IVP)
DNTB	*Dictionary of New Testament Background* (IVP)
DPL	*Dictionary of Paul and His Letters* (IVP)
DSB	Daily Study Bible (Westminster John Knox)
DSS	Dead Sea Scrolls
EBC	Expositor's Bible Commentary (Zondervan)
ECC	Eerdmans Critical Commentary
EDB	*Eerdmans Dictionary of the Bible*
EGGNT	Exegetical Guides to the Greek New Testament (Eerdmans)

Epworth	Epworth Commentary Series
EvBC	Everyman's Bible Commentary (Moody)
FOTL	The Forms of the Old Testament Literature (Eerdmans)
GAP	Guides to the Apocrypha and Pseudepigrapha (Sheffield)
GBS	German Bible Society
G/K	Goodrick/Kohlenberger
GNT	Greek New Testament
GTJ	*Grace Theological Journal*
HALOT	L. Koehler and W. Baumgartner. *A Hebrew-Aramaic Lexicon of the Old Testament.* 3d ed. Brill, 1994–2002.
HCOT	Historical Commentary on the Old Testament (Peeters)
Hermeneia	Hermeneia: A Critical and Historical Commentary (Fortress)
IBC	Interpretation: A Bible Commentary for Teaching and Preaching (Westminster John Knox)
IBR	Institute for Biblical Research (Baker)
IBT	Interpreting Biblical Texts (Abingdon)
ICC	International Critical Commentary (T & T Clark)
IES	Israel Exploration Society
ISBE	*International Standard Bible Encyclopedia.* Edited by G. W. Bromiley. 4 vols. Eerdmans, 1979–1988.
ITC	International Theological Commentary (Eerdmans/Handsel)
IVP	InterVarsity Press
IVPNTC	IVP New Testament Commentary
JEDP	Documentary hypothesis sources
JETS	*Journal of the Evangelical Theological Society*
JPS	Jewish Publication Society
JPSTC	Jewish Publication Society Torah Commentary
JSNT	Journal for the Study of the New Testament
LEC	Library of Early Christianity (Westminster John Knox)

LXX	Septuagint; Greek translation of the Old Testament
Mentor	Mentor Old Testament Commentary (Christian Focus)
MT	Masoretic Text
NA^{26}	*Nestle-Aland Novum Testamentum Graece.* 26th ed. GBS, 1979.
NA^{27}	*Nestle-Aland Novum Testamentum Graece.* 27th ed. GBS, 1993.
NAC	New American Commentary (Broadman & Holman)
NBC	*New Bible Commentary* (IVP)
NBD	*New Bible Dictionary* (IVP)
NCBC	New Century Bible Commentary (Eerdmans/Sheffield)
NCC	The New Communicator's Commentary (Word/Thomas Nelson)
NIB	The New Interpreter's Bible (Abingdon)
NIBCNT	New International Bible Commentary on the New Testament (Hendrickson)
NIBCOT	New International Bible Commentary on the Old Testament (Hendrickson)
NICNT	New International Commentary on the New Testament (Eerdmans)
NICOT	New International Commentary on the Old Testament (Eerdmans)
NIDNTT	*New International Dictionary of New Testament Theology* (Zondervan)
NIDOTTE	*New International Dictionary of Old Testament Theology and Exegesis* (Zondervan)
NIGTC	New International Greek Testament Commentary (Eerdmans)
NIVAC	The NIV Application Commentary (Zondervan)
NIVTDNTW	*NIV Theological Dictionary of New Testament Words* (Zondervan)
NT	New Testament

NTC	New Testament in Context Commentaries (Trinity)
NTG	New Testament Guides (Cornell/Sheffield Academic Press)
NTL	New Testament Library (Westminster John Knox)
NTT	New Testament Theology (Cambridge University Press)
OT	Old Testament
OTG	Old Testament Guides (Cornell/Sheffield Academic Press)
OTL	Old Testament Library (Westminster John Knox)
PCA	Presbyterian Church in America
Pillar	The Pillar New Testament Commentary (Eerdmans)
Q	Siglum for the Synoptic sayings-source
SBL	Society of Biblical Literature
SIL	Summer Institute of Linguistics
TBT	*The Bible Translator*
TDNT	*Theological Dictionary of the New Testament* (Eerdmans)
TJ	*Trinity Journal*
TMSTJ	*The Master's Seminary Theological Journal*
TNTC	Tyndale New Testament Commentaries (Eerdmans)
TOTC	Tyndale Old Testament Commentaries (IVP)
TWOT	*Theological Wordbook of the Old Testament*
UBS	United Bible Societies
UBS^4	B. Aland, et al., eds. *The Greek New Testament.* 4th ed. UBS, 1993.
WBC	Word Biblical Commentary (Thomas Nelson)
WBComp	Westminster Bible Companion
WEC	Wycliffe Exegetical Commentary (Moody)
WTJ	*Westminster Theological Journal*
ZIBBC	*Zondervan Illustrated Bible Backgrounds Commentary*

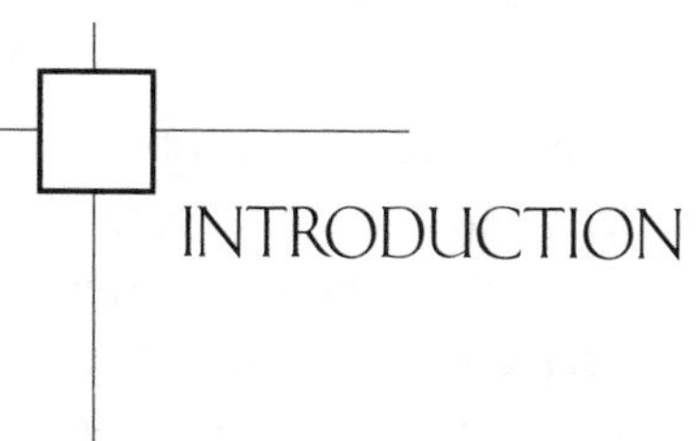

INTRODUCTION

In the late springtime of 1992, while I was fishing through the "missionary" basket where departing Moody Bible Institute students left behind items they didn't care to take home for summer, I discovered a copy of Douglas Moo's edited *Annotated Bibliography of the Bible and the Church.*[1] Having just begun to build a personal reference library in preparation for attending Dallas Theological Seminary, I was immediately interested, especially because it contained sections on the best available commentaries at that time.

When I arrived at Dallas Theological Seminary, I found that the school bookstore had surveys that had been compiled by the Old Testament and the New Testament departments. Comparing Moo's book and the surveys, I began to get a better idea of which commentaries I should purchase—and purchase I did. Over the next several years, I continued to acquire other surveys and sources, periodically refining my list and adding additional categories to cover other examples of extrabiblical literature.

Now, after ten years of analyzing and reviewing books, I can safely say that I have received an additional theological education. However, one maxim I have continued to observe is that I should maintain only a library that will continue to be useful, even if only a few pages of a certain book clarifies an answer that I am seeking.

What are the salient features of this survey? About 40 percent of the total books mentioned in this survey are commentaries, which

1. Douglas Moo, *Annotated Bibliography of the Bible and the Church,* 2d ed. (Alumni Publications, 1986).

comprise the largest single category. Given the high cost of most commentaries, it is imperative that readers derive from each volume as much value as possible. Therefore, commentaries mentioned herein are noted in each biblical book in two categories: Technical and Semitechnical for the student trained in the original languages, and Exposition for the informed layman or pastor who has more general biblical training. Technical, or exegetical, commentaries concentrate principally on the interpretation of the original languages *in the main text,* whereas semitechnical commentaries generally relegate grammatical, textual, and historical problems to footnotes. Because the main text of semitechnical works are primarily expositional, they can also be used by the informed layman.

Commentaries geared toward application are subsumed under the exposition rubric. These include titles from Zondervan's NIV Application Commentary (NIVAC), InterVarsity's Bible Speaks Today (BST), IVP New Testament Commentary (IVPNTC), the Interpretation series from Westminster John Knox (IBC), and the New Communicator's Commentary (NCC), previously published by Word and now by Thomas Nelson.

Furthermore, given the wide range of theological perspectives in most categories, each entry is further delineated by the following codes:

- E = Evangelical
- E/Cr = Evangelical/Critical
- C/M = Conservative/Moderate
- L/Cr = Liberal/Critical

What this means is that commentaries on a specific biblical book may run the gamut from evangelicals who affirm "the idea that Scripture in the original manuscripts does not affirm anything that is contrary to fact"[2] to Liberal/Critical scholars who believe that the Bible contains clear errors and may or may not affirm what it says about itself and God. Between these two perspectives exist varying degrees of inerrancy where the Bible could be in error concerning some mi-

2. Wayne Grudem, *Bible Doctrine* (Zondervan, 1999), 487.

nor historical facts (Evangelical/Critical), or that it only affirms what is normative in faith and practice rather than in historical or scientific detail (Conservative/Moderate).[3] The titles are listed alphabetically, and boldfaced entries represent titles that I highly recommend and consider the "best of the best." The full names of series mentioned can be found under "Abbreviations."

That said, a paradigm of the previously mentioned criteria follows.

Matthew

Technical, Semitechnical

L/Cr	1.	Boring, Eugene. NIB, vol. 8 (Abingdon, 1995).
E	**2.**	**Carson, D. A. EBC, vol. 8 (Zondervan, 1984).**
C/M	**3.**	**Davies, W. D., and Dale Allison. ICC, 3 vols. (T & T Clark, 1988–97).**
E/Cr	4.	Gundry, Robert. *Matthew,* 2d ed. (Eerdmans, 1994).
E/Cr	**5.**	**Hagner, Donald. WBC, 2 vols. (Word, 1993–94).**
L/Cr	6.	Harrington, Daniel. *Sacra Pagina* (Liturgical, 1991).
L/Cr	7.	Hill, David. NCBC (Eerdmans, 1981).

3. The gospel of Matthew is an example of how these criteria can be applied. For example, although no explicit references to Matthew as the author of the gospel exist, Craig Keener accepts on the basis of the earliest patristic materials that the author is indeed Matthew. His approach is evangelical. Donald Hagner, WBC, 2 vols. (Word/Nelson, 1993–94), on the other hand, takes this lack of surety one step further by positing that, in spite of the possibility that Matthew was largely responsible for the gospel's material, it was probably finished by a fellow Jewish Christian. Although this possible conclusion does not bear directly on the issue of inerrancy, "Gospel According to Matthew and One of His Followers" does call into question the absolute veracity of the text and is, thus, Evangelical/Critical. As for W. D. Davies and Dale Allison's massive work, *A Critical and Exegetical Commentary on the Gospel According to St. Matthew,* ICC, 3vols. (T & T Clark, 1988–97), historical issues are addressed ad hoc, ad infinitum. Thus, we can accept on face value what Matthew affirms about faith and God, but the historical events must be evaluated independently. This earns them the Conservative/Moderate moniker. Finally, Ulrich Luz's first two volumes of a projected three-volume project in the Hermeneia series (Fortress, 2001–) is so thoroughly form and redaction-critical that virtually any assertion by any so-called author is to be regarded with a thorough-going skepticism. In this approach, Luz even goes so far as to suggest that Matthew was written in the mid-second century. Thus, he is classified as Liberal/Critical.

E 8. Keener, Craig (Eerdmans, 1999).
L/Cr 9. Luz, Ulrich. *Hermeneia,* 3 vols. (Fortress, 1998–).

Expositional (Partial list)

E 1. Blomberg, Craig. NAC (Broadman & Holman, 1993).
E/Cr 2. France, Richard. TOTC (Eerdmans, 1988).
E 3. Green, Michael. BST (IVP, 2001).
E 4. Keener, Craig. IVPNTC (IVP, 1997).
E 5. Morris, Leon. Pillar (Eerdmans, 1992).

A Special Studies section, which includes particularly useful monographs, augments each book list of commentaries. Asterisked footnotes throughout the survey generally indicate forthcoming titles to appear and provide a capsule summary of the present and future possibilities of what might actually constitute an ideal library. Numbered footnotes, however, offer more detail on a particular book or subject.

The rest of the survey covers resources for other biblical and theological disciplines, including Biblical Hebrew, New Testament Greek, Systematic Theology, and Church History. Here, too, outstanding entries are listed in bold. In addition, a list of computer resources and Internet sites are offered.

Finally, I have included a few special features to elucidate further specific recommendations. "On Commentary Series" provides the big picture of the individual titles alluded to in each biblical book. Please read "Building a 'Must-Have' Personal Reference Library." When approaching the daunting task of assembling a library (which might cost the equivalent of a good second-hand car), it is advisable to develop a consumer strategy. This might not be a consumer report, but it might help steer you clear of unnecessary frills.

Also for your benefit, "The Ultimate Commentary Collection" charts the best exegetical and expositional commentaries for each book. Here, I have done my best to list the primary exegetical choice first followed by the best expositional commentary.

For sake of brevity, all subtitles are omitted unless they are absolutely necessary to explain a book's contents. Since this volume is primarily a buyer's guide, I have omitted the name of the city of the publisher. Often, I will simply add a short note for explanation.

Appraisal

First, although I have not read all of the approximately 1,600 books listed in this survey, I rely principally on the consensus of other published bibliographies and surveys. Second, each quarter I photocopy reviews from twenty-five theological journals (British journals also inform me of books of which I might be otherwise unaware).[4] Third, I receive review copies from more than a dozen publishers.

When I receive a new book, I first check the endorsements. An author's reputation has already raised the level of anticipation attending the release of a new book. The reputation of the author's endorsers adds further weight to how well professors, pastors, and other interested professionals might receive it. Generally, subsequent reviews of new books appearing in journals follow the suit of endorsements (if the reviewer is of the same persuasion as the endorser and the author).

Next, I'll turn to the table of contents and select sample sections to peruse. From these, I am able to discern the general thrust of the authors' approach and how they have handled a particular interpretative issue. Bibliographies and indices are also of great interest to me. I often refer to the author index to note which commentators the author cites most often. If the richness of citation matches an informed and current bibliography, things are looking good.

Finally, I scan each book's bibliography religiously to spot titles that are being mentioned continually by different authors. Thus, this survey attempts to represent the best books available in each category.

---

4. Periodicals worth considering are the *Ashland Theological Journal, Bibliotheca Sacra, Catholic Biblical Quarterly, Churchman, Denver Journal* (online at denver-journal.densem.edu), *Expository Times, Interpretation, Journal of Biblical Literature, Journal of the Evangelical Theological Society, Religious Studies Review, Review and Expositor, Themelios, Trinity Journal, and the Westminster Theological Journal.*

A Word on Exegetical Forecasting

Though recommending forthcoming commentaries may seem a bit presumptuous, my rationale is as follows. Of the more than seventy new evangelical titles slated to appear in the next few years (delays, however, are inevitable), more than half are from scholars who have already written one or more studies. For instance, D. A. Carson has written two semitechnical commentaries (Matthew and John) as well as several other books. He is scheduled to write two technical commentaries (Hebrews and 1–3 John), and two semitechnical works (Galatians and Revelation), which will ultimately place him in the exalted company of F. F. Bruce, C. K. Barrett, and I. Howard Marshall as a premier commentator on the New Testament. Peter O'Brien finds himself in such company with his recent, outstanding semitechnical effort on Ephesians, technical commentaries on Philippians and Colossians/Philemon, and a forthcoming commentary on Hebrews (Pillar). I think it fair to say that we can expect more of the same from these men (although, admittedly, this is not always the case). But bear in mind that it is possible for a commentary to be reassigned or delayed significantly.

In many instances, you will discover that a particular book, such as Genesis or Romans, is already well served. A small percentage (5 percent to 10 percent) of the books in this survey may also be currently out of print, but some publishers such as Good Books and Wipf & Stock specialize in reprinting discontinued titles. Occasionally, the original publisher will reprint one of their backlisted titles. I think it important to mention these inasmuch as they can often be obtained secondhand (see Internet Web Sites: Used Books) or can be found in theological libraries for purposes of study.

You might want to consult the used booksellers if you would like to sell some of your library to finance newer acquisitions. The best of new commentaries, of course, will still take into account the old masters, but they will especially focus on commentators of the last twenty-five years.

These are the methods by which I keep this survey current, in both reassessing aging titles and assessing the new titles that have emerged. The purpose of my survey is to evaluate the length and breadth of current scholarship; it is not intended as a history of interpretation.

In an effort to keep this survey as current and useful as possible, please send any suggestions or criticisms to me at the following address or telephone number.

JOHN GLYNN
81 Perry Avenue
Stoughton, MA 02072
781-341-4515

1

BUILDING A "MUST-HAVE" PERSONAL REFERENCE LIBRARY

How do you build a basic working reference library? Which books do you absolutely require when you find yourself in the perplexing position in which you can find no satisfactory solution to an apparent exegetical conundrum?

While perusing the libraries of various pastors, I have observed that ministers often either do not possess the essential tools necessary for quality inductive Bible study or simply could make better choices. Many such mini-libraries are cluttered with titles destined to gather dust or disseminate inferior information. Paradoxically, I have also witnessed fully equipped libraries accumulated by those who never end up in full-time ministry.

Thus, in attempting to determine a list of titles for an ideal "must-have" personal reference library, one must discern between the "must-have" volumes and the "dare-not" titles for the benefit of the occasional pathological bibliophile (such as myself) who lies in perpetual danger of sacrificing his final semester's tuition (if a pending Bible college or seminary graduate) in the pursuit of the "ideal" reference set. With this concern in view, I have tried to construct a recommendation geared for the layman, the student, and the pastor of a church, each of whom lacks a nearby Bible college or seminary library on which to fall back. First, every Christian should purchase a core group of resources for the benefit of his or her own study.

For Laymen

To learn how to conduct an inductive Bible study, I would recommend that the informed layman begin by reading Duvall and Hays.[1] For more advanced students, a more excellent guide is Klein, Blomberg, and Hubbard.[2] Then, having learned how to conduct an inductive Bible study, both layman and student must acquire the minimum number of basic tools. The start-up cost of the following titles is approximately **$350 retail.**

1. Barker, Kenneth, ed. *Zondervan NIV Study Bible, 10th Anniversary Edition* (Zondervan, 2002). Thought for thought.[3]
2. Brisco, Thomas. *Holman Bible Atlas* (Broadman & Holman, 1999).
3. Elwell, Walter, ed. *Baker Encyclopedia of the Bible,* 4 vols. (Baker, 1992).[4]
4. Erickson, Millard. *Christian Theology,* 2d ed. (Baker, 1998); **or** Grudem, Wayne. *Systematic Theology* (Zondervan, 1994).
5. Goodrick, Edward, and John Kohlenberger. *Zondervan NIV Exhaustive Concordance* (Zondervan, 1981). Lists every occurrence of word.
6. Marshall, I. Howard, et al., eds. *New Bible Dictionary,* 3d ed. (IVP, 1996).
7. *New Living Translation* (Tyndale, 1996). Provides general nuance; dynamic equivalence (thought for thought).
8. *English Standard Version* (Crossway, 2001). The ESV, an

1. Scott Duvall and Daniel Hays, *Grasping God's Word* (Zondervan, 2001); and idem, *Grasping God's Word Workbook* (Zondervan, 2001).
2. William Klein, Craig Blomberg, and Robert Hubbard, *Introduction to Biblical Interpretation* (Word, 1993).
3. More than 80 percent of 20,000 footnotes have been revised, rewritten, or replaced, and introductions and other features have been significantly expanded. The *Zondervan KJV Study Bible* (2002) has undergone a similar refurbishment, while the *Today's NIV Bible* (Zondervan), a 7 percent correction of the NIV dealing mostly with semantic and gender issues, awaits completion.
4. Advanced students purchase *ISBE* instead.

outstanding translation, is like a cross between the NASB and the RSV.[5]

9. Wenham, Gordon, et al., eds. New Bible Commentary: Twenty-First Century Edition (IVP, 1994).

For Bible College and Seminary Students

Assuming that the previously mentioned titles have been secured, the next order of business for the prospective ministry student is to begin assembling language resources that will facilitate study while he or she is in school. For first-year Greek students, whether in Bible college or seminary, at least a basic grammar, a workbook, and a copy of the Greek New Testament will be required texts.[6] Once you have ascertained which school you will be attending, you might want to "get a leg up" by calling the school bookstore to determine if a standard text is used in all beginning Greek courses.

Many professors will also require the purchase of the *BDAG* lexicon (see the following list), if not a Greek-English concordance and an exhaustive concordance to the Greek New Testament (which lists every occurrence of a Greek word). In any case, all of these tools will continue to be of value in future ministry and can be obtained for around **$200.**

The titles that I suggest for a basic Greek reference set are as follows:

1. Bauer, Walter, Frederick Danker, William Arndt, and F. Wilbur Gingrich. *A Greek-English Lexicon of the New Testament,* 3d ed. (University of Chicago, 2000).
2. Guthrie, George, and Scott Duvall. *Biblical Greek Exegesis*

5. *The Holman Christian Standard Bible* (HCSB) by Broadman & Holman Publishers strives for the middle ground between the NASB and the NIV at an eighth-grade level.
6. Either E. Nestle, and Kurt Aland, eds., *Novum Testamentum Graece,* 27th ed. (GBS, 1993), which gives the most comprehensive listings of variant readings, or Barbara Aland, et al., eds., *The Greek New Testament,* 4th ed. (UBS, 1993), which is the same text with a concise dictionary and a shorter evaluation of variants.

(Zondervan, 1998). Intermediate, advanced; selected readings, grammatical and semantic diagramming, how-to-do exegeticals; companion to Daniel Wallace's *Greek Grammar Beyond the Basics* (Zondervan, 1996).

3. Kohlenberger, John, Edward Goodrick, and James Swanson. *The Exhaustive Concordance to the Greek New Testament* (Zondervan, 1995). UBS[4] text.
4. Kohlenberger, John, Edward Goodrick, and James Swanson. *The Greek-English Concordance to the New Testament* (Zondervan, 1997). NIV text; G/K numbering system.
5. Mounce, William. *Basics of Biblical Greek* (Zondervan, 1993). Includes interactive study aid CD.[7]
   ———. *Basics of Biblical Greek: Workbook* (Zondervan, 1994).

Then you will need to acquire a basic set of language helps to fertilize your growing knowledge of the New Testament in its original tongue. Elementary helps include an analytical lexicon to the GNT, which indicates every form of a Greek word found in the New Testament and provides its lexical root and basic definition.[8]

An interlinear Greek-English New Testament also proves to be of inestimable help in a pinch, especially when double-checking your own translation and comparing the various ways Greek words have been translated in English versions.[9] A sister-companion to an interlinear translation is Timothy and Barbara Friberg, *Analytical Greek New Testament,* which parses the GNT word by word and has placated many of the frantic nights when paradigm memorization failed me.[10] Nevertheless, learning New Testament Greek is nothing of which

7. Mounce is presently being condensed.
8. Either William Mounce, *The Analytical Lexicon to the GNT* (Zondervan, 1992), which features the G/K numbering system, or the Friberg, Friberg, and Miller, *Analytical Lexicon of the GNT* (Baker, 1999), which is based on the NA[27] and UBS[4] texts.
9. Options include J. D. Douglas, ed., *The New Interlinear Greek-English New Testament* (Tyndale, 1990), which is based on the NA[26], the UBS[4] corrected, and the NRSV texts.
10. Timothy and Barbara Friberg, *Analytical Greek New Testament* (Baker, 1981).

to be afraid (which, for that matter, is also true of Hebrew). By exercising diligence, one can master both of the sacred languages, eventually rendering some helps anachronistic.

Two other Greek helps will produce dividends later in one's pastorate, yet they will be most beneficial during second and third year Greek while the student is preparing the daunting exegetical paper. These resources are an intermediate Greek grammar, to explain the interrelationship of Greek words in phrases and sentences (syntax),[11] and the word-study reference edited by Colin Brown, *The New International Dictionary of New Testament Theology*.[12]

A student can borrow reference titles from other students or photocopy relevant passages in the school library. However, the same tools that *assist* in learning while one is in training are the same tools that enable the minister to *persist* in learning when the graduate moves on.

Some of the tools you can sell second-hand (e.g., first-year grammars, AGNT, and analytical lexicons) before departing school. Thus, the "must-have" cost of a library for a Bible college or seminary graduate (with Greek training) is to date approximately **$1,200.**

The same basic components will ensure future proficiency for Hebrew study: a *BHS* Hebrew Bible,[13] a basic grammar and workbook, a lexicon, a Hebrew-English concordance, and an exhaustive concordance. Depending on the specific requirements of your school's language department, I recommend the following:

11. Daniel Wallace, *Greek Grammar Beyond the Basics* (Zondervan, 1996). For pastors, a helpful supplement to Wallace with some variegation of syntactical categories is Richard Young, *Intermediate New Testament Greek* (Broadman & Holman, 1994).
12. Colin Brown, ed., *The New International Dictionary of New Testament Theology,* 4 vols. (Zondervan, 1975–1978).
13. K. Elliger and W. Rudolph, eds., *Biblia Hebraica Stuttgartensia,* 5th ed. (GBS, 1997). The *Biblia Hebraica Quinta* is currently in preparation and ultimately will be superior to *BHS.*

1. *Brown-Driver-Briggs Hebrew and English Lexicon* (Hendrickson, 1996). Strong's coded.[14]
2. Even-Shoshan, Abraham *A New Concordance of the Old Testament,* 2d ed. (Baker, 1989).
3. Kohlenberger, John, and James Swanson, eds. *The Hebrew-English Concordance to the Old Testament* (Zondervan, 1999).
4. Pratico, Gary, and Brad Van Pelt. *Basics of Biblical Hebrew* (Zondervan, 2001).[15]
   ———. *Basics of Biblical Hebrew: Workbook* (Zondervan, 2001).

For Hebrew, the suggested counterparts are as follows:

1. Kohlenberger, John, ed. *The NIV Hebrew-English Interlinear Old Testament* (Zondervan, 1987).
2. Owens, John. *Analytical Key to the Old Testament,* 4 vols. (Baker, 1989–92).
3. VanGemeren, Willem, ed. *The New International Dictionary of Old Testament Theology and Exegesis,* 5 vols. (Zondervan, 1997). G/K numbering system.
4. Waltke, Bruce, and Michael O'Connor. *An Introduction to Biblical Hebrew Syntax* (Eisenbrauns, 1990).

Worth mentioning are features contained in both Owens and the NIDOTTE. Owens actually does double duty as a Hebrew-English Old Testament (RSV) and a parsing guide. Passage by passage, it parses *every* Hebrew word in the Old Testament, identifies the page number

---

14. Although *BDB* is often a requirement in many seminaries, many pastors find William Holladay, *A Concise Hebrew and Aramaic Lexicon of the Old Testament* (Eerdmans, 1971), to be far more practical as a quick reference to Hebrew words, and it's still in print for the same price. If you have the *NIDOTTE,* however, you don't really need either of them.
15. Other options include Allen Ross, *Introducing Biblical Hebrew* (Baker, 2000); and Duane Garrett, *A Modern Grammar for Classical Hebrew* (Broadman & Holman, 2002). For second-year Hebrew and rusty pastors, *From Exegesis to Exposition* (Baker, 1999) by Robert Chisholm is useful for exegetical papers and sermon preparation.

where it appears in *BDB*, supplies the root for verb forms, and lists the frequency of occurrences of each word. This feature makes it a valuable tool for exegetical papers. The *NIDOTTE* does much the same as its New Testament counterpart (providing the ancient Near Eastern, OT, LXX, Qumran, Rabbinic, and NT background to each Hebrew word). But it does one better by including a volume on topical entries (such as biblical concepts, places, persons, and events) and an index of semantic fields. Its contributors are evangelical.

The cost to date for the Hebrew-Greek graduate, which includes the basic reference set ($575.00), Greek grammars and language helps ($575.00), and the Hebrew grammars and language helps ($850.00), is **$2,000.**

For Pastors

Students in seminary and Bible college should plan to acquire a working set of commentaries while they are still in school. By scanning for book sales on bulletin boards, trolling the used-book room at the school bookstore, and taking advantage of the occasional publisher discounts, significant savings can be realized.

But why, you might ask, should I burden myself with so many books that I will rarely read from cover to cover? First, commentaries equip the pastor with a ready answer to any biblical question. One never knows when an inquiry concerning Obadiah or Jude could come your way. Otherwise, you could end up ruing the day for lack of references.[16]

Second, commentaries can furnish comprehensive coverage against shaky sermons, if, in a weak moment, the pastor's usual caution gives way to a homiletic flight of fancy. Commentaries suggest not only a range of possible solutions to problem passages but also a wealth of theological, literary, and cultural background material to ensure that the general tenor of a pulpit message remains sound.

16. I am not suggesting that a pastor replace an already existing working library. First, as a general rule, libraries need to become fully equipped (expanded). Then, older commentaries and references can be updated as needed. Computer options enable the user both to update language and reference helps and to save enormous time in sermon preparation.

The kind of commentaries one buys must be reflective of the training that one has received. For the seminary-trained professional, a mix-and-match, hodge-podge approach to commentary collecting is still the best route to follow because many complete testament or Bible series are uneven in quality and might cover a wider theological spectrum than that with which you are comfortable.

A pastor should have two technical (or one technical and one semitechnical) commentaries on each book of the Bible and an exposition commentary to provide a general overview of each book (with an eye toward application) if the budget allows. The pastor can assume that approximately two-thirds of his "must-have" library will consist of commentaries and commentary sets. Thus, the cost for a library of 100–120 commentaries alone can be expected to approach **$3,200.**

I recommend both the technical Word Biblical Commentary series (WBC) and the semitechnical New International Commentary series on both testaments published by Eerdmans (NICOT, NICNT). It would be better to substitute deficient titles in either series with available titles from Eerdmans's New International Greek Testament Commentary (NIGTC), the Eerdmans Critical Commentary (ECC), Broadman & Holman's whole-Bible New American Commentary (NAC), the newly emerging Apollos Old Testament Commentary (IVP), and the Baker Exegetical Commentary on the New Testament (BECNT) series.

For Bible college or M.A. students with two to three years of Greek background, the best combination is WBC (Word/Thomas Nelson) and NIGTC (Eerdmans) series in the New Testament. For those with less Greek background, NICNT (Eerdmans), Pillar New Testament Commentary (Eerdmans), and BECNT (Baker) are to be preferred. In the Old Testament, a combination of the NICOT (Eerdmans), the NAC (Broadman & Holman), Hendrickson's The New International Biblical Commentary on the Old Testament (NIBCOT), the Apollos Old Testament Commentary (IVP), and another IVP series, the Tyndale Old Testament Commentary (TOTC), would be your best choices. Depending on the number of paperbacks purchased (TOTC and NIBCOT), the overall commentary costs for Greek-only ministers comes to approximately **$2,500–$3,000.**

Finally, for the pastor or layman without training in the original languages, several very worthwhile preaching, application, and expositional commentary series are available.[17] Of these, the best combination for the New Testament is The NIV Application Commentary (NIVAC) by Zondervan, the Pillar series by Eerdmans, and a collection of four other series.[18] The Old Testament is best covered by the NIVAC, the TOTC (IVP), and The Bible Speaks Today series (BST), also by IVP. The estimated price for a solid expositional library is approximately **$1,300.**

Now that I have gone to the wire (and the limits of your expense account) in championing the fat commentary bookcase, I am compelled by the ghosts of Hebrew and Greek professors to extend a caveat. Commentaries are not intended to take the place of your own intensive Bible study (and use of language helps and references where applicable) as illustrated in hermeneutics texts. They are meant to be an *aid* to study, such as gaining a perspective on background, or analyzing phrases with cultural, historical, or theological nuance, or as a last line of defense in double-checking the integrity of your own conclusions.

Owning and soaking in your own message is vital to your own growth and that of your congregation. The last thing you need is a videotaped sermon rented from a commentary (at the expense of the Holy Spirit). Having said all that, and having spent this much money, following are thirteen more titles that you should obtain.

---

17. Expositional as opposed to technical, exegetically based commentaries often succeed better at providing the general theological and applicational thrust of a given passage or biblical book. Therefore, they can be equally valuable to the seminary-trained pastor. Indeed, some series such as the NIVAC (Zondervan), Interpretation (Westminster John Knox), the IVP New Testament Commentary (IVPNTC), and The New Communicator's Commentary by Thomas Nelson are designed specifically for preachers. Also, the New Interpreter's Bible commentary series (Abingdon) follows each block of commentary with a very helpful "Reflections" section.
18. The Tyndale New Testament Commentary (TNTC) from Eerdmans, Black's New Testament Commentary (BNTC) from Hendrickson Publishers, the NAC (Broadman & Holman), and the IVPNTC series (IVP).

1. Alexander, Desmond, et al., eds. *New Dictionary of Biblical Theology* (IVP, 2000). Three parts: introductory articles, individual book theologies, 215 (A–Z) topics.
2. Dillard, Raymond, and Tremper Longman. *Introduction to the Old Testament* (Zondervan, 1995).[19]
3. Elwell, Walter, ed. *Baker Theological Dictionary of the Bible* (Baker, 1994, 2001). Formerly *Evangelical Dictionary of Biblical Theology,* **or** Elwell, Walter, ed. *Evangelical Dictionary of Theology,* 2d ed. (Baker, 2001).
4. Kaiser, Walter. *A History of Israel* (Broadman & Holman, 1998).
5. Keener, Craig. *The IVP Bible Background Commentary: New Testament* (IVP, 1993).[20]
6. Porter, Stanley, and Lee McDonald. *Early Christianity and Its Sacred Literature* (Hendrickson, 2000). Moderate.
7. Walton, John, Victor Matthews, and Mark Chavalas. *The IVP Bible Background Commentary: Old Testament* (IVP, 2000).

The first of four volumes is slated for the Old Testament, and the four-volume set is for key background and theological information on the New Testament.[21]

---

19. For courses requiring more survey than introductory material, choose Andrew Hill and John Walton, *A Survey of the Old Testament,* 2d ed. (Zondervan, 2000); or Colin Smith, *Unfolding the Bible Story,* 4 vols. (Moody, 2002), whose two Old Testament volumes are ideal for two-semester surveys.
20. For a comprehensive, single-volume treatment of the cultural, political, and religious environment during New Testament times, another alternative is Everett Ferguson, *Background of Early Christianity,* 2d ed. (Eerdmans, 1993).
21. Of the four NT volumes, the *DLNTD* and the *DNTB* are particularly outstanding, although some people have difficulty with the moderate tone of many articles. All told, even as an encyclopedia segmented into biblical sections (e.g., the *DPL* deals strictly with Pauline material while limiting its interaction with material germane to the *DJG*), it will ultimately surpass *ISBE* as the standard primary reference. Sometimes this approach leads to redundancy, but do you really mind having four different articles on the Holy Spirit by four different authors with contrasting perspectives? Correspondingly, the article by J. Albert Harrill on slavery in the *DNTB* updates the article by A. A. Rupprecht in the

1. Baker, David, and Desmond Alexander, eds. *Dictionary of the Old Testament: The Pentateuch* (IVP, 2002).
2. Davids, Peter, and Ralph Martin, eds. *Dictionary of the Later New Testament and Its Developments* (IVP, 1997).
3. Evans, Craig, and Stanley Porter, eds. *Dictionary of New Testament Backgrounds* (IVP, 2000). Highly academic (i.e., Qumran documents, apocryphal writings, etc.).
4. Green, Joel, Scot McKnight, and Howard Marshall, eds. *Dictionary of Jesus and the Gospels* (IVP, 1992).
5. Hawthorne, Gerald, Ralph Martin, and Daniel Reid, eds. *Dictionary of Paul and His Letters* (IVP, 1993).

Exegetical and Bible Study Computer Programs

Purchasing a combination exegetical and Bible study computer program supplies many of the references recommended earlier at a significantly reduced cost with the bonus of several additional titles. For those who prefer to trip the references *fantastique* in CD-ROM, two Windows-compatible options excel. For a superior, purely exegetical program, Hermeneutika's recent *BibleWorks for Windows 5.0* ($250 CBD at 800-CHRISTIAN, $300 retail)[22] is extremely user friendly with context-sensitive pop-up windows and almost four hours of online instructional videos. This edition has 122 reference works and helps (although ninety of these are foreign translations and references in twenty-eight languages, making this collection unique), including an advanced search engine for complex constructions, twenty English translations (featuring the excellent new *English Standard Version*), the *TWOT,* the unabridged *BDB* lexicon, an abridged Liddell-Scott lexicon, Louw-Nida, the Friberg and Miller revised analytical lexicon (2000) and *AGNT2* morphological data base. In addition, *BibleWorks* recently offered both *HALOT* and *BDAG* as add-on modules. To supplement *BibleWorks* further, consider also the electronic

---

DPL. In other instances, original articles have been either reproduced or moderately recast (e.g., Richard Bauckham's entry on the Apocryphal Gospels in *DJG* by Stanley Porter in *DNTB).* In this case, it gives you the rare insight of seeing an editor at work, deleting some parts and embellishing others.

22. *See* Computer Resources: Optimal Package for highlights.

editions of the *NIDNTT* and *NIDOTTE* (Zondervan), now available on the same CD as the *Zondervan Theological Dictionaries.* Both modules together ($270 retail) are available from CBD for $130.

Another Windows-compatible option is the new software platform edition of Logos Research System's *Scholar's Library* ($599 retail, $449 CBD),[23] which also features a simpler interface[24] but on a much larger scale than *BibleWorks.* It combines more than 230 volumes in a combination exegetical and pastoral Bible study program. About forty of these are exegetical works, sixty-five are pastoral studies from the *Leadership Journal,* about thirty-five would fall under the rubric of a *Christian Home Library* (home schooling texts, discipleship, etc.), and the remaining more than ninety would constitute an extensive biblical study base. In addition to the new software platform mentioned earlier, herein lies the principal advantage of *Scholar's Library,* not to mention the bonus of pastoral studies.

Personally, I prefer *BibleWorks* for exegetical study because of its ease of use, sophisticated concordance function, and layout, but for around a hundred dollars more, it's difficult to argue against *Scholar's Library* as a primary choice. First, one of the special features of *Scholar's Library* is its brand new software platform, the *Libronix Digital Library System.* This system enables the user to do rapid passage, word, or exegetical studies in which all research is paralleled on the desktop by the passage and related references. Second, *Scholar's Library* also has the advantage of being able to be expanded with other Libronix-compatible titles such as the *Essential IVP Reference Collection,*[25] Thomas Nelson's sixty-two-volume WBC series on two CD-ROMS ($500 CBD, $1,000 retail), and the forty-six-volume NAC series (Broadman & Holman; thirty-one titles, presently available through Logos for $499, 800-87BIBLE, $660 retail).

This system makes this search mechanism doubly effective, whereas

---

23. Ibid.
24. To quote the promotional literature, ". . . it actually acts as your personal assistant looking up relevant articles, organizing content around your specific target passage or topic, automatically collecting material, and generating reports tailored to your specific study."
25. *See* Computer Resources: Optimal Package for highlights.

in *BibleWorks* you would have to conduct searches on at least two different platforms. Although this new feature is not a replacement for more complex, original-language constructions, it brings up a host of links for more simple searches. You can also limit your search to a particular book or series.

For instance, in the WBC series, one could match and compare commentary on words and phrases such as "the angel of the Lord" in Greek, Hebrew, English, and seven other languages for that matter (i.e., Gen. 16:7; Exod. 3:2; Num. 22:22; 1 Kings 19:7; 2 Kings 1:3; 2 Sam. 24:16; 1 Chron. 21:30; Ps. 34:7; Isa. 37:36; Matt. 1:20, 28:2; Luke 2:9). As for the NAC, its addition to your library not only fulfills the ultimate ambition of possessing one exegetical and one semi-technical commentary per biblical book but also, because of its conservative Southern Baptist slant, provides an alternative interpretation to the more liberal and moderate offerings in WBC. Hundreds of other potential Libronix add-ons are also available. However, if one does opt for *BibleWorks,* these series (NAC and WBC) are also available as separate modules and would still function together with the IVP collection as a single system.[26]

Perhaps then, the ideal combo is either *BibleWorks*[27] or *Scholar's Library,* the *Zondervan Theological Dictionaries,* the WBC series, and the other latest offerings: *The Essential IVP Reference Collection* ($170.00 retail, $136 CBD) and the NAC ($2,100 total CBD),[28] creating a virtual bookcase of 210–240 immediately practical volumes on 9–12 disks. This fact substantially reduces by half the cost of a complete print library and for the first time makes it possible for missionaries to travel fully equipped with a combo computer programs and print library (fifteen to twenty-five books). As for Macintosh, the best

26. A search on the obscure phrase "arm of the Lord" in just the IVP, WBC, and NAC series yielded twenty-two hits in nine different commentaries and references (excluding Bibles).
27. Note that *BibleWorks* alone is still more than satisfactory, especially when supplemented by *HALOT, BDAG,* and the *Essential IVP Reference Collection,* which is redundant by four volumes in *Scholar's Library* but still well worth the price.
28. This price includes the eventual cost of upgrading the series to include yet-to-be published titles.

available program is *Accordance* (Oaktree Software), which is compatible with Mac versions of the *NIDOTTE* and *NIDNTT*.

Optimal Package

1. *BibleWorks for Windows 5.0* (Hermeneutika). 800-74-BIBLE.
2. Clendenen, Ray, gen. ed. The New American Commentary Series, 46 vols. (Broadman & Holman). Libronix and Logos compatible, available from Logos Research Systems. 800-87BIBLE.
3. Metzger, Bruce, ed. Word Biblical Commentary Series (Thomas Nelson). Libronix and Logos compatible. 800-251-4000.
4. Scholar's Library: Logos Bible Software Series X (Logos Research Systems. See *Libronix Integrated Digital Library System* under Computer Resources: References for add-ons. Libronix and Logos compatible. 800-875-6467.
5. *The Essential IVP Reference Collection* (IVP, 2001). Libronix and Logos compatible (Libronix). 630-734-4321.
6. VanGemeren, Willem, and Colin Brown, gen. eds. *Zondervan Theological Dictionaries* (Zondervan, 2002). *NIDOTTE* and *NIDNTT* bundled together. STEP compatible. 800-727-1309.

The "must-have" cost of a personal biblical reference library is as follows:

Seminary-trained student (about 165 volumes):	**$5,700**[29]
Bible college with Greek (about 145 volumes):	**$4,400**
Computer programs (15–25 print resources):	**$2,900**
Layman (about 120 volumes):	**$2,300**

29. Retail cost. Taking advantage of discounts, used books, and selling of the language helps that are designed specifically for seminary use should reduce each number by 40 percent. Consider this a wise investment. A library that is approximately the same cost as a semester of school will help you retain three to four years of learning. Second, the average time a pastor spends on preparing a weekly message or two (over a period of thirty to forty years) amply justifies the initial down payment. In my mind, that's the best way to stretch your ministry dollar.

2 ON COMMENTARY SERIES

For specific recommendations on whole sets, I recommend both the Word Biblical Commentary (WBC) and Eerdmans's New International Greek Testament Commentary (NIGTC), which are technical. Also, excellent choices are the semitechnical New International Commentary on both testaments, also published by Eerdmans (NICOT, NICNT); Baker Exegetical Commentary on the New Testament (BECNT), a key emerging series to watch from Baker Book House;[1] and the nascent Apollos Old Testament Commentary (IVP),[2] which is formatted like the WBC with a theological emphasis in the explanation section following each pericope. It is also advisable to consult commentaries from series that generally run moderate-liberal in their persuasion.

The WBC series, formerly published by Word and now carried by Thomas Nelson, has a fairly equal combination of evangelical and moderate (with some liberal) commentators. A commentary with an evangelical bias would typically subscribe to the belief that all Scripture is absolutely inerrant, that is, the Bible is written with full historical and scientific accuracy on all matters that it affirms and thus is completely truthful. A moderate view would affirm that the inerrancy

1. Titles to date include Darrell Bock's opus on the gospel of Luke (volume 2 was a 1996 *Christianity Today* Best Books selection), Thomas Schreiner on Romans, and Grant Osborne on Revelation.
2. Specifically intended for pastors, Apollos follows the format of the WBC series with special emphasis on theological reflection and applicational possibilities in the corresponding "Explanations" section. As such, it is more scholarly than the applicational series mentioned below, with some commentaries indicating an evangelical/critical slant (i.e., Gordon McConville on Deuteronomy).

of Scripture is restricted to its theological content rather than its historical or scientific statements. A moderate, for instance, could hold that the actual author of 2 Peter is someone other than the apostle himself but that its theological truths are still consistent with the rest of Scripture. A liberal view, however, would generally assert that Scripture's claim to divine origin is dubious (i.e., the JEDP documentary hypothesis of Pentateuchal redaction).

In recent years, evangelicals have been forced to play catch-up in writing commentaries that supply the advanced philology, text-critical notes, theological implications, socioliterary background, and extrabiblical parallels that have characterized liberal scholarship for decades. A particularly noteworthy liberal commentary series are Hermeneia (Augsburg Fortress) and The Old Testament Library (OTL)[3] and the New Testament Library (NTL), both from Westminster John Knox. Series of mixed theological persuasion (including liberal, evangelical, and moderate commentators) that deserve mention are the Eerdmans Critical Commentary (ECC), the revising ICC series (T & T Clark), and the Anchor Bible (Doubleday).

Other options include the new wave of commentaries that exclusively address cultural and literary backgrounds. Rather than following the verse-by-verse format of the traditional grammatical-historical commentaries, these generally exposit blocks of text. This format includes the New Testament in Context (NTC) by Trinity Press International and the socio-rhetorical commentaries published by Eerdmans.

Some of the series that I include are semitechnical as well as expositional, namely, Broadman & Holman's whole-Bible New American Commentary (NAC)[4] and the Pillar New Testament

---

3. The Old Testament Library was inaugurated by Westminster, but since merging with John Knox, the name of the publisher is Westminster John Knox. Also, titles in the Interpretation series were originally published by John Knox, but are now also available through Westminster John Knox. I have tried to make these distinctions throughout the book, including the WBC volumes.
4. Particularly outstanding in the NAC series and able to be used as a semitechnical commentary include David Garland on 2 Corinthians, Duane Garrett on Hosea and Amos, Robert Bergen on 1–2 Samuel, Daniel Block on Judges and Ruth, David Howard on Joshua, Dennis Cole on Numbers, and Mark Rooker on Leviticus.

Commentary (Pillar) series, which are designed specifically for the serious student and the general reader alike. As such, these commentaries usually are better than more technical treatments for grasping the overall flow of the passage. In some cases, I have included them under Technical, Semitechnical references.

For expositional recommendations in addition to those mentioned earlier, I would also recommend the NIV Application Commentary (NIVAC),[5] the Tyndale Old Testament Commentary (TOTC), The Bible Speaks Today (BST), the Black's New Testament Commentary (BNTC), and an emerging series to watch from Hendrickson Publishers, the New International Biblical Commentary on the Old Testament (NIBCOT).

The following overview presents a list of series arranged according to my recommendations:

Evangelical and Technical, Semitechnical[6]

1. New International Greek Testament Commentary (NIGTC)
2. New International Commentary (NICOT, NICNT)
3. Baker Exegetical Commentary (BECNT)
4. Pillar New Testament Commentaries (Pillar)
5. Apollos Old Testament Commentary (Apollos)

Mixed, Technical, Semitechnical[7]

1. Word Biblical Commentaries (WBC)
2. International Critical Commentary (ICC)

---

5. The NIVAC series is the best homiletic set current. It breaks the interpretation into three categories: original meaning, bridging contexts, and contemporary significance, thus following the accepted pattern for preparing sermons.
6. Note that the Anchor, Hermeneia, Interpretation, NIB, NICNT, NICOT, NIGTC, NIVAC, NTL, OTL, Pillar, and TNTC are all printed on acid-free paper, promising years of durability and clarity.
7. The commentaries of Milgrom, Christensen, Klein, McCarter, Cogan, Hobbs, Japhet, Williamson, Fox, Clines, Seow, Murphy, Andersen, Freedman, Barrett, Cranfield, Thrall, Best, Johnson, Achtemeier, Smalley, and Schnackenburg are among those of the moderate-to-liberal persuasion (primarily in the Hermeneia, OTL, Anchor, ICC, and WBC series) that are considered as desirable selections for conservatives.

3. The Anchor Bible (AB)
4. Eerdmans Critical Commentary (ECC)
5. Black's New Testament Commentaries (BNTC), formerly Harper's New Testament Commentaries (HNTC)
6. Sacra Pagina
7. Abingdon New Testament Commentaries (ANTC), Abingdon Old Testament Commentaries (AOTC)
8. New Century Bible Commentary (NCBC)
9. New Testament in Context (NTC)[8]

Liberal, Technical

1. Hermeneia, Continental
2. Old Testament Library (OTL), New Testament Library (NTL)

Exposition

1. New American Commentary (NAC)
2. Tyndale Old Testament Commentary (TOTC)
3. New International Biblical Commentary: OT and NT (NIBCOT, NIBCNT)
4. New Interpreter's Bible (NIB)[9]
5. Tyndale New Testament Commentary (TNTC)
6. Expositors Bible Commentary (EBC)
7. Believer's Church Bible Commentary (BCBC)
8. Daily Study Bible (DSB)

Preaching and Application

1. The NIV Application Commentary (NIVAC)
2. The Bible Speaks Today (BST)

---

8. The NTC abbreviation is used for this series rather than the New Testament Commentary by William Hendriksen and Simon Kistemaker (Baker) because of more recommended titles.
9. Especially Walter Kaiser on Leviticus, Choon-Leong Seow on Kings, Leslie Allen on Chronicles, Ralph Klein on Ezra/Nehemiah, Clinton McCann on Psalms, Raymond Van Leeuwen on Proverbs, Christopher Seitz on Isaiah 40–66, Kathryn Pfister-Darr on Ezekiel, Alan Culpepper on Luke, Gail O'Day on John, Robert Wall on Acts, Tom Wright on Romans, and Richard Hays on Galatians.

3. IVP New Testament Commentary (IVPNTC)
4. Interpretation (IBC)
5. New Communicator's Commentary (NCC)

3 OLD TESTAMENT INTRODUCTION, SURVEY, AND THEOLOGY

Old Testament Introduction

1. Archer, Gleason. *A Survey of Old Testament Introduction,* rev. ed. (Moody, 1994).
2. Dillard, Raymond, and Tremper Longman. *Introduction to the Old Testament* (Zondervan, 1994). Historical, theological, and literary background.
3. Dumbrell, William. *The Faith of Israel,* 2d ed. (Baker, 2002). Especially theology.
4. Harrison, R. K. *Introduction to the Old Testament* (Prince, 1996).
5. LaSor, William, David Hubbard, and Frederic Bush. *Old Testament Survey,* 2d ed. (Eerdmans, 1996).

Old Testament Survey*

1. **Arnold, Bill, and Bryan Beyer. *Encountering the Old Testament* (Baker, 1999).** Includes multimedia, interactive CD-ROM,

* Forthcoming are the following four *Exploring the Old Testament* books from IVP: Gordon Wenham, *Pentateuch;* Philip Satterthwaite, *History Books;* Ernest Lucas, *Psalms and Wisdom;* and Gordon McConville, *The Prophets.* Happily, with the emergence of IVP's *Exploring the Old Testament* and Colin Smith's two Old Testament volumes (he has also authored two New Testament survey companions), both college and seminary professors now have the option of tailoring their courses with textbooks designed for simplicity, especially if their respective institutions advocate the two-semester approach. Of particular interest to me is Colin Smith's method for inviting future retention of significant personages, themes, and events. He specifically focuses on key chapters, assigning appropriate biblical and theological correlations to each (i.e., Law for Exodus 20).

companion reader (*see under* Old Testament Background: Ancient Near East Parallels).

2. **Hill, Andrew, and John Walton. *A Survey of the Old Testament,* 2d ed. (Zondervan, 2000).**
3. Smith, Colin. *Unfolding the Bible Story,* 2 vols. (Moody, 2002).

Introduction to the Pentateuch

1. **Alexander, Desmond. *From Paradise to the Promised Land,* 2d ed. (Baker, 2002).**
2. Hamilton, Victor. *Handbook on the Pentateuch* (Baker, 1982).
3. **Sailhamer, John. *The Pentateuch as Narrative* (Zondervan, 1992).**
4. **Wenham, Gordon. *Exploring the Old Testament: A Guide to the Pentateuch* (IVP, 2003).**
5. *See* Critical Introductions.

Introduction to the Historic Books

1. **Hamilton, Victor. *Handbook on the Historical Books* (Baker, 2001).**
2. **Howard, David. *An Introduction to the Old Testament Historical Books* (Moody, 1993).**
3. Nelson, Richard. IBT (Abingdon, 1998). Second Samuel 24 as test case.

Introduction to the Wisdom Literature*

1. Berry, Donald. *An Introduction to Wisdom and Poetry of the Old Testament* (Broadman & Holman, 1995).
2. Bullock, Hassell. *An Introduction to the Old Testament Poetic Books,* rev. ed. (Moody, 1988).

   ———. *Encountering the Book of Psalms* (Baker, 2001).
3. **Clifford, Richard. IBT (Abingdon, 1998).** Outstanding critical introduction.
4. Crenshaw, James. *The Psalms, An Introduction* (Eerdmans, 2001).

* Forthcoming: Gerald Wilson, IBT (Abingdon).

———. *Old Testament Wisdom,* rev. ed. (Westminster John Knox, 1998).

5. **Murphy, Roland. *The Tree of Life,* 3d ed. (Eerdmans, 2002).**

Introduction to Prophetic Literature

1. Bullock, Hassell. *An Introduction to the Old Testament Prophetic Books* (Moody, 1986).
2. **Chisholm, Robert. *Handbook on the Prophets* (Baker, 2002).**
3. **Petersen, David. *The Prophetic Literature* (Westminster John Knox, 2002).** Includes Elijah, Elisha, etc.
4. Rofé, Alexander. *Introduction to Prophetic Literature* (Sheffield Academic Press, 1997).
5. VanGemeren, Willem. *Interpreting the Prophetic Word* (Zondervan, 1990).

Critical Introductions

1. Anderson, Bernhard. *Understanding the Old Testament,* 4th ed., abridged and updated (Prentice-Hall, 2000).
2. Birch, Bruce, et al. *A Theological Introduction to the Old Testament* (Abingdon, 1999).
3. Blenkinsopp, Joseph. *The Pentateuch,* ABRL (Doubleday, 1992). Especially interpretation, 1800 to present.
4. Childs, Brevard. *Introduction to the Old Testament as Scripture* (Fortress, 1979). Moderate.
5. Crenshaw, James. *Old Testament Story and Faith* (Hendrickson, 1992).
6. Drane, John. *Introducing the Old Testament,* rev. ed. (Fortress, 2001).
7. Eissfeldt, Otto. *The Old Testament* (Harper, 1965). Classic JEDP, dated.
8. Flanders, Henry, Robert Crapps, and David Smith. *People of the Covenant,* 3d ed. (Oxford University Press, 1988).
9. Fretheim, Terence. *The Pentateuch,* IBT (Abingdon, 1996).
10. Rendtorff, Rolf. *The Old Testament: An Introduction* (Fortress, 1986).

11. Schmidt, Werner. *Old Testament Introduction,* 2d ed. (Westminster John Knox, 2000).
12. Whybray, Norman. *Introduction to the Pentateuch* (Eerdmans, 1995). As single author fiction.

Principal Old Testament Theologies

1. **Barr, James. *The Concept of Biblical Theology* (Fortress, 1999).**
2. Brueggemann, Walter. *Theology of the Old Testament* (Fortress, 1997). Employs metaphor and imagery of the courtroom.
3. Clements, Ronald. *Wisdom in Theology* (Eerdmans, 1992). Exilic developments.
4. Gerstenberger, Erhard. *Theologies of the Old Testament* (Fortress, 2002).
5. **House, Paul. *Old Testament Theology* (IVP, 1998).**
6. **Kaiser, Walter. *Toward an Old Testament Theology* (Zondervan, 1978).**
7. Knierim, Rolf. *The Task of Old Testament Theology* (Eerdmans, 1995).
8. Martens, Elmer. *God's Design,* 3d ed. (Bibal, 1998).
9. Ollenburger, Ben, et al., eds. *The Flowering of Old Testament Theology* (Eisenbrauns, 1992).
10. Perdue, Leo. *Wisdom and Creation* (Abingdon, 1994). Wisdom theology.
11. Preuss, Horst. *Old Testament Theology,* OTL, 2 vols. (Westminster John Knox, 1995–96). Liberal focus on Yahweh.
12. Robertson, Palmer. *The Christ of the Covenants* (Presbyterian & Reformed, 1981).
13. Sailhamer, John. *Introduction to Old Testament Theology* (Zondervan, 1995).
14. Smith, Ralph. *Old Testament Theology* (Broadman & Holman, 1994). Useful historical overview.
15. von Rad, Gerhard. *Old Testament Theology,* 2 vols. (Westminster John Knox, 2001). Liberal, salvation-history approach.

Supplemental Theologies

1. Brown, Michael. *Israel's Divine Healer* (Zondervan, 1995).
2. **Carroll R., M. Daniel, and Richard Hess, eds. *Israel's Messiah in the Bible and the Dead Sea Scrolls* (Baker, 2003).**
3. Gowan, Donald. *Theology of the Prophetic Books* (Westminster John Knox, 1998).
4. Greenspahn, Frederick. *When Brothers Dwell Together* (Oxford University Press, 1994). Refutes primogeniture.
5. Hildebrandt, Wilf. *An Old Testament Theology of the Spirit of God* (Hendrickson, 1995).
6. Johnston, Philip, and Peter Walker, eds. *The Land of Promise* (IVP, 2000).
7. McEntire, Mark. *The Blood of Abel* (Mercer, 1999). OT violence.
8. Niehaus, Jeffrey. *God at Sinai* (Zondervan, 1996).
9. Penchansky, David, and Paul Redditt, eds. *Shall Not the Judge of the Earth Do What Is Right?* (Eisenbrauns, 2000).
10. **Satterthwaite, Philip, Richard Hess, and Gordon Wenham, eds. *The Lord's Anointed: Interpretations of Old Testament Messianic Texts* (Baker, 1996).**
11. Seitz, Christopher. *Word Without End* (Eerdmans, 1998).
12. Wisdom, Jeffrey. *Blessings for the Nations and the Curse of the Law* (Mohr, 2001).

Biblical Theologies of Both Testaments

1. Childs, Brevard. *Biblical Theology of the Old and New Testaments* (Fortress, 1992).
2. Goldsworthy, Graeme. *According to Plan* (IVP, 2002). Introductory.
3. **Hafemann, Scott, ed. *Biblical Theology* (IVP, 2002).**
4. Kraftchick, Steven, et al., eds. *Biblical Theology* (Abingdon, 1995).
5. Scobie, Charles. *An Approach to Biblical Theology* (Eerdmans, 2002).
6. Sun, H., et al., eds. *Problems in Biblical Theology* (Eerdmans, 1997).

7. Zuck, Roy, and Darrell Bock, eds. *Biblical Theology of the New Testament* (Moody, 1994).
8. Zuck, Roy, Eugene Merrill, and Darrell Bock, eds. *Biblical Theology of the Old Testament* (Moody, 1992).

4 OLD TESTAMENT COMMENTARIES

Genesis*

Technical, Semitechnical[1]

C/M 1. Cassuto, Umberto. *A Commentary on Book of Genesis,* 2 vols. (Magnes, 1961, 1964). Covers 1:1–13:5. Alternative to Documentary Hypothesis.

L/Cr 2. Fretheim, Terence. NIB, vol. 1 (Abingdon, 1994). Appreciation for literary facets; particularly plots, structure, and sequence.

E 3. Hamilton, Victor. NICOT, 2 vols. (Eerdmans, 1990, 1995). Especially comparative Semitics.

C/M 4. Sarna, Nahum. JPSTC (JPS, 1989). Incorporates rabbinic exegesis.

L/Cr 5. von Rad, Gerhard. OTL, rev. ed. (Westminster, 1973). Theological interpretation.

---

* Forthcoming: David Baker, Apollos (IVP); and Theodore Hiebert, AOTC (Abingdon).

1. Genesis may be the beginning of all things, but commentary writing itself began with targums and tannaitic midrash beginning in the immediate postexilic period. This tradition carried over into the early church fathers, who provided us with the nearest glimpse of how New Testament writings (and the Old Testament in light of the New) were to be interpreted. Since then, there has been no end to commentary writing. Here, I list nineteen, most of which are from 1987 on. The place for a scholar to start is Wenham, Westermann, and Hamilton. For the pastor, a combination of Wenham, Waltke, and Walton would be ideal. Walton's commentary is especially fresh with applicational possibilities and is faithful to the original intent of the NIVAC series like only a few others. It even contains an illustration index. David Baker's forthcoming commentary should be obtained.

E/Cr 6. Wenham, Gordon. WBC, 2 vols. (Word, 1987, 1994). Especially form, structure, setting.

L/Cr 7. Westermann, Claus. Continental, 3 vols. (Fortress, 1984–86). Tradition-critical.

Exposition

E/Cr 1. Atkinson, David. *The Message of Genesis 1–11,* BST (IVP, 1990).

E/Cr 2. Baldwin, Joyce. *The Message of Genesis 12–50,* BST (IVP, 1986).

L/Cr 3. Brueggemann, Walter. IBC (John Knox, 1982). Especially theology.

E 4. Eveson, Philip. *The Book of Origins* (Evangelical Press, 2001).

E/Cr 5. Hartley, John. NIBCOT (Hendrickson, 2001). Editing from Moses to time of Solomon.

E/Cr 6. Kidner, Derek. TOTC (IVP, 1967). Day-age creation view.

E 7. Leupold, Herbert. *Exposition of Genesis* (Baker, 1942).

E 8. Mathews, Kenneth. NAC, 2 vols. (Broadman & Holman, 1996–).

E 9. Ross, Allen. *Creation and Blessing* (Baker, 1988). Thorough expositional study guide.

E 10. Sailhamer, John. EBC, vol. 2 (Zondervan, 1990).

E 11. Waltke, Bruce, with Cathi Fredericks. *Genesis* (Zondervan, 2001). Especially theology, somewhat semitechnical.

E 12. Walton, John. NIVAC (Zondervan, 2001).

Special Studies

E/Cr 1. Alexander, Desmond. *Abraham in the Negev* (Paternoster, 1997). Genesis 20–22.

E 2. Arnold, Bill. *Encountering the Book of Genesis* (Baker, 1998). College-level introduction.

L/Cr 3. Bailey, Lloyd. *Noah: The Person and the Story in History and Tradition* (University of South Carolina, 1989).

L/Cr 4. Carr, David. *Reading the Fractures of Genesis* (Westminster John Knox, 1996).

L/Cr 5. Clifford, Richard. *Creation Accounts in the Ancient Near East and in the Bible* (Catholic Biblical Association, 1994).

L/Cr 6. Hendel, Ronald. *The Text of Genesis 1–11* (Oxford University Press, 1998). LXX instructive to original reading.

E/Cr 7. Hess, Richard, Philip Satterthwaite, and Gordon Wenham, eds. *He Swore an Oath* (Baker, 1994). Themes from Genesis 12–50.

E 8. Hess, Richard, and David Tsumura, eds. *I Studied Inscriptions from Before the Flood* (Eisenbrauns, 1994).

E 9. Sheridan, Mark. *Genesis 12–50.* ACCS (IVP, 2002). Patristic commentary.

L/Cr 10. Thompson, Thomas. *The Historicity of the Patriarchal Narratives* (Trinity Press International, 2002).

L/Cr 11. Westermann. Claus. *Genesis: An Introduction* (Fortress, 1992). Three commentary introductions combined.

C/M 12. Williamson, Paul. *Abraham, Israel and the Nations* (Sheffield Academic Press, 2000). Genesis 15 and 17 as separate covenants.

Exodus*

Technical, Semitechnical

L/Cr 1. Brueggemann, Walter. NIB, vol. 1 (Abingdon 1994).

* Forthcoming: Douglas Stuart, NAC (Broadman & Holman); Desmond Alexander, Apollos (IVP); Alec Motyer, BST (IVP); Thomas Dozeman, NIBCOT (Hendrickson); Dennis Olson, AOTC (Abingdon); and Sean McBride, Hermeneia (Fortress). Eugene Carpenter, Bethel College in Mishawaka, Indiana, has completed a massive conservative tome (approximately nine hundred manuscript pages) originally intended for the NICOT series. I have received an advance copy from Dr. Carpenter, and his coverage of the philological and textual details is exhaustive in addition to clarifying the theology of the text. This commentary fulfills a long-felt need because Exodus is currently served by a superfluity of liberal/critical scholars in the Technical, Semitechnical category. Wait, also, for Stuart and Alexander, although Enns (NIVAC) is a "should have."

L/Cr 2. Cassuto, Umberto. *A Commentary on the Book of Exodus* (Magnes, 1967).

L/Cr 3. Childs, Brevard. OTL (Westminster, 1974). Canonical approach with history of interpretation for each passage.

L/Cr 4. Durham, John. WBC (Word, 1987). Source-critical, dubious about historicity.

L/Cr 5. Houtman, Cornelis. HCOT, 3 vols. (Peeters, 1993–2000). Written sixth century B.C., historical-critical. Especially the "Book of the Covenant" (20:22–23:19) in vol. 3.

L/Cr 6. Propp, Brian. AB, 2 vols. (Doubleday, 1999, 2003). JEDP, excellent on textual criticism (with DSS readings), social background. Narrative study the principal focus of which is folktale analysis. Impractical for pastors.

C/M 7. Sarna, Nahum. JPSTC (JPS, 1991). Incorporates rabbinic exegesis.

Exposition

E 1. Cole, Alan. TOTC (IVP, 1973).

E 2. Currid, John. *Exodus,* 2 vols. (Evangelical Press, 2000–02).

E 3. Enns, Peter. NIVAC (Zondervan, 2000).

L/Cr 4. Fretheim, Terence. IBC (John Knox, 1991). Creation theology.

E 5. Kaiser, Walter. EBC, vol. 2 (Zondervan, 1989).

C/M 6. Larrson, Göran. *Bound for Freedom* (Hendrickson, 1999).

E 7. Mackay, John. *Exodus* (Christian Focus, 2001).

Special Studies

L/Cr 1. Coats, George. *Exodus 1–18,* FOTL (Eerdmans, 1999).

E 2. Enns, Peter. *Exodus Retold* (Harvard University Press, 1995).

C/M 3. Gowan, Donald. *Theology in Exodus* (Westminster John

Knox, 1994). Especially Exodus 3–4, intertestamental, rabbinic development.

C/M **4. Jackson, Bernard. *The Semiotics of Biblical Law* (Sheffield Academic Press, 2000).**

L/Cr 5. Loewenstamm, Samuel. *The Evolution of the Exodus Tradition* (Magnes, 1992). Distributed by Eisenbrauns.

E **6. Sprinkle, Joe. *The Book of the Covenant* (JSOT Press, 1994).** Exodus 20:22–23:33.

Leviticus*

Technical, Semitechnical

L/Cr 1. Budd, Philip. NCBC (Eerdmans, 1996). Exilic, postexilic.

L/Cr 2. Gerstenberger, Erhard. OTL (Westminster, 1996). Leviticus as postexilic; from 1986–87 German edition.

E/Cr **3. Hartley, John. WBC (Word, 1992).** Includes history of interpretation.

L/Cr 4. Levine, Baruch. JPSTC (JPS, 1989). Documentary hypothesis view; recent linguistic, archaeological data.

C/M **5. Milgrom, Jacob. AB, 3 vols. (Doubleday, 1991, 2000, 2001).**

E/Cr **6. Wenham, Gordon. NICOT (Eerdmans, 1979).** Includes rhetorical analysis, NT parallels. Influenced by anthropologist Mary Douglas.

Exposition

C/M 1. Balentine, Samuel. IBC (Westminster, 2003).

E 2. Harris, R. Laird. EBC, vol. 2 (Zondervan 1990). Detailed philology and biblical theology.

E **3. Harrison, R. K. TOTC (IVP, 1980).**

E **4. Kaiser, Walter. NIB, vol. 1 (Abingdon, 1994).**

C/M 5. Knight, George A. DSB (Westminster, 1981).

E 6. Noordtzij, A. BSC (Zondervan, 1982).

E **7. Rooker, Mark. NAC (Broadman & Holman, 2000).**

---

* Forthcoming: Roy Gane, NIVAC (Zondervan—with Numbers).

E **8.** **Ross, Allen.** ***Holiness to the Lord: A Guide to the Exposition of the Book of Leviticus*** **(Baker, 2002).**

Special Studies

C/M 1. Douglas, Mary. *Leviticus as Literature* (Oxford University Press, 2000).

L/Cr 2. Gammie, John. *Holiness in Israel* (Fortress, 1989).

L/Cr 3. Gorman, Frank. ITC (Eerdmans, 1997).

L/Cr 4. Grabbe, Lester. OTG (Sheffield Academic Press, 1993).

Numbers*

Technical, Semitechnical

E **1.** **Ashley, Timothy. NICOT (Eerdmans, 1993).** Especially philology and theology.

L/Cr 2. Budd, Philip. WBC (Word, 1984). Form/redaction-critical, history of interpretation.

L/Cr 3. Davies, Eryl. NCBC (Eerdmans, 1995). Redaction-critical.

L/Cr 4. Levine, Baruch. AB, 2 vols. (Doubleday 1993, 2000). Documentary view, comparative study of priestly terms, especially volume 2.

C M **5.** **Milgrom, Jacob. JPSTC (JPS, 1990).**

Exposition

E 1. Allen, Ronald. EBC, vol. 2 (Zondervan 1990).

E 2. Brown, Raymond. BST (IVP, 2002).

E **3.** **Cole, R. Dennis. NAC (Broadman & Holman, 2000).**

L/Cr 4. Dozeman, Thomas. NIB, vol. 2 (Abingdon, 1998).

E **5.** **Harrison, R. K.** ***Numbers*** **(Baker, 1993).**

L/Cr 6. Olson, Dennis. IBC (John Knox, 1996).

---

* Forthcoming: Moshe Weinfeld, Hermeneia (Fortress); and John Sailhamer, WBC (Thomas Nelson). Sailhamer has been assigned the replacement volume for Budd in the WBC series. Certainly, this commentary should be much anticipated because Sailhamer has already demonstrated proficiency in his commentary on Genesis and his exposition of the Pentateuch (both above).

E 7. Philip, James. NCC (Word, 1987).

E/Cr 8. Wenham, Gordon. TOTC (IVP, 1981). Especially structure, anthropology, and priestly ritual.

Special Studies

C/M 1. Douglas, Mary. *In the Wilderness* (Oxford, 2001).

E 2. Moore, Michael. *The Balaam Tradition* (Scholars, 1990).

L/Cr 3. Nelson, Richard. *Raising Up a Faithful Priest* (Westminster John Knox, 1993).

L/Cr 4. Sakenfeld, Katharine. *Journeying with God,* ITC (Eerdmans, 1995).

E/Cr 5. Wenham, Gordon. OTG (Sheffield Academic Press, 1997). Outstanding introduction.

Deuteronomy*

Technical, Semitechnical

C/M 1. Christensen, Duane. *Deuteronomy 1–21:9,* WBC, rev. ed. (Thomas Nelson, 2001). Deuteronomy a poem in five concentric units.[2]

———. *Deuteronomy 21:10–34:12,* WBC (Thomas Nelson, 2002).

L/Cr 2. Clements, Ronald. NIB, vol. 2 (Abingdon, 1998).

E 3. Craigie, Peter. NICOT (Eerdmans, 1976). Ugaritic, ANE background.

L/Cr 4. Mayes, A. D. H. NCBC (Eerdmans, 1979). Theological, literary developments.

E/Cr 5. McConville, J. Gordon. Apollos (IVP, 2002).

L/Cr 6. Nelson, Richard. OTL (Westminster, 2002).

L/Cr 7. Tigay, Jeffrey. JPSTC (JPS, 1995). Source-critical.

---

* Forthcoming: Norbert Lohfink and G. Braulik, Hermeneia (Fortress), and Daniel Block, NIVAC (Zondervan). Use Block with Christensen and McConville.

2. Christensen's frequent allusions to the numerical theory of his mentor Casper Labuschagne (see the review by Richard Taylor in *JETS* 44 [2001] 727–29) means that in addition to his redaction history these can be skipped over safely. All told, that leaves about 600 pages of commentary, which is more than anyone else, except Weinfeld.

L/Cr 8. Weinfeld, Moshe. AB, 2 vols. (Doubleday, 1991, 2002).[3]

Exposition[4]

E 1. Brown, Raymond. BST (IVP, 1993).
L/Cr 2. Brueggeman, Walter. AOTC (Abingdon, 2001).
E 3. Merrill, Eugene. NAC (Broadman & Holman, 1994). Somewhat semitechnical.
C/M 4. Miller, Patrick. IBC (John Knox, 1990). NT, contemporary, theological application.
L/Cr 5. Payne, David. DSB (Westminster, 1985).
E 6. Ridderbos, Herman. BSC (Zondervan, 1984).
E/Cr 7. Thompson, John. TOTC (IVP, 1974).
E 8. Wright, Christopher. NIBCOT (Hendrickson, 1996). Ethical implications.

Special Studies

C/M 1. Christensen, Duane, ed. *A Song of Power and the Power of Song* (Eisenbrauns, 1993).
C/M 2. Knight, George A. *The Song of Moses* (Eerdmans, 1995). Deuteronomy 32.
L/Cr 3. Lohfink, Norbert. *Theology of the Pentateuch* (Fortress, 1994).
E/Cr 4. McConville, J. Gordon. *Grace in the End* (Zondervan, 1993). Theology.
E/Cr 5. McConville, J. Gordon, and J. Gary Millar. *Time and Place in Deuteronomy* (Sheffield Academic Press, 1994).
E/Cr 6. Millar, Gary. *Now Choose Life* (Eerdmans, 1999). Theology and ethics.
L/Cr 7. Olson, Dennis. *Deuteronomy and the Death of Moses* (Fortress, 1994).

---

3. Especially textual criticism. Weinfeld's analysis, which advocates multiple redactions interspersed with reconstructions of cultic history, obscures its value for referencing early Jewish and medieval interpretation.
4. Alongside Block (when it comes out), one will be well repaid by Merrill's contribution.

L/Cr 8. Rofé, Alexander. *Deuteronomy: Issues and Interpretation* (T & T Clark, 2001).

Joshua*

Technical, Semitechnical

L/Cr 1. Boling, Robert, and G. E. Wright. AB (Doubleday, 1982). Dated interpretation of archaeology.

E/Cr 2. Butler, Trent. WBC (Word, 1983). Literary-critical.

L/Cr 3. Nelson, Richard. OTL (Westminster, 1997). Especially Old Greek, Deuteronomistic history.

E 4. Woudstra, Marten. NICOT (Eerdmans, 1981).

Exposition[5]

L/Cr 1. Auld, Graeme. DSB (Westminster, 1984). With Judges, Ruth.

E 2. Hess, Richard. TOTC (IVP, 1996). Especially archaeology.

E 3. Howard, David. NAC (Broadman & Holman, 1998). Especially theology and philology.

Special Studies

L/Cr 1. Auld, Graeme. *Joshua Retold* (T & T Clark, 1998). Especially LXX-MT divergence, Deuteronomic redaction.

L/Cr 2. Hamlin, E. ITC (Eerdmans, 1983).

---

* Forthcoming: Graeme Auld (T & T Clark); Kyle McCarter, Hermeneia (Fortress); and Robert Hubbard, NIVAC (Zondervan). When Woudstra is supplemented with Howard, Hess, or Hubbard (to come), you'll have all of the bases covered, albeit in a more expositional fashion than usual. For more technical details, use Butler's commentary.

5. Hess's commentary, one of the best in the Tyndale series, is particularly strong on historical and archaeological background. Howard brings the strengths he exhibited in his *Introduction to the Old Testament Historical Books* (Moody, 1993) to his commentary. Throughout, he is keen to bring out the theology in the text. The strength of the commentary is the in-depth philological investigations that accompany every word or phrase of significance in the text. For comparisons with conquest accounts you would need to consult the monograph of Younger. For reference to cognate literature on border descriptions, land grants, and place-name lists, the commentary of Hess is needed.

C/M 3. Merling, David. *The Book of Joshua* (Andrews University Press, 1997). Especially archaeology.

L/Cr 4. Polzin, Robert. *Moses and the Deuteronomist* (Indiana University Press, 1993). Deuteronomy through Judges.

E 5. Younger, Lawson. *Ancient Conquest Accounts* (Sheffield Academic Press, 1990).

Judges*

Technical, Semitechnical

E 1. Block, Daniel. NAC (Broadman & Holman, 1999). With Ruth.[6]

L/Cr 2. Boling, Robert. AB (Doubleday, 1975). Significant redaction based on pre-monarchical traditions, though reflecting many actual events.

C/M 3. Lindars, Barnabas. *Judges 1–5* (T & T Clark, 1995). Examination of versions, targums, ancient-medieval sources.

L/Cr 4. Soggin, J. Alberto. OTL (Westminster, 1981). Survey of Continental scholarship.

Exposition

L/Cr 1. Auld, Graeme. DSB (Westminster, 1984). With Joshua and Ruth.

E 2. Brensinger, Terry. BCBC (Herald, 1999). Especially Judges 19–21.

E 3. Cundall, Arthur. TOTC (IVP, 1968). With Ruth.

L/Cr 4. Olson, Dennis. NIB, vol. 2 (Abingdon, 1998).

E 5. Wilcock, Michael. BST (IVP, 1992).

E 6. Wood, Leon. *The Distressing Days of the Judges* (Zondervan, 1975; Wipf & Stock, 2000).

---

* Forthcoming: Trent Butler, WBC (Thomas Nelson); and A. D. H. Mayes, ICC (T & T Clark). Use Butler with Block and Younger.

6. Block's commentary is almost as good as his two-volume work on Ezekiel, which, both in my mind and in the mind of many others, is the best Old Testament commentary extant.

E 7. **Younger, Lawson. NIVAC (Zondervan, 2002).** With Ruth.[7]

Literary Perspectives

E 1. **Bluedorn, Wolfgang. *Yahweh versus Baalism* (Sheffield Academic Press, 2001).** Gideon-Abimelech.

L/Cr 2. **Klein, Lillian. *The Triumph of Irony in the Book of Judges* (Almond, 1988).**

C/M 3. **O'Connell, Robert. *The Rhetoric of the Book of Judges* (Brill, 1996).**

L/Cr 4. **Schneider, Tammi. *Berit Olam* (Liturgical, 2000).**

E/Cr 5. **Webb, Barry. *The Book of Judges* (Sheffield Academic Press, 1987).** Structural coherence, replay of key motifs.

L/Cr 6. Yee, Gale. *Judges and Method* (Fortress, 1995; Wipf & Stock, 1999). Numerous methods applied to select passages.

Ruth

Technical, Semitechnical

E 1. **Block, Daniel. NAC (Broadman & Holman, 1998).** With Judges.

E/Cr 2. **Bush, Frederic. WBC (Word, 1996).** With Esther, especially ANE background.

L/Cr 3. **Campbell, Edward. AB (Doubleday, 1975).** Especially theology and archaeology.

E 4. **Hubbard, Robert. NICOT (Eerdmans, 1988).** Especially literary criticism.

L/Cr 5. **Sasson, Jack. *Ruth*, 2d ed. (Sheffield Academic Press, 1989).** Supports MT, especially ANE background.

---

7. Younger's commentary uses most of his thirty-page introduction to address the book's literary features. In the commentary proper he focuses almost exclusively on its original context rather than its application. That Younger heavily references all of the major exegetical commentaries and monographs on Judges and Ruth and defers from mentioning expositional commentaries ought to tell you just what sort of "popular" commentary this is. It, too, is a hallmark of erudition if not a faithful representative of the series to which it belongs.

Exposition

E 1. **Atkinson, David. BST (IVP, 1983).** Especially kinsman-redeemer issue.

E/Cr 2. Harris, J. Gordon, Cheryl Brown, and Michael Moore. NIBCOT (Hendrickson, 2000).

E 3. Morris, Leon. TOTC (IVP, 1968).

E 4. Roop, Eugene. BCBC (Herald, 2002).

L/Cr 5. Sakenfeld, Katharine. IBC (Westminster John Knox, 1999).

E 6. Younger, Lawson. NIVAC (Zondervan, 2002). With Judges.

Literary Perspectives

L/Cr 1. Fewell, Danna, and David Gunn. *Compromising Redemption* (Westminster John Knox, 1990).

E/Cr 2. Gow, Murray. ***The Book of Ruth*** **(Apollos, 1992).** Contribution of rhetoric to structure.

L/Cr 3. Korpel, Marjo. *The Structure of the Book of Ruth* (Van Gorcum, 2001).

C/M 4. Larkin, Katrina. ***Ruth and Esther,*** **OTG (Sheffield Academic Press, 1996).**

L/Cr 5. Nielsen, Kirsten. OTL (Westminster, 1997). Narrative-critical commentary, especially intertextualism.

L/Cr 6. Trible, Phyllis. *God and the Rhetoric of Sexuality* (Fortress, 1978). Feminist.

L/Cr 7. van Wolde, E. J. *Ruth and Naomi* (SCM, 1998). Narrative-critical commentary.

Samuel*

Technical, Semitechnical

C/M 1. Anderson, Arnold. WBC (Word, 1989). Second Samuel only.

---

* Forthcoming: David Tsumura, NICOT (Eerdmans); and Bill Arnold, NIVAC (Zondervan). The wealth of background knowledge that Tsumura brings would perfectly countenance the discourse analysis of Bergen. Keep Klein on 1 Samuel and McCarter on 2 Samuel.

E 2. **Bergen, Robert. NAC (Broadman & Holman, 1996).** Somewhat semitechnical, especially discourse analysis, linguistics.

L/Cr 3. Hertzberg, H. OTL (Westminster, 1964).

C/M 4. **Klein, Ralph. WBC (Word, 1983).** 1 Samuel only; survey of previous work and canonical approach.

L/Cr 5. **McCarter, P. Kyle. AB, 2 vols. (Doubleday, 1980, 1984).** Especially textual criticism, relationship to Greek and DSS.

Exposition

E/Cr 1. **Arnold, Bill. NIVAC (Zondervan, 2003).**

E/Cr 2. **Baldwin, Joyce. TOTC (IVP, 1988).**

L/Cr 3. Brueggemann, Walter. IBC (John Knox, 1990). Theological insights, Samuel as literature.

C/M 4. Evans, Mary. NIBCOT (Hendrickson, 2000). Detailed endnotes.

E 5. **Gordon, Robert. *1 and 2 Samuel* (Zondervan, 1988).**

E 6. Youngblood, Ronald. EBC, vol. 3 (Zondervan, 1992).

Special Studies

L/Cr 1. Brueggemann, Walter. *David's Truth,* 2d ed. (Fortress, 2002).

L/Cr 2. Eslinger, Lyle. *Kingdom of God in Crisis* (Almond, 1985). First Samuel 1–2.

L/Cr 3. Fokkelman, J. P. *Narrative Art and Poetry in the Books of Samuel,* 4 vols. (Van Gorcum, 1981–93). Ca. 2,000 pages.

L/Cr 4. Halpern, Baruch. *David's Secret Demons* (Eerdmans, 2001).

E/Cr 5. **Klement, Herbert. *II Samuel 21–24* (Lang, 2000).**

L/Cr 6. Polzin, Robert. *Samuel and the Deuteronomist* (Indiana University Press, 1993). 1 Samuel.
———. *David and the Deuteronomist* (Indiana University Press, 1993). Second Samuel.

L/Cr 7. Schniedewind, William. *Society and the Promise to David* (Oxford University Press, 1999). 2 Samuel 7:7–17.

E 8. Wallace, Ronald. *Hannah's Prayer and Its Answer* (Eerdmans, 2002). First Samuel 1–7.

Kings*

Technical, Semitechnical

C/M 1. Cogan, Mordechai. AB (Doubleday, 2001). 1 Kings.

C/M 2. Cogan, Mordechai, and Hayim Tadmor. AB (Doubleday, 1988). 2 Kings, especially helpful on philological, historical issues, Assyrian context of later monarchy, particularly Hezekiah.

E/Cr 3. DeVries, Simon. WBC (Word, 1985). 1 Kings; especially for compositional history of the text and textual criticism.

L/Cr 4. Fritz, Volkmar. *1 and 2 Kings.* Continental (Fortress, 2003). Brief.

L/Cr 5. Gray, John. OTL (Westminster, 1963). Especially ANE background.

E/Cr 6. Hobbs, T. R. WBC (Word, 1985). 2 Kings; especially literary, historical, and theological issues. Sees as "tragic drama" of covenant failure.

L/Cr 7. Montgomery, James, and J. S. Gehman. ICC (T & T Clark, 1951).

C/M 8. Mulder, M. HCOT (Peeters, 1998). 1 Kings 1–11.

Exposition

L/Cr 1. Auld, Graeme. DSB (Westminster, 1986).

L/Cr 2. Brueggemann, Walter. *1 and 2 Kings* (Smyth and Helwys, 2000). Contains CD that duplicates content.

* Forthcoming: David Howard, NICOT (Eerdmans); Gus Konkel, NIVAC (Zondervan); and Robert Wilson, Hermeneia (Fortress). Wait for Howard and use with any of the recommended expositional commentaries. Keep Cogan on 1 Kings and Hobbs on 2 Kings.

E **3. House, Paul. NAC (Broadman & Holman, 1995).** Theological and literary synthesis.

L/Cr 4. Jones, Gwilym. NCBC, 2 vols. (Eerdmans, 1984). Historical-critical issues and textual criticism.

L/Cr 5. Nelson, Richard. IBC (1987). Rich in its theological insight.

E **6. Provan, Iain. NIBCOT (Hendrickson, 1995).** Like House, with excursuses on canonical connections. Does not address MT, LXX issue adequately.

———. OTG (Sheffield Academic Press, 1997). Conservative apologetic emphasizing literary features.

L/Cr 7. Rice, Gene. ITC (Eerdmans, 1990). 1 Kings.

C/M **8. Seow, Choon-Leong. NIB, vol. 3 (Abingdon, 1999).**

E **9. Wiseman, Donald. TOTC (IVP, 1993).** Especially archaeological studies.

Special Studies

L/Cr 1. Fretheim, Terence. WBComp (Westminster John Knox, 1999). Study guide emphasizing rhetoric and purpose.

E **2. Gallagher, William.** ***Sennacherib's Campaign to Judah*** **(Brill, 1999).** 2 Kings 18–19.

E/Cr **3. Hauser, Alan, and Russell Gregory.** ***From Carmel to Horeb*** **(Almond, 1990).** 1 Kings 12–2 Kings 2.

L/Cr **4. Knoppers, Gary.** ***Two Nations Under God,*** **2 vols. (Scholars, 1993–94).** Historical-critical.

C/M 5. Laato, Timo. *Josiah and David Redivivus* (Almqvist and Wiksell, 1992). Messianic expectations in 2 Kings 14–25.

L/Cr 6. Long, Burke. FOTL, 2 vols. (Eerdmans, 1984, 1991). Genre and form analysis.

E 7. Moore, Rick. *God Saves* (Sheffield Academic Press, 1990). 2 Kings 5–6.

L/Cr 8. Sweeney, Marvin. *King Josiah of Judah* (Oxford University Press, 2000). 2 Kings 22–23. 2 Chronicles 34–35.

Chronicles*

Technical, Semitechnical

E/Cr **1. Braun, Roddy. WBC (Word, 1986).** 1 Chronicles only.

E/Cr **2. Dillard, Raymond. WBC (Word, 1987).** 2 Chronicles only, with greatest debt to Rudolf (1955) and Williamson (1976–82).

L/Cr **3. Japhet, Sara. OTL (Westminster John Knox, 1993).** Theological and sensitive to Chronicles as history.

C/M 4. Johnstone, William. *1 and 2 Chronicles,* 2 vols. (Sheffield Academic Press, 1997). Especially literary and rhetorical features.

L/Cr 5. Myers, Jacob. AB (Doubleday, 1965).

Exposition

E/Cr **1. Allen, Leslie. NIB, vol. 3 (Abingdon, 1999).** Almost literal recasting of NCC.

———. NCC (Word, 1987).

E/Cr **2. Hill, Andrew. NIVAC (Zondervan, 2003).**

C/M 3. McConville, Gordon. DSB (Westminster, 1984).

E 4. Payne, Barton. EBC, vol. 4 (Zondervan, 1988).

E 5. Sailhamer, John. EvBC (Moody, 1983).

E **6. Selman, Martin. TOTC, 2 vols. (IVP, 1994).** Especially theology.

E 7. Stewart, Andrew. *A House of Prayer* (Presbyterian & Reformed, 2002). 2 Chronicles.

E 8. Thompson, John. NAC (Broadman & Holman, 1994). Especially genealogies.

C/M 9. Tuell, Steven. IBC (John Knox, 2001). Especially theology, fourth century B.C. composition, link with Ezra/Nehemiah.

E 10. Wilcock, Michael. BST (IVP, 1987).

---

* Forthcoming: Ralph Klein, Hermeneia (Fortress); and Andrew Hill, NIVAC (Zondervan). Use Hill with Japhet, as I suspect his commentary on Chronicles will be a bargain given his thoroughness on Malachi (464 pp.). Otherwise, Selman is excellent. Japhet's commentary, which supports her contention that 1–2 Chronicles was essentially written by a single author with a peculiar literary style, is a model of erudition.

C/M 11. **Williamson, Hugh. NCBC (Eerdmans, 1982).** Essentially historical with creative theological development.

Special Studies

E 1. Crockett, William. *A Harmony of Samuel, Kings, and Chronicles* (Baker, 1956).

L/Cr 2. DeVries, Simon. FOTL (Eerdmans, 1989).

L/Cr 3. Endres, John, William Millar, and John Burns, eds. *Chronicles and Its Synoptic Parallels in Samuel, Kings, and Related Biblical Texts* (Liturgical, 1998).

L/Cr 4. Graham, Patrick, Kenneth Hoglund, and Steven McKenzie, eds. *The Chronicler as Historian* (Sheffield Academic Press, 1997).

E/Cr 5. Kelly, Brian. *Retribution and Eschatology in Chronicles* (Sheffield Academic Press, 1996). Postexilic.

E 6. Newsome, John. *A Synoptic Harmony of Samuel, Kings, and Chronicles* (Baker, 1986).

L/Cr 7. Schniedewind, William. *The Word of God in Transition* (Sheffield Academic Press, 1995). Redaction-critical.

C/M 8. Thiele, Edwin. *The Mysterious Numbers of the Hebrew Kings* (Kregel, 1994).

Ezra/Nehemiah*

Technical, Semitechnical

L/Cr 1. Blenkinsopp, Joseph. OTL (Westminster, 1988). Especially Persian background.

L/Cr 2. Clines, David. NCBC (Eerdmans, 1984). Especially introductions. With Esther.

E 3. Fensham, F. Charles. NICOT (Eerdmans, 1982). Especially historical and archaeological background.

C/M 4. Williamson, Hugh. WBC (Word, 1985). Ezra and Nehemiah independent of Chronicles; takes archaeology into account.

* Forthcoming: Shemaryahu Talmon, Hermeneia (Fortress); Hannah Harrington, NICOT (Eerdmans); and Douglas Green, NIVAC (Zondervan). Williamson is a superior exegetical commentary. Use with Harrington and Klein.

Exposition

E 1. Breneman, Mervin. NAC (Broadman & Holman, 1993). With Esther.

E 2. Brown, Raymond. BST (IVP, 1998). Nehemiah only.

E 3. Kidner, Derek. TOTC (IVP, 1979). Especially for relating exposition to theology.

L/Cr 4. Klein, Ralph. NIB, vol. 3 (Abingdon, 1999). Posits traditional date, emphasizes message.[8]

E/Cr 5. McConville, Gordon DSB (Westminster, 1985). With Esther.

L/Cr 6. Throntveit, Mark. IBC (John Knox, 1992). Especially theology, proposes multiple chiasmuses.

E 7. Yamauchi, Edwin. EBC, vol. 4 (Zondervan, 1988).

Special Studies

L/Cr 1. Davies, Gordon. Berit Olam (Liturgical, 1999). Rhetorical analysis.

L/Cr 2. Eskanazi, Tamara. *In an Age of Prose* (Scholars, 1988).

L/Cr 3. Grabbe, Lester. *Ezra and Nehemiah* (Routledge, 1998).

L/Cr 4. Hoglund, Kenneth. *Achaemenid Imperial Administration in Syria-Palestine and the Missions of Ezra and Nehemiah* (Scholars, 1992). Reconstructing society from archaeology.

L/Cr 5. Holmgren, Fredrick. ITC (Eerdmans, 1987).

E 6. Ingram, Chip. *Holy Ambition* (Moody, 2002). Illuminating application of Nehemiah.

---

8. The clear-cut expositional leader is Ralph Klein's entry in the NIB, vol. 3 (Abingdon, 1999). This is the best volume in the series and can supply your expositional needs with excellent commentaries on 1–2 Kings and 1–2 Chronicles by Choon-Leong Seow and Leslie Allen, respectively. Seow is noted for his Hebrew grammar and exegesis of Ecclesiastes. Allen is noted for commentaries on Psalms 101–150, Ezekiel, and Joel, Obadiah, Jonah, and Micah. He is also author (with Timothy Laniak on Esther) of a forthcoming commentary on Ezra/Nehemiah, NIBCOT (Hendrickson). His NIB entry is essentially a barely disguised rehash of his earlier NCC entry with an updated bibliography and a smattering of post-1987 footnotes, but it is still superior. Purchasing this volume is a bargain at seventy dollars for these three commentaries, with the additional bonus of a commentary on Esther.

L/Cr 7. Van Wijk-Bos, Johanna. WBComp (Westminster John Knox, 1998). With Esther.

L/Cr 8. Weinberg, Joel. *The Citizen-Temple Community* (Sheffield Academic Press, 1992). Political and economic background.

Esther*

Technical, Semitechnical

L/Cr 1. Berlin, Adele. JPSTC (JPS, 2001). Draws from Greek literature of Persian period for context.

E/Cr 2. Bush, Frederic. WBC (Word, 1995). Especially ANE background, literary analysis that divides books into acts, scenes, and episodes. With Ruth.

L/Cr 3. Clines, David. NCBC (Eerdmans, 1984). With Ezra/Nehemiah.

L/Cr 4. Fox, Michael. *Character and Ideology in the Book of Esther,* 2d ed. (Eerdmans, 2001). Commentary. Especially text-critical, literary features, including characters and motifs.

L/Cr 5. Levenson, Jon. OTL (Westminster John Knox, 1997). Especially biblical theology. Assesses LXX, MT divergence, also comments on additions.

L/Cr 6. Moore, Carey. AB (Doubleday, 1971).

Exposition

E/Cr 1. Baldwin, Joyce. TOTC (IVP, 1984). Same as above.

L/Cr 2. Bechtel, Carol. IBC (Westminster John Knox, 2002).

E 3. Jobes, Karen. NIVAC (Zondervan, 1999). Strong introduction, theology.[9]

---

* Forthcoming: Jonas Greenfield, Hermeneia (Fortress); Robert Hubbard, NICOT (Eerdmans); and Eugene Roop, *Ruth, Jonah, Esther* BCBC (Herald). Wait for Hubbard and use with Jobes. Fox is heavy wading, but it is by far the best commentary on Esther available.

9. I think you would be delighted how well Karen Jobes treats the literary and theological nuances of Esther. It is a model for the goals of the NIVAC series, which is to provide an overview of its exegesis and suggest possible applications.

E/Cr 4. McConville, Gordon. DSB (Westminster, 1985). With Ezra/Nehemiah.

L/Cr 5. White Crawford, Sidnie. NIB, vol. 3 (Abingdon, 1999). As fiction with historical elements, includes five additions.

Special Studies

C/M 1. Day, Linda. *Three Faces of a Queen* (Sheffield Academic Press, 1995). Comparison of Esther with two Greek versions.

E 2. Laniak, Timothy. *Shame and Honor in the Book of Esther* (Scholars, 1998).

L/Cr 3. Larkin, Katrina. *Ruth and Esther,* OTG (Sheffield Academic Press, 1996).

Job*

Technical, Semitechnical

L/Cr 1. Clines, David. WBC, 2 vols. (Word, 1989; Thomas Nelson, 2002). Literary study.

L/Cr 2. Dhorme, Edouard. *A Commentary on the Book of Job* (Thomas Nelson, 1984).

L/Cr 3. Gordis, Robert. *The Book of Job* (KTAV, 1978). Interpretation of difficult words and phrases.

C/M 4. Habel, Norman. OTL (Westminster, 1985). Literary background.

E/Cr 5. Hartley, John. NICOT (Eerdmans, 1988). Especially ANE background.

L/Cr 6. Newsom, Carol. NIB, vol. 4 (Abingdon, 1995). Persian date with earlier sources.

L/Cr 7. Pope, Marvin. AB, 2d ed. (Doubleday, 1965). ANE parallels.

L/Cr 8. Rowley, H. H. NCBC (Eerdmans, 1970).

* Forthcoming: Michael Coogan, Hermeneia (Fortress); Dennis Magary, NIVAC (Zondervan); and Gerald Wilson, NIBCOT (Hendrickson). Clines and Hartley are more than adequate exegetically. Look for Magary or Wilson as an exposition.

E 9. Smick, Elmer. EBC, vol. 4 (Zondervan, 1988). Technical for series.

Exposition

E 1. Alden, Robert. NAC (Broadman & Holman, 1994).

E/Cr 2. Andersen, Francis. TOTC (IVP, 1976). Linguistic study.

E 3. Atkinson, David. BST (IVP, 1991).

L/Cr 4. Gibson, John. DSB (Westminster, 1985).

L/Cr 5. Janzen, Gerald. IBC (John Knox, 1989). Existential and theological.

Special Studies

L/Cr 1. Perdue, Leo, and Clark Gilpin, eds. *The Voices from the Whirlwind* (Abingdon, 1992).

L/Cr 2. Van der Lugt, P. *Rhetorical Criticism and the Poetry of the Book of Job* (Brill, 1995).

L/Cr 3. van Wolde, Ellen. *Mr. and Mrs. Job* (SCM, 1997).

E-L/Cr 4. Zuck, Roy, ed. *Sitting with Job* (Baker, 1988). Collected essays.

Psalms*

Technical, Semitechnical

E/Cr 1. Allen, Leslie. *Psalms 101–150,* rev. ed., WBC (Thomas Nelson, 2002).

C/M 2. Anderson, Alan. NCBC, 2 vols. (Eerdmans, 1972). Valuable survey of scholarship now dated on literary, shaping issues.

E/Cr 3. Craigie, Peter. *Psalms 1–50,* WBC (Word, 1983).

---

* Forthcoming: Gordon Wenham, Apollos (IVP); and Richard Clifford, AOTC (Abingdon). Craigie, Tate, and Allen are still the technical commentaries of choice, which has improved with Allen's revision of Psalms 101–150. Add to these Wenham. For exposition, McCann, Mays, Broyles, Wilcock, and Kidner are all quite good. If push came to shove, I would choose Wilson.

L/Cr **4. Kraus, Hans-Joachim. Continental, 2 vols. (Augsburg, 1988–89).** Form-critical, surveys continental scholarship.

E/Cr **5. Tate, Marvin. *Psalms 51–100,* WBC (Word, 1990).**

L/Cr **6. Terrien, Samuel. ECC (Eerdmans, 2002).** Especially theology, exhaustive.

L/Cr 7. Weiser, Artur. OTL (Westminster, 1962). Usage of Psalms in Covenant Renewal Festival.

Exposition

E/Cr **1. Broyles, Craig. NIBCOT (Hendrickson, 1999).** Especially strong on theology and relationship to rest of canon.

E 2. Kidner, Derek. TOTC, 2 vols. (IVP, 1973, 1975). Especially theology and attention to musical features, dated in regards to form criticism.

E 3. Leupold, Herbert. *Exposition of the Psalms* (Wartburg Press, 1959).

L/Cr **4. Mays, James. IBC (John Knox, 1994).** Theologically profound, history of interpretation.

L/Cr 5. McCann, Clinton. NIB, vol. 4 (Abingdon, 1995). Especially sensitive to form, theology, and key words.

E 6. VanGemeren, Willem. EBC, vol. 5 (Zondervan, 1991).

E **7. Wilcock, Michael. BST, 2 vols. (IVP, 2001).** Meaning of Psalms discerned through pattern and order (i.e., Psalms 1–2 summons to obedience; 146–50 the consequent expression of praise and confidence in God).

E 8. Williams, Donald. NCC, 2 vols. (Word, 1986–89).

E **9. Wilson, Gerald. NIVAC, 2 vols. (Zondervan, 2002–).**

Shaping of the Psalms[10]

L/Cr 1. Anderson, Bernhard. *Out of the Depths,* 3d ed. (Westminster John Knox, 2000).

L/Cr 2. Avishur, Yitzhak. *Studies in Hebrew and Ugaritic Psalms* (Magnes, 1994).

10. Because Special Studies on Psalms fell into the two following categories, I have taken the liberty to delineate accordingly.

C/M 3. Bellinger, William. *A Hermeneutics of Curiosity and Readings of Psalm 61* (Mercer, 1995).

E 4. Creach, Jerome. *Yahweh as Refuge and the Editing of the Hebrew Psalter* (Sheffield Academic Press, 1996).

L/Cr 5. deClaisse-Walford, Nancy. *Reading from the Beginning* (Mercer University Press, 1997).

C/M 6. Eaton, J. *Psalms of the Way and the Kingdom* (Sheffield Academic Press, 1995). Surveys key commentators of Psalms 1, 19, 119 (Torah) and 93, 97, 99 (Kingship).

L/Cr 7. Gerstenberger, Erhard. FOTL, 2 vols. (Eerdmans, 1988, 2001). Includes Lamentations.[11]

E 8. Howard, David. *The Structure of Psalms 93–100* (Eisenbrauns, 1997).

E 9. Howard, David, and Patrick Miller, eds. *The Psalms in Recent Research* (Eisenbrauns, 2002).

L/Cr 10. McCann, Clinton, ed. *The Shape and Shaping of the Psalter* (Sheffield Academic Press, 1993).

C/M 11. Schaeffer, Konrad. Berit Olam (Liturgical, 2001). Especially "A School of Prayer" in introduction.

L/Cr 12. Westermann, Claus. *The Living Psalms* (Eerdmans, 1989).

E 13. Wilson, Gerald. *The Editing of the Hebrew Psalter* (Scholars, 1985). Groundbreaking study.

Theology of the Psalms

E/Cr 1. Broyles, Craig. *The Conflict of Faith and Experience in the Psalms* (Sheffield Academic Press, 1989).

C/M 2. Davidson, Robert. *The Vitality and Richness of Worship* (Eerdmans, 1998). Commentary.

C/M 3. Fløysvik, Ingvar. *When God Becomes My Enemy* (Concordia Academic Press, 1997). Complaint Psalms: 6; 44; 74; 88; 90.

---

11. Gerstenberger's second volume on Psalms with Lamentations focuses on the songs and prayers in Psalms in light of their sociohistorical setting and is meant for advanced students.

E 4. Futato, Mark. *Transformed by Praise* (Presbyterian & Reformed, 2002).

L/Cr 5. Kraus, Hans-Joachim. *Theology of the Psalms,* Continental (Fortress, 1986).

L/Cr 6. Lohfink, Norbert, and Erich Zenger. *The God of Israel and the Nations* (Liturgical, 2000). Isaiah, Psalms 25; 33; 87; 90–106.

L/Cr 7. Mays, James. *The Lord Reigns* (Westminster John Knox, 1994).

L/Cr 8. McCann, Clinton. *A Theological Introduction to the Book of Psalms* (Abingdon, 1993).

C/M 9. Mitchell, David. *The Message of the Psalter* (Sheffield Academic Press, 1997).

L/Cr 10. Zenger, Erich. *A God of Vengeance?* (Westminster John Knox, 1996). Advocacy of enmity psalms for worship.

Proverbs*

Technical, Semitechnical

L/Cr 1. Clifford, Richard. OTL (Westminster John Knox, 1999). Especially structure and context.

L/Cr 2. Fox, Michael. AB, 2 vols. (Doubleday, 2000, 2003). Frequent LXX citings, numerous excursuses, lack of reference to Clifford and Murphy in volume 1.

L/Cr 3. McKane, William. OTL (Westminster, 1970). Evolution of secular wisdom to Biblical proverbs.

L/Cr 4. Murphy, Roland. WBC (Thomas Nelson, 1998). Especially literary context and theological application.

L/Cr 5. Whybray, Norman. NCBC (Eerdmans, 1994). Especially textual criticism, literary context.

---

* Forthcoming: Andrew Steinmann (Concordia); Bruce Waltke, NICOT (Eerdmans); and Paul Koptak, NIVAC (Zondervan). Fox, Waltke, and Koptak will probably be your best choices. Waltke's recent commentary on Genesis is superb and will fulfill a need for a full, evangelical treatment here.

Exposition

E 1. Alden, Robert. *Proverbs* (Baker, 1983).

E 2. Atkinson, David. BST (IVP, 1996). Topical.

E 3. Garrett, Duane. NAC (Broadman & Holman, 1993). With Ecclesiastes and Song of Songs. Summary of interpretative options. Suggests theological application.

E/Cr 4. Hubbard, David. NCC (Word, 1989).

E 5. Kidner, Derek. TOTC (IVP, 1964). Especially introduction to themes.

L/Cr 6. Perdue, Leo. IBC (Westminster John Knox, 2000). Attributes to immediate postexilic period. Wise versus fools reflect political tensions between pro-Persians and malcontents.

E/Cr 7. Van Leeuwen, Raymond. NIB, vol. 5 (Abingdon, 1997). Especially role of context in determining meaning.

Special Studies*

L/Cr 1. Camp, Claudia. *Wisdom and the Feminine in the Book of Proverbs* (Almond, 1985).

E 2. Estes, Daniel. *Hear, My Son* (IVP, 2001). Proverbs 1–9.

E 3. Heim, Martin. *Like Grapes of Gold Set in Silver* (de Gruyter, 2001). Proverbs 10–22.

E 4. Longman, Tremper. *How to Read Proverbs* (IVP, 2002).

5. McCreesh, Thomas. *Biblical Sound and Sense* (Sheffield Academic Press, 1992). Poetics of 10–29.

L/Cr 6. Perry, S. *Wisdom Literature and the Structure of Proverbs* (Penn State University Press, 1993).

E/Cr 7. Van Leeuwen, Raymond. *Context and Meaning in Proverbs 25–27* (Scholars, 1988).

L/Cr 8. Washington, Harold. *Wealth and Poverty in the Instruction of Amenemope and the Hebrew Proverbs* (Scholars, 1994).

---

* Forthcoming: Thomas McCreesh, Berit Olam (Liturgical).

L/Cr 9. Westermann, Claus. *Roots of Wisdom* (Westminster John Knox, 1995).

L/Cr 10. Whybray, Norman. *The Composition of the Book of Proverbs* (Sheffield Academic Press, 1994).
———. *The Book of Proverbs: A Survey of Modern Study* (Brill, 1995).

E-L/Cr 11. Zuck, Roy, ed. *Learning from the Sages* (Baker, 1995). Compendium of journal articles.

Ecclesiastes*

Technical, Semitechnical

L/Cr 1. Crenshaw, James. OTL (Westminster, 1987). Literary features.

L/Cr 2. Fox, Michael. *A Time to Tear Down and a Time to Build Up* (Eerdmans, 1999).

L/Cr 3. Gordis, Robert. *Koheleth, the Man and His World,* 3d ed. (Schocken, 1968). Especially philology.

L/Cr 4. Loader, J. *Ecclesiastes.* Text and Interpretation (Eerdmans, 1986).

E/Cr 5. Longman, Tremper. NICOT (Eerdmans, 1997). Linguistic, literary, and typology study.

L/Cr 6. Murphy, Roland. WBC (Word, 1992). Lengthy introduction, theologically profound, as challenge to conventional wisdom.

L/Cr 7. Seow, Choon-Leong. AB (Doubleday, 1997). Non-Solomonic author, Persian period, summary of scholarship.

Exposition

L/Cr 1. Brown, William. IBC (John Knox, 2000). Late third to fourth centuries.

L/Cr 2. Davidson, Robert. DSB (Westminster, 1986). With Songs.

E 3. Eaton, Michael. TOTC (IVP 1983). Qohelet as apologetic for faithlessness.

---

* Forthcoming: T. Kruger, Hermeneia (Fortress); and Michael Fox (JPS). Pick Seow, Longman, and Provan (with Songs as a bonus).

E/Cr **4. Hubbard, David. NCC (Word, 1992).** With Songs.
E 5. Kaiser, Walter. EvBC (Moody, 1979).
E **6. Kidner, Derek. BST (IVP, 1976).**
E 7. Leupold, Herbert. *Exposition of Ecclesiastes* (Baker, 1952).
E **8. Provan, Iain. NIVAC (Zondervan, 2001).** With Songs. Concentrates on bringing out message.
L/Cr 9. Towner, Sibley. NIB, vol. 5 (Abingdon, 1997). Brief but helpful.
L/Cr **10. Whybray, Norman. NCBC (Eerdmans, 1989).** Hellenistic author.
E 11. Wright, J. Stafford. EBC, vol. 5 (Zondervan, 1991).

Special Studies

L/Cr 1. Farmer, Kathleen. ITC (Eerdmans, 1991).
E **2. Fredericks, Daniel. *Qohelet's Language* (Mellon, 1986).** Possibly preexilic.
———. *Coping with Transcience* (Sheffield Academic Press, 1993).
L/Cr 3. Ogden, Graham. *Qoheleth* (Sheffield Academic Press, 1987). Commentary on structure, argument, and word meaning.
L/Cr 4. Schoors, A., ed. *Qohelet in the Context of Wisdom* (Peeters, 1998).
L/Cr 5. Whitley, Charles. *Koheleth* (de Gruyter, 1979). Post-Maccabean composition. Highlights literary features.
E-L/Cr 6. Zuck, Roy, ed. *Reflecting with Solomon* (Baker 1994). Collected essays.

Song of Solomon*

Technical, Semitechnical

L/Cr 1. Bloch, A., and C. Bloch. *Song of Songs* (University of California, 1998).

* Forthcoming: Duane Garrett, Paul House, and David Hubbard, WBC (Thomas Nelson, 2003). When it is published, use it together with Longman and Gledhill. I especially like Gledhill, which is one of the best in the BST series.

L/Cr 2. Gordis, Robert. *The Song of Songs and Lamentations,* rev. ed. (KTAV, 1974).

L/Cr 3. Keel, Othmar. Continental (Fortress, 1994). Interpretation of images.

E 4. Longman, Tremper. NICOT (Eerdmans, 2001). Linguistic, literary, typology study.

L/Cr 5. Murphy, Roland. Hermeneia (Fortress, 1990). Egypt-Mesopotamia link.

L/Cr 6. Pope, Marvin. AB (Doubleday, 1977). Especially comparative customs, history of interpretation.

L/Cr 7. Snaith, John. NCBC (Eerdmans, 1993). Explores link to Egyptian songs.

Exposition

E 1. Carr, Lloyd. TOTC (IVP, 1984).

C/M 2. Davidson, Robert. DSB (Westminster, 1986). With Ecclesiastes.

E 3. Gledhill, Tom. BST (IVP, 1994).

E 4. Glickman, S. *A Song for Lovers* (IVP, 1976).

E/Cr 5. Hubbard, David. NCC (Word, 1992). With Ecclesiastes.

E 6. Kinlaw, Dennis. EBC, vol. 5 (Zondervan, 1991).

E 7. Provan, Iain. NIVAC (Zondervan, 2001). With Ecclesiastes.

L/Cr 8. Weems, Renita. NIB, vol. 5 (Abingdon, 1997). Feminist.

Special Studies

L/Cr 1. Brenner, Athalya, ed. *A Feminist Companion to the Song of Songs* (Sheffield Academic Press, 1993).

L/Cr 2. Falk, Marcia. *The Song of Songs* (HarperSanFrancisco, 1990).

L/Cr 3. Fox, Michael. *The Song of Songs and the Ancient Egyptian Love Songs* (University of Wisconsin, 1985). Detailed comparison.

L/Cr 4. LaCocque, Andre. *Romance, She Wrote* (Trinity Press International, 1998). Proposes female author.

Isaiah*

Technical, Semitechnical

L/Cr 1. Baltzer, Klaus. *Deutero-Isaiah,* Hermeneia (Fortress, 2001). 40–55, postexilic liturgical drama (fifth century).

L/Cr 2. Beuken, W. *Isaiah Part II,* vol. 2, HCOT (Peeters, 2000). Covers chapters 28–39. Multiredactions for Isaiah. Some parts recast in light of Babylonian conquest of Jerusalem.

L/Cr 3. Blenkinsopp, Joseph. AB, 3 vols. (Doubleday, 2000, 2002–3). Serial interpretation.

L/Cr 4. Childs, Brevard. OTL (Westminster John Knox, 2000). Replacement for Kaiser and Westermann. Canonical approach, especially literary features, theology, history of interpretation.

L/Cr 5. Clements, R. E. NCBC (Eerdmans, 1980). 1–39.

L/Cr 6. Kaiser, Otto. OTL, 2 vols. (Westminster, 1983², 1974). 1–39, late date.

C/M 7. Koole J. HCOT, 3 vols. (Peeters, 1997–1999). 40–66.

E 8. Oswalt, John. NICOT, 2 vols. (Eerdmans, 1986, 1998).[12]

L/Cr 9. Westermann, Claus. OTL (Westminster, 1969). 40–66.

L/Cr 10. Whybray, R. N. NCBC (Eerdmans, 1981). 40–66.

---

* Forthcoming: Andrew Bartelt and Paul Raabe, *First Isaiah,* ECC (Eerdmans); Shalom Paul, *Second Isaiah,* ECC (Eerdmans); Richard Schultz, Apollos (IVP); Larry Walker, NAC, 2 vols. (Broadman & Holman); Trent Butler, Holman Old Testament Commentary (Broadman & Holman); and John Oswalt, NIVAC (Zondervan). Meanwhile, stick with Oswalt's semitechnical two-volume commentary and Motyer's *Prophecy of Isaiah.* In view of the excellence of his monograph (*see* Special Studies), obtain Schultz when it is released.

12. Moderate and liberal scholars alike often criticize Oswalt on two points: being cavalier in response to alternatives and not adequately addressing matters of form and structure concerning Isaiah. Ironically, Brevard Childs (whose introduction is unsurprisingly short in view of his contention that the final reading of Isaiah is that which is to be regarded as authoritative), does a far better job of consistently engaging these scholars over the course of his exposition. Nevertheless, a need for a technical, semitechnical, and conservative commentary on Isaiah that interacts with Beuken, Koole, Childs, and Blenkinsopp, etc., still exists. Shalom Paul on Isaiah 40–66 promises to be conservative in light of his earlier work on Amos.

C/M 11. Wildberger, Hans. Continental, 3 vols. (Fortress, 1991, 1996, 2002). 1–39, form-critical.

E 12. Young, Edward. *The Book of Isaiah,* 3 vols. (Eerdmans, 1965–72). Amillennial.

Exposition

E/Cr 1. Goldingay, John. NIBCOT (Hendrickson, 2001). Especially literary structure.

E 2. Grogan, Geoffrey. EBC, vol. 6 (Zondervan, 1986).

L/Cr 3. Hanson, Paul. IBC (John Knox, 1995). 40–66, overall unity.

E 4. McKenna, David. NCC, 2 vols. (Word, 1993–94).

E 5. Motyer, Alec. *The Prophecy of Isaiah* (IVP, 1993). Premillennial, connection of text to structure.
———. TOTC (IVP, 1999). Questionable literary divisions.

E/Cr 6. Oswalt, John. NIVAC (Zondervan, 2003).

E 7. Ridderbos, Herman. BSC (Zondervan, 1985).

L/Cr 8. Seitz, Christopher. NIB, vol. 6 (Abingdon, 2001). Single author (40–66) from immediate post-exile, connects servant to Jesus. Especially literary features.
———. IBC (John Knox, 1993). 1–39, somewhat semitechnical.

E 9. Webb, Barry. BST (IVP, 1996). All-around but brief.

E 10. Wolf, Herbert. *Interpreting Isaiah* (Zondervan, 1985).

Special Studies

E/Cr 1. Broyles, Craig, and Craig A. Evans, eds. *Writing and Reading the Scroll of Isaiah,* 2 vols. (Brill, 1997).

L/Cr 2. de Waard, Jan. *A Handbook on Isaiah* (Eisenbrauns, 1997).

E 3. Ma, Wonsuk. *Until the Spirit Comes* (Sheffield Academic Press, 1999). Spirit passages.

L/Cr 4. Miller, P. *Rhetoric and Redaction in Trito-Isaiah* (Brill, 1995).

C/M **5. O'Connell, Robert. *Concentricity and Continuity* (Sheffield Academic Press, 1994).**

L/Cr 6. Polaski, Donald. *Authorizing an End* (Brill, 2001). Isaiah. 24–27.

E **7. Schultz, Richard. *The Search for Quotation* (Sheffield Academic Press, 1999).** Analysis of prophetic parallels with five Isianic passages.

L/Cr 8. Sweeney, Marvin. *Isaiah 1–39.* FOTL (Eerdmans, 1996). Redaction-critical.

L/Cr 9. van Ruiten, J., ed. *Studies in the Book of Isaiah* (Peeters, 1997).

E **10. Wegner, Paul. *An Examination of Kingship and Messianic Expectation* (Mellon, 1992).**

L/Cr **11. Williamson, Hugh. *The Book Called Isaiah: Deutero-Isaiah's Role in Composition and Redaction* (Oxford University Press, 1994).**

———. *Variations on a Theme* (Paternoster, 1998).

Jeremiah*

Technical, Semitechnical

C/M 1. Bright, John. AB (Doubleday, 1965). Especially introduction.

L/Cr 2. Brueggemann, Walter. ITC (Eerdmans, 1997). Especially theology.

L/Cr 3. Carroll, Robert. OTL (Westminster, 1986). Text as ideological creation. Comments on literary reconstruction.

E/Cr 4. Craigie, Peter, Page Kelley, and Joel Drinkard. WBC (Word, 1991), 1–25.

C/M **5. Holladay, William. Hermeneia, 2 vols. (Fortress, 1986, 1989).** Datable to time of Jeremiah, wealth of textual, exegetical notes.

---

* Forthcoming: Pamela Scalise, NICOT (Eerdmans); Terence Fretheim (Smyth and Helwys); and Trent Butler, NIBCOT (Hendrickson). Scalise drew particular praise for her responsibilities in the WBC commentary on Jeremiah 26–52, which bodes well. Use with Dearman and Lundblom (see below). I also recommend sticking with Thompson, which, though dated, is still worth having.

L/Cr 6. Jones, Douglas. NCBC (Eerdmans, 1992).

E 7. Keown, Gerald, Pamela Scalise, and Thomas Smothers. WBC (Word, 1995). Covers chapters 26–52.

L/Cr 8. Lundblom, Jack. AB, 2 vols. (Doubleday, 1999–).[13]

L/Cr 9. McKane, William. ICC, 2 vols. (T & T Clark, 1986, 1996). Especially textual criticism, Baruch core with Deuteronomic redaction.

E/Cr 10. Thompson, J. A. NICOT (Eerdmans, 1980).

Exposition

L/Cr 1. Clements, Ronald. IBC (John Knox, 1988). Form critical.

C/M 2. Davidson, Robert. DSB, vol. 1 (Westminster, 1985). 1–20.

E 3. Dearman, Andrew. NIVAC (Zondervan, 2002). With Lamentations.

E 4. Guest, John. NCC (Word, 1988). With Lamentations.

E 5. Harrison, R. K. TOTC (IVP, 1973). With Lamentations.

E 6. Huey, F. NAC (Broadman & Holman, 1993). With Lamentations.

E 7. Kidner, Derek. BST (IVP, 1987).

L/Cr 8. McKeating, Henry. Epworth (Epworth, 1999).

L/Cr 9. Miller, Patrick. NIB, vol. 6 (Abingdon, 2001).

E 10. Ryken, Philip. *Jeremiah and Lamentations* (Crossway, 2001).

Special Studies

E/Cr 1. Biddle, Mark. *Polyphony and Symphony in Prophetic Literature: Rereading Jeremiah 7–20* (Mercer University Press, 1996).

---

13. Lundblom's first volume on Jeremiah 1–20 is particularly valuable because he believes these particular chapters are written by Jeremiah. (He holds that the ministry of Jeremiah was stimulated by the discovery of the Torah in 622 B.C.) The first edition of Lundblom's earlier work on Jeremiac rhetoric has drawn substantial notice and is considered a standard in the field. Others have pointed to Jeremiah's prayers, sermons, and biographical accounts as devices that set Jeremiah apart from all the other prophets.

L/Cr 2. Curtis, A., and T. Römer. *The Book of Jeremiah and Its Reception* (Leuven University Press, 1997).

C/M 3. Diamond, Pete, Kathleen O'Connor, and Louis Stulman, eds. *Troubling Jeremiah* (Sheffield Academic Press, 1999).

E/Cr 4. Friebel, Kelvin. *Jeremiah's and Ezekiel's Sign Acts* (Sheffield Academic Press, 1999).

E/Cr 5. Hill, J. *Friend or Foe?* (Brill, 1999). Babylon.

L/Cr 6. King, Philip. *Jeremiah: An Archaeological Companion* (Westminster John Knox, 1993).

L/Cr 7. Lundblom, Jack. *Jeremiah,* 2d ed. (Eisenbrauns, 1997). Rhetoric.

———. *The Early Career of the Prophet Jeremiah* (Mellen, 1993).

C/M 8. McConville, Gordon. *Judgment and Promise* (Eisenbrauns, 1993). Anti-Deuteronomic redaction.

C/M 9. O'Connor, Kathleen. *The Confessions of Jeremiah* (Scholars, 1988). Fine treatment of laments in 1–25.

C/M 10. Parke-Taylor, G. *The Formation of the Book of Jeremiah* (Society of Biblical Literature, 2000).

C/M 11. Stulman, Louis. *Order Amid Chaos* (Sheffield Academic Press, 1998).

L/Cr 12. Thompson, Henry. *The Book of Jeremiah: An Annotated Bibliography* (Scarecrow, 1997).

Lamentations*

Technical, Semitechnical

L/Cr 1. Berlin, Adele. OTL (Westminster John Knox, 2002). Especially background, architecture, theology.

---

* Forthcoming: Look for Duane Garrett, Paul House, and David Hubbard, WBC (Thomas Nelson); and Robert Hubbard, NICOT (Eerdmans). Use either one with Provan (if you can get it), which packs an enormous amount of information into 142 pages (a little more than a page per line). Renkema is superb at 641 pages but might also be difficult to obtain. Adele Berlin builds on the strength of her earlier work, *The Dynamics of Biblical Parallelism* (Indiana University Press, 1985), to dissect the complex acrostic patterns of Lamentations' five poems; focusing on the hope that can be found in the midst of human suffering.

L/Cr 2. **Hillers, Delbert. AB, rev. ed. (Doubleday, 1992).** Especially philology, poetry, and structure.

E 3. **Provan, Iain. NCBC (Eerdmans, 1991).** Especially literary features.

C/M 4. **Renkema, J. HCOT (Peeters, 1998).** Especially insights on poetic structure.

Exposition

L/Cr 1. Davidson, Robert. DSB, vol. 2 (Westminster, 1985). With Jeremiah. 21–52.

E 2. Dearman, Andrew. NIVAC (Zondervan, 2002).With Jeremiah.

C/M 3. **Dobbs-Allsopp, F. IBC (Westminster John Knox, 2000).**[14]

E 4. Ellison, Henry. EBC, vol. 6. (Zondervan, 1986).

E 5. Harrison, R. K. TOTC (IVP, 1973). With Jeremiah.

E 6. Huey, F. NAC (Broadman & Holman, 1993). With Jeremiah.

E 7. Kaiser, Walter. *A Biblical Approach to Personal Suffering* (Moody, 1982).

C/M 8. O'Connor, Kathleen. NIB, vol. 6 (Abingdon, 2001).

E 9. Ryken, Philip. *Jeremiah and Lamentations* (Crossway, 2001).

Special Studies

L/Cr 1. **Dobbs-Allsopp, F. *Weep, O Daughter of Zion* (Pontifical Biblical Institute, 1993).**

L/Cr 2. Linafelt, Tod. *Surviving Lamentations* (University of Chicago, 1999).

L/Cr 3. Martin-Achard, Robert, and S. Paul Re'emi. ITC (Eerdmans, 1984). Includes Amos.

---

14. Dobbs-Allsopp, the author of a major monograph and seven journal articles on Lamentations in the last ten years, builds on his earlier work. He goes somewhat against the supposed intentions of the Interpretation series by not providing easily discernable segments devoted to application, yet weaves in such an impressive array of mostly secular literature (especially on the Holocaust) that its just as delightful to read as it is to study.

L/Cr 4. **Salters, Robin. *Jonah and Lamentations,* OTG (Sheffield Academic Press, 1994).**

L/Cr 5. **Westermann, Claus. *Lamentations* (Fortress, 1994).** Recent history of interpretation.

Ezekiel

Technical, Semitechnical

E/Cr 1. **Allen, Leslie. WBC, 2 vols. (Word, 1990, 1994).** Especially text criticism, theology, and ANE background. Volume 1 replacement for Brownlee.

E 2. **Block, Daniel. NICOT, 2 vols. (Eerdmans, 1997, 1998).**[15]

L/Cr 3. Eichrodt, Walther. OTL (Westminster, 1970). Emends text and posits expansions from traditio-historical approach. Also, ANE background, literary analysis.

C/M 4. Greenberg, Moshe. AB, 3 vols. (Doubleday, 1983, 1997–). As holistic final form essentially from prophet.

L/Cr 5. **Zimmerli, Walther. Hermeneia, 2 vols. (Fortress, 1979–1983).** Form/tradition-critical.

Exposition

E 1. Alexander, Ralph. EBC, vol. 6 (Zondervan, 1986). Especially the excursus on the millennial temple.

L/Cr 2. Blenkinsopp, Joseph. IBC (John Knox, 1990).

L/Cr 3. Clements, Ronald. WBComp (Westminster John Knox, 1996).

15. Block's two-volume exegesis is the best commentary on any book of the Old Testament, even better than Wenham on Genesis, Milgrom on Leviticus, Japhet on 1–2 Chronicles, and his own work on Judges/Ruth. In a recent review, Gordon Matties (author of the monograph on the following page) said, "Daniel Block's massive commentary will become a standard for Ezekiel studies for years to come. . . . A commentary as massive as this one that advocates profoundly at every turn *for* Ezekiel and his God, and *against* our own biases, complicity with evil, and idolatries, deserves our deepest respect" (*Ashland Theological Journal* 33 [2001]: 111–12). Block leaves no stone unturned whether it be on textual/grammatical and historical issues, ANE comparative literature, overall literary structures, analysis of symbols as a means of speech, and a theology that points to the restoration of Israel in both a temporal and an eternal sense.

E 4. Cooper, Lamar. NAC (Broadman & Holman, 1994). Dispensational.

E/Cr 5. Craigie, Peter. DSB (Westminster, 1983).

E 6. Duguid, Iain. NIVAC (Zondervan, 2000). 568 pages of exposition.

E 7. Feinberg, Charles. *The Prophecy of Ezekiel* (Moody, 1969). Dispensational.

E 8. Lind, Millard. BCBC (Herald, 1996).

C/M 9. Pfister Darr, Katheryn. NIB, vol. 6 (Abingdon, 2001).

E 10. Stuart, Douglas. NCC (Word, 1989).

E 11. Taylor, John. TOTC (IVP, 1979).

E 12. Wright, Christopher. BST (IVP, 2001). Organized into groups of related chapters with some omissions.

Special Studies

L/Cr 1. Bodi, Daniel. *The Book of Ezekiel and the Poem of Erra* (Vandenhoeck and Ruprecht, 1991).

L/Cr 2. Davis, Ellen. *Swallowing the Scroll* (Almond, 1989). Discourse analysis.

E 3. Duguid, Iain. *Ezekiel and the Leaders of Israel* (Brill, 1994).

E/Cr 4. Friebel, Kelvin. *Jeremiah's and Ezekiel's Sign-Acts* (Sheffield Academic Press, 1999).

L/Cr 5. Galumbush, Julie. *Jerusalem in the Book of Ezekiel* (Scholars, 1992). Especially Ezekiel 16; 23.

L/Cr 6. Hals, Ronald. FOTL (Eerdmans, 1989). Excellent genre analysis.

C/M 7. Lapsey, Jacqueline. *Can These Bones Live?* (de Gruyter, 2000). Especially 3–48.

E 8. Matties, Gordon. *Ezekiel 18 and the Rhetoric of Moral Discourse* (Scholars, 1990).

L/Cr 9. McKeating, Henry. OTG (Sheffield Academic Press, 1993).

E-L/Cr 10. Odell, Margaret, and John Strong, eds. *The Book of Ezekiel* (SBL, 2000).

E 11. Renz, Thomas. *The Rhetorical Function of the Book of Ezekiel* (Brill, 1999).

L/Cr 12. Stevenson, Kalinda. *The Vision of Transformation* (Scholars, 1996). 40–48.

Daniel*

Technical, Semitechnical

L/Cr 1. Collins, John. Hermeneia (Fortress, 1993). Late composition.

E/Cr 2. Goldingay, John. WBC (Word, 1989). Amillennial, apocalypse-midrash, valuable (including nonbiblical) cross-references, late composition.

L/Cr 3. Hartman, Louis, and Alexander Dilella. AB (Doubleday, 1978). Maccabean edit.

L/Cr 4. Lacocque, Andre. *The Book of Daniel* (John Knox, 1979). Late-date.

E/Cr 5. Lucas, Ernest. Apollos (IVP, 2002). Canonical approach, compositional issues in epilogue.

L/Cr 6. Montgomery, James. ICC (Charles Scribner's Sons, 1927). Especially philology, textual data.

L/Cr 7. Porteous, Norman. OTL, 2d ed. (Westminster, 1979). With supplement updating 1965 edition.

E 8. Young, Edward. *The Prophecy of Daniel* (Eerdmans, 1949; Wipf & Stock, 2000). Addresses millennial debates. Amillennial.

Exposition

E/Cr 1. Baldwin, Joyce. TOTC (IVP, 1978). Amillennial, all-around exposition.

---

* Forthcoming: Eugene Carpenter (Tyndale); and T. Mitchell, NICOT (Eerdmans). Goldingay and Collins are both excellent. However, both propose a late date ranging from the end of the Persian period to the Hasmonean period (333–167 B.C.). Mitchell's comprehension of the Babylonian and Persian background should prove a worthy counterpart to Goldingay. You should use both of them with dispensationalist Miller to obtain a balanced theological perspective. Miller also suggests the authorship of Daniel. Baldwin is still superior but shows its age. Go with Goldingay, Mitchell, and Lucas, but watch for Carpenter's commentary on Daniel, which will be bound together with Ezekiel (semitechnical) in a new eighteen-volume series from Tyndale.

E **2. Brensinger, Terry. BCBC (Herald, 1999).** Amillennial.
E 3. Ferguson, Sinclair. NCC (Word, 1988). Amillennial.
L/Cr 4. Gowan, Donald. AOTC (Abingdon, 2001).
E 5. Longman, Tremper. NIVAC (Zondervan, 1999). Amillennial.
E **6. Miller, Stephen. NAC (Broadman & Holman, 1994).** Dispensational.
L/Cr 7. Redditt, Paul. NCBC (Sheffield Academic Press, 2000). Final form 160 B.C.
L/Cr 8. Towner, Sibley. IBC (Westminster, 1984). Late composition.
E **9. Wallace, Ronald. BST (IVP, 1979).** Millennial.
E 10. Wood, Leon. *A Commentary on Daniel* (Zondervan, 1973; Wipf & Stock, 2000). Dispensational.

Special Studies

L/Cr 1. Collins, John. *Daniel with an Introduction to Apocalyptic Literature,* FOTL (Eerdmans, 1984).
L/Cr 2. Collins, John, and Peter Flint, eds. *Book of Daniel,* vol. 1 (Brill, 2001).
L/Cr 3. Fewell, Danna. *Circle of Sovereignty* (Abingdon, 1991).
L/Cr 4. Meadowcroft, T. *Aramaic Daniel and Greek Daniel* (Sheffield Academic Press, 1995).
L/Cr 5. Van der Woude, Adam, ed. *The Book of Daniel in the Light of New Findings* (Leuven University Press, 1993).

Minor Prophets

Entire Twelve Books*

L/Cr 1. Achtemeier, Elizabeth. IBC (John Knox, 1986). Micah–Malachi.
———. *Minor Prophets I,* NIBCOT (Hendrickson, 1996). Hosea–Micah, especially Hosea, Joel.
E 2. Boice, J. M. *The Minor Prophets,* 2 vols. (Baker, 2001).

* Forthcoming: Duane Christensen and Pamela Scalise, *Minor Prophets II,* NIBCOT (Hendrickson—with Nahum–Malachi).

E/Cr 3. Craigie, Peter. *Twelve Prophets,* DSB, 2 vols. (Westminster, 1984–85).

E 4. Gaebelein, Frank., ed. EBC, vol. 7 (Zondervan, 1985). With Daniel.

E 5. Kaiser, Walter. NCC (Word, 1992). Micah–Malachi.

E-L/Cr 6. Keck, Leander, ed. NIB, vol. 7 (Abingdon, 1996). With Daniel.

L/Cr 7. Limburg, James. IBC (John Knox, 1988). Hosea–Jonah.

E/Cr 8. McComiskey, Thomas, ed. *The Minor Prophets,* 3 vols. (Baker, 1992–98).[16]

E 9. Prior, David. *Joel, Micah, and Habakkuk,* BST (IVP, 1999).

E 10. Smith, Gary. *Hosea/Amos/Micah,* NIVAC (Zondervan, 2001).[17]

E 11. Smith, Ralph. WBC (Word, 1984). Micah–Malachi.

E 12. Stuart, Douglas. WBC (Word, 1987). Hosea–Jonah.

Special Studies

L/Cr 1. Achtemeier, Elizabeth. *Preaching from the Minor Prophets* (Eerdmans, 1998).

E 2. Chisholm, Robert. *Interpreting the Minor Prophets* (Zondervan, 1990).

L/Cr 3. Floyd, Michael. *Minor Prophets, Part 2.* FOTL (Eerdmans, 1999).

---

16. I recommend certain commentaries in McComiskey's three-volume set (noted later under individual volumes) because it is uneven in quality. As an example of the varying ranges of coverage, the three chapters each of Jonah, Nahum, and Habakkuk receive treatments of 47, 64, and 65 pages, respectively (176 total) whereas Waltke's 173-page treatment of the seven chapters in Micah is as good as any exposition anywhere. Only Andersen/Freedman's 720-page treatment exceeds its quality exegetically. The Hermeneia-like size of the three-volume series lends itself to study.

17. Forthcoming NIVAC titles (Zondervan): David Baker, *Joel/Obadiah/Malachi;* James Bruckner, *Jonah/Nahum/Habakkuk/Zephaniah;* and Mark Boda, *Haggai/Zechariah.* I recommend that you purchase most of the current and forthcoming NIVAC commentaries.

E/Cr 4. Gordon, Robert, ed. *The Place Is Too Small for Us* (Eisenbrauns, 1995). Recent scholarship.

L/Cr 5. Griffin, William. *The Gods of the Prophets* (Sheffield Academic Press, 1997). Statistical analysis of Joel with Isaiah 1–3; Hosea 4–8; Nahum; Malachi; and Zechariah 12–14.

E 6. Matthews, Victor. *Social World of the Hebrew Prophets* (Hendrickson).

E 7. Smith, Gary. *The Prophets as Preachers* (Broadman & Holman, 1994).

L/Cr 8. Sweeney, Marvin. *The Twelve Prophets,* Berit Olam, 2 vols. (Liturgical, 2001).

Minor Prophets
(Individual Books)[18]

(Except where indicated, Technical, Semitechnical, and Expositional commentaries, as well as Special Studies, are subsumed under one category.)

Hosea

C/M 1. Andersen, Francis, and David Freedman. AB (Doubleday, 1980). Especially textual problems, unity, poetics. Written by Hosea.

L/Cr 2. Davies, Graham. NCBC (Eerdmans, 1992). Especially textual criticism, later redactions.

C/M 3. Macintosh, A. A. ICC (T & T Clark, 1997). Judean redactors reflecting 750–720 B.C. Especially Rabbinics,

18. Once relegated to one- or two-volume treatments of the entire Minor Prophets, individual books in recent years (see following) have presented some astonishingly full treatments. Among these are A. A. Macintosh on Hosea (704 pp.), Paul Raabe on Obadiah (336 pp.), Francis Andersen and David Freedman on Micah (720 pp.), Andersen on Habakkuk (456 pp.), and Andrew Hill on Malachi (464 pp.). By contrast, Douglas Stuart and Ralph Smith covered the entire corpus in 793 pages for the WBC series.

textual criticism, influence of DSS, new archaeology. One hundred-page introduction.[19]

L/Cr 4. Mays, James. OTL (Westminster, 1969). Form critical. Added material by later authors. Especially theology.

L/Cr 5. McKeating, Henry. CBC (Cambridge, 1971). Includes Amos, Micah.

L/Cr 6. Wolff, Hans. Hermeneia (Fortress, 1974). Form critical, later redactions.

Evangelical Commentaries[20]

1. **Garrett, Duane. NAC (Broadman & Holman, 1997).** Includes Joel and excursuses.
2. Guenther, Allen. BCBC (Herald, 1998).

E/Cr 3. Hubbard, David. TOTC (IVP, 1990).

4. Kidner, Derek. BST (IVP, 1987).
5. **McComiskey, Thomas. "Hosea."** ***The Minor Prophets,*** **vol. 1. Edited by Thomas McComiskey (Baker, 1992).**

---

19. Macintosh is conservative in the sense that he believes that the book is essentially a unity flowing from the prophet's own hand. He attributes its well-known linguistic difficulties to the novelty of Hosea's Northern Kingdom dialect. In a lengthy excursus, he suggests that Gomer's promiscuity is "after the fact," which is one of the few places where some redaction has taken place. His concession to redaction includes the possibility that Hosea was further emendated to adjust its message to a successive audience.

20. Some strictly evangelical commentaries on Hosea exist of which one can avail himself, although some of them are bundled together with one or two other books. Duane Garrett, the author of a recent grammar on classical Hebrew (Broadman & Holman), goes one step further here by explicating the literary features of the text along with its philology. Douglas Stuart's shorter treatment of Hosea joins Jonah as his most cohesive exegesis of the first half of the Minor Prophets. Andrew Dearman's forthcoming commentary in the NICOT series is anxiously anticipated. David Hubbard's Tyndale entry is a bargain (234 pp., $12.95 paper), as is McComiskey in volume 1 of his *Minor Prophets.* I should also mention Gary Smith's expositional treatment of Hosea, which, although brief (he understandably devotes half of the book to Amos), is a model of thoughtful exposition, especially the theological implications of Hosea's relationship with Gomer. With Garrett, Dearman, and Smith, you would be set on Hosea for a lifetime, and if you already have Stuart and Hubbard, you should at least obtain Garrett.

6. **Stuart, Douglas. WBC (Word, 1987).** Especially covenantal background.

Joel

L/Cr 1. Achtemeier, Elizabeth. NIB, vol. 7 (Hendrickson, 1996).
E/Cr 2. Allen, Leslie. NICOT (Eerdmans, 1976).
L/Cr 3. Barton, John. OTL (Westminster, 2001). With Obadiah.
L/Cr 4. Crenshaw, James. AB (Doubleday, 1995). Especially literary structure.
E/Cr 5. Dillard, Raymond. "Joel," *The Minor Prophets,* vol. 1. Edited by Thomas McComiskey (Baker, 1992).
E 6. Garrett, Duane. NAC (Broadman & Holman, 1997).
E 7. Patterson, Richard. EBC, vol. 7 (Zondervan, 1985).
E 8. Stuart, Douglas. WBC (Word, 1987).
L/Cr 9. Wolff, Hans (*see* Joel, Amos below). Form critical.

Amos*

C/M 1. Andersen, Francis, and David Freedman. AB (Doubleday, 1989). Primarily authentic. In addition to an 178-page introduction, each of four sections receives literary introduction. Emphasizes poetics and linguistics. Somewhat obtuse.

---

* Forthcoming: M. Daniel Carroll R., NICOT (Eerdmans). Use with Paul and Smith if you can get it. If you can't get Smith's fuller treatment, his entry on Amos in the NIVAC series (which includes Hosea and Micah) occupies more than half of the book. Denver Seminary professor M. Daniel Carroll R.'s forthcoming commentary promises to be superb. In referring to the commentaries of Shalom Paul, Francis Andersen, David Freedman, and Jörg Jeremias in his review of Jeremias's *The Book of Amos,* Carroll R. writes that they ". . . argue that the literary cohesiveness and poetic touches point away from the hypothetical stages of production long argued by some critics. . . . The literary arguments are now being bolstered by more finds from the Ancient Near East that could also add solid historical grounds for the substantial authenticity of this prophetic book. In other words, whatever might have been the actual original product of the prophet Amos and the process of the shaping of the book that bears his name, the critical paradigm seems to be losing some of its ability to credibly explain all sorts of data" (*Denver Journal* 1, no. 0110 [1998]). I am also indebted to Carroll R. for the preceding annotations from a prepublication portion of *Writing on Amos.*

L/Cr 2. Gowan, Donald. NIB, vol. 7 (Abingdon, 1996).

L/Cr 3. Jeremias, Jörg. OTL (Westminster John Knox, 1998). Mostly postdates the fall of Judah. Several redactional stages. An attempt to balance form/redaction-critical and canonical approaches. Against most critical interpretations, recognizes the role of structure in the message.

L/Cr 4. Mays, James. OTL (Westminster, 1969). Form critical.

E 5. McComiskey, Thomas. EBC, vol. 7 (Zondervan, 1986).

E 6. Motyer, Alec. BST (IVP, 1974). Appreciation for Amos as literature.

E 7. Niehaus, Jeffrey. "Amos," *The Minor Prophets*, vol. 1. Edited by Thomas McComiskey (Baker, 1992). Covenant lawsuit.

C/M 8. Paul, Shalom. Hermeneia (Fortress, 1991). Especially ANE parallels and literary background. Numerous excursuses, 68-page bibliography.

E 9. Smith, Billy. NAC (Broadman & Holman, 1995). Particularly textual and theological issues.

E 10. Smith, Gary. Mentor, rev. ed. (Christian Focus, 1998). Features "Theological Developments" following each block of exposition. Update of 1989 Zondervan edition includes new, sociorhetorical insights.

———. *Hosea/Amos/Micah*, NIVAC (Zondervan, 2001).

L/Cr 11. Wolff, Hans (*see* Joel, Amos below). Analysis of genre, style, and composition for each pericope. Six-stage redaction from time of Amos to postexilic. Scarce discussion of literary structure.

Special Studies

E 1. Carroll R., M. Daniel. *Amos, the Prophet and His Oracles* (Westminster John Knox, 2002).

E 2. Hasel, Gerhard. *Understanding Amos* (Baker, 1991).

E-L/Cr 3. Thompson, Henry. *The Book of Amos: An Annotated Bibliography* (Scarecrow, 1997).

E-L/Cr 4. Watts, John. *Vision and Prophecy in Amos,* 2d ed. (Mercer, 1997).

Obadiah

E/Cr 1. Allen, Leslie. NICOT (Eerdmans, 1976).

E 2. Baker, David, Desmond Alexander, and Bruce Waltke. TOTC (IVP, 1988).

L/Cr 3. Barton, John. OTL (Westminster John Knox, 2001).

L/Cr 4. Ben Zvi, Ehud. *A Historical-Critical Study of the Book of Obadiah* (de Gruyter, 1996).

L/Cr 5. Coggins, Richard, and S. Re'emi. ITC (Eerdmans, 1985). With Nahum, Esther.

E/Cr 6. Raabe, Paul. AB (Doubleday, 1996). How apostrophe determines meaning.

C/M 7. Watts, John. *Obadiah* (Eerdmans, 1969; Alpha Pub., 1981).

L/Cr 8. Woolf, Hans. Continental (Fortress, 1986). Form-critical.

Jonah*

E/Cr 1. Allen, Leslie. NICOT (Eerdmans, 1976). Nonliteral Jonah, especially literary features, theology.

E 2. Baker, David, Desmond Alexander, and Bruce Waltke. TOTC (IVP, 1988).

E 3. Ellison, H. EBC, vol. 7 (Zondervan, 1985).

L/Cr 4. Limburg, James. OTL (Westminster/John Knox, 1993). Targumic, rabbinic developments, modern motifs in art, literature.

E 5. Nixon, Rosemary. *The Message of Jonah*. BST (IVP, 2003).

E 6. Page, Frank. NAC (Broadman & Holman, 1995). Sensitivity to genre, literary issues.

L/Cr 7. Sasson, Jack. AB (Doubleday, 1990). Especially text-critical, philological analysis, parallel ANE, Jewish sources. Postexilic, composite unity.

---

* Forthcoming: James Kugel, Hermeneia (Fortress); and Yvonne Sherwood, BBC (Blackwell). Jonah has not been particularly well served by evangelicals, at least in terms of providing a full-length exegetical commentary, as most of the currently available evangelical commentaries run less than a hundred pages. To put it into perspective, the slightly longer 2 Peter (61 verses to 48) has received a 2,101-page treatment from Richard Bauckham.

L/Cr 8. Simon, Uriel. JPSTC (JPS, 2000).

E 9. Stuart, Douglas. WBC (Word, 1987).

L/Cr 10. Trible, Phyllis. NIB, vol. 7 (Abingdon, 1996). Rhetorical-critical.

L/Cr 11. Woolf, Hans. Continental (Fortress, 1986).

Special Studies

L/Cr 1. Fretheim, Terence. *The Message of Jonah* (Augsburg, 1977). Theological.

L/Cr 2. Magonet, J. *Forms and Meaning,* 2d ed. (Almond, 1983).

L/Cr 3. Sherwood, Yvonne. *A Biblical Text and Its Afterlives* (Cambridge University Press, 2000). History of interpretation.

L/Cr 4. Trible, Phyllis. *Rhetorical Criticism* (Fortress, 1994). Jonah.

Micah

C/M 1. Andersen, Francis and David Freedman. AB (Doubleday, 2000). Especially history of interpretation, 67-page bibliography.

L/Cr 2 Ben Zvi, Ehud. FOTL (Eerdmans, 2000). Literary analysis.

L/Cr 3. Hillers, Delbert. Hermeneia (Fortress, 1983). Sociological concerns, extensive textual notations.

L/Cr 4. Mays, James. OTL (Westminster, 1976). Redaction/form-critical.

L/Cr 5. McKane, William. ICC (T & T Clark, 1998). Excellent textual-linguistic analysis, limited background.

L/Cr 6. Wolff, Hans. Continental (Fortress, 1990). Redaction/form critical, many textual notes.

———. *Micah the Prophet* (Augsburg, 1981).

Evangelical Commentaries

E/Cr 1. Allen, Leslie. NICOT (Eerdmans, 1976). Especially theology, some sections later additions.

E 2. Barker, Kenneth. NAC (Broadman & Holman, 1999). Dispensational, with Nahum-Zephaniah.

E 3. Jacobs, Mignon. *The Conceptual Coherence of the Book of Micah* (Sheffield Academic Press, 2001).

E 4. McComiskey, Thomas. EBC, vol. 7 (Zondervan 1986).

E 5. Smith, Gary. *Hosea, Amos, Micah,* NIVAC (Zondervan, 2001).

E 6. Waltke, Bruce. "Micah." *The Minor Prophets,* vol. 2. Edited by Thomas McComiskey (Baker, 1993).

Nahum

E 1. Armerding, Carl. EBC, vol. 7 (Zondervan, 1985).

E 2. Bailey, Waylon. NAC (Broadman & Holman, 1999).

E 3. Baker, David. TOTC (IVP, 1988).

E/Cr 4. Longman, Tremper. "Nahum." *The Minor Prophets,* vol. 2. Edited by Thomas McComiskey (Baker, 1993).

E 5. Maier, Walter. *The Book of Nahum* (Concordia, 1959).

L/Cr 6. Roberts, J. OTL (Westminster, 1991). Especially textual, grammatical concerns.

E 7. Smith, Ralph. WBC (Word, 1984).

L/Cr 8. Spronk, K. HCOT (Peeters, 1999). Especially philological, literary analysis, Nahum as pseudonym, and well-structured unity based on strophic analysis.

Habakkuk

C/M 1. Andersen, Francis. AB (Doubleday, 2001). Exhaustive. Helpful excursuses.

E 2. Armerding, Carl. EBC, vol. 7 (Zondervan, 1985).

E 3. Bailey, Waylon. NAC (Broadman & Holman, 1999).

E 4. Baker, David. TOTC (IVP, 1988).

E/Cr 5. Bruce, F. F. "Habakkuk." *The Minor Prophets,* vol. 2. Edited by Thomas McComiskey (Baker, 1993).

L/Cr 6. Gowan, Donald. *The Triumph of Faith in Habakkuk* (John Knox, 1976).

E 7. Haak, Robert. *Vetus Testamentum Supplement* (Brill, 1992). Political background.

L/Cr 8. Roberts, J. OTL (Westminster, 1991).

Zephaniah

E 1. **Bailey, Waylon. NAC (Broadman & Holman, 1999).**

E 2. **Baker, David. TOTC (IVP, 1988).**

C/M 3. **Ball, Ivan. *Zephaniah: A Rhetorical Study* (Bibal Press, 1988).**

L/Cr 4. **Ben Zvi, Ehud. *A Historical-Critical Study of the Book of Zephaniah* (de Gruyter, 1993).**

L/Cr 5. **Berlin, Adele. AB (Doubleday, 1994).** Especially rabbinic sources, literary cohesion, canonical interpretation. Fictive author.

E 6. **House, Paul. *Zephaniah: A Prophetic Drama* (Almond Press, 1988).**

E 7. Motyer, Alec. "Zephaniah," *The Minor Prophets,* vol. 3. Edited by Thomas McComiskey (Baker, 1998).

L/Cr 8. **Roberts, J. OTL (Westminster, 1991).** Especially textual, grammatical concerns.

E 9. **Robertson, O. Palmer. NICOT (Eerdmans, 1990).** Especially theology.

E 10. Smith, Ralph. WBC (Word, 1984).

C/M 11. **Vlaardingerbroek, J. HCOT (Peeters, 1999).**

E 12. Walker, Larry. EBC, vol. 7 (Zondervan, 1985).

Haggai

E/Cr 1. Baldwin, Joyce. TOTC (IVP, 1972). Especially theology.

E 2. Merrill, Eugene. *Haggai, Zechariah, Malachi* (Moody, 1994).

L/Cr 3. **Meyers, Carol, and Eric Meyers. AB, 2 vols. (Doubleday, 1987, 1993).** Especially historical background, parallels.

L/Cr 4. **Petersen, David. OTL, 2 vols. (Westminster, 1984).** Especially historical, literary features.

E 5. **Verhoef, Pieter. NICOT (Eerdmans, 1986).** Especially theology.

E 6. Wolf, Herbert. EvBC (Moody, 1976). With Malachi.

L/Cr 7. **Wolff, Hans. Continental (Fortress, 1988).** Form critical.

Zechariah*

E/Cr 1. **Baldwin, Joyce. TOTC (IVP, 1972).** Especially authorship and literary features in introduction.

E 2. Barker, Kenneth. EBC, vol. 7 (Zondervan, 1985).

C/M 3. Conrad, Edgar. *Zechariah* (Sheffield Academic Press, 1999).

L/Cr 4. Larkin, Katrina. *The Eschatology of Second Zechariah* (Kok Pharos, 1994).

E 5. Leupold, Herbert. *Exposition of Zechariah* (Baker, 1969). Amillennial.

C/M 6. Love, Mark. *The Evasive Text* (Sheffield Academic Press, 2000). Chapters 1–8.

E 7. **McComiskey, Thomas. "Zechariah,"** ***The Minor Prophets,*** **vol. 3. Edited by Thomas McComiskey (Baker, 1998).**

E 8. **Merrill, Eugene.** ***Haggai, Zechariah, Malachi*** **(Moody, 1994).** Dispensational, eye to the NT.

L/Cr 9. **Meyers, Carol, and Eric Meyers. AB, 2 vols. (Doubleday, 1987, 1993).** Excellent historical and linguistic analysis.

L/Cr 10. Ollenburger, Ben. NIB, vol. 7 (Abingdon, 1996).

L/Cr 11. **Petersen, David. OTL, 2 vols. (Westminster, 1984, 1995).** Dates 9–14 and Malachi to Persian period. Especially socioreligious, literary background.

E 12. Unger, Merrill. *Zechariah* (Zondervan, 1963). Dispensational.

Malachi†

E/Cr 1. Baldwin, Joyce. TOTC (IVP, 1972).

---

* Forthcoming: Douglas Stuart, NICOT (Eerdmans—amillennial). Try to get Merrill secondhand (*see* Internet Web Sites: Used Books) because it is the best available dispensational treatment of Zechariah, and use it with Stuart.

† Forthcoming: Ray Clendenen, NAC (Broadman & Holman); and Adam van der Woude, Hermeneia (Fortress). Moderate liberals, commenting on the uniqueness of an evangelical entry in the *Anchor Bible* series, commend the evenhandedness with which Hill comments on the text, aware of all of the pertinent literature while defending a conservative position.

C/M **2. Glazier-McDonald, Beth. *Malachi* (Scholars, 1987).** Literary-historical perspective.

E **3. Hill, Andrew. AB (Doubleday, 1998).** Exceptional, well-balanced commentary. Thoughtful interaction with breadth of scholarship.

E 4. Kaiser, Walter. *God's Unchanging Love* (Baker, 1984).

E 5. Merrill, Eugene. *Haggai, Zechariah, Malachi* (Moody, 1994). Dispensational.

L/Cr 6. Redditt, Paul. NCBC (Eerdmans, 1995).

E 7. Smith, Ralph. WBC (Word, 1984).

E 8. Stuart, Douglas. "Malachi," *The Minor Prophets,* vol. 3. Edited by Thomas McComiskey (Baker, 1998).

E 9. Verhoef, Pieter. NICOT (Eerdmans, 1986). Especially structural analysis.

E 10. Wolf, Herbert. EvBC (Moody, 1976).

Combination Volumes

Joel, Amos

L/Cr 1. Coggins, Richard. NCBC (Sheffield Academic Press, 2000). Brought together in second century B.C.

E 2. Finley, Thomas. WEC (Moody, 1990). Includes Obadiah.[21]

E/Cr 3. Hubbard, David. TOTC (IVP, 1989). Especially literary features.

L/Cr 4. Wolff, Hans. Hermeneia (Fortress, 1977). Six redactional stages.

Obadiah, Jonah, Micah

E/Cr 1. Allen, Leslie. NICOT (Eerdmans, 1976). Includes Joel, nonliteral Jonah, later additions to Micah.

E 2. Baker, David, Desmond Alexander, and Bruce Waltke. TOTC (IVP, 1988).

---

21. The commentaries of Thomas Finley, Richard Patterson, and Eugene Merrill (Moody) more than adequately covered all but Hosea, Jonah, and Micah, and might be difficult to obtain secondhand (*see* Internet Web Sites: Used Books).

E 3. Finley, Thomas. EvBC (Moody, 1996). Without Jonah, includes Joel.

E/Cr 4. Mason, Rex. *Micah, Nahum, Obadiah,* OTG (Sheffield Academic Press, 1991). Introduction.

E 5. Smith, Billy, and Frank Page. NAC (Broadman & Holman, 1995). Includes Amos, excludes Micah.

L/Cr 6. Wolff, Hans. Continental (Augsburg, 1986). Without Micah, form critical.

Nahum, Habakkuk, Zephaniah*

E 1. Baker, David. TOTC (IVP, 1988).

E 2. Barker, Kenneth, and Waylon Bailey. NAC (Broadman & Holman, 1999). Includes Micah.

E/Cr 3. Mason, Rex. *Zephaniah, Habakkuk, Joel,* OTG (Sheffield Academic Press, 1994).

E 4. Patterson, Richard. WEC (Moody, 1991).

L/Cr 5. Roberts, J. J. M. OTL (Westminster/John Knox, 1991). Especially textual criticism, philology, historical background.

E 6. Robertson, O. Palmer. NICOT (Eerdmans, 1990). Especially theology.

Haggai, Zechariah, Malachi†

E/Cr 1. Baldwin, Joyce. TOTC (IVP, 1972). Especially Zechariah and theology.

L/Cr 2. Coggins, Richard. OTG (Sheffield Academic Press, 1987).

---

* Forthcoming: Thomas Renz, NICOT (Eerdmans), which is a replacement for Robertson. Use together with Barker/Bailey and Bruckner (forthcoming), or try to get Patterson secondhand.

† Forthcoming: Ray Clendenen on Malachi and George Klein on Haggai/Zechariah, NAC (Broadman & Holman); Paul Hanson, Hermeneia (Fortress); Mignon Jacob's replacement for Verhoef on Haggai and Malachi; and Douglas Stuart on Zechariah (both NICOT, Eerdmans). Jacobs, Stuart, Clendenen/Klein, and Merrill (if you can get it) will serve you best. If not, Baldwin still excels, and Boda should meet expectations.

E/Cr 3. Mason, Rex. CBC (Cambridge University Press, 1973). Especially Zechariah's use of earlier tradition.

E 4. Merrill, Eugene. *Haggai, Zechariah, Malachi* (Moody, 1994). Dispensational, especially Zechariah.

L/Cr 5. Meyers, Carol, and Eric Meyers. AB, 2 vols. (Doubleday, 1987, 1993). Without Malachi, attention to parallels.

L/Cr 6. Petersen, David. OTL, 2 vols. (Westminster, 1984, 1995). Zechariah 9–14 to Malachi 1–4 dated to Persian period. Especially socioreligious, literary background. Expert on prophetic literature.

L/Cr 7. Redditt, Paul. NCBC (Eerdmans, 1995). Redaction-critical.

L/Cr 8. Tollington, Janet. *Tradition and Invention in Haggai and Zechariah 1–8* (Sheffield Academic Press, 1993).

E 9. Verhoef, Pieter. NICOT (Eerdmans, 1987). Especially Haggai and theology, without Zechariah.

5

OLD TESTAMENT BACKGROUND

Primary References

1. **Baker, David, and Desmond Alexander, eds. *Dictionary of the Old Testament: The Pentateuch* (IVP, 2002).**
2. **Boardman, John, et al., eds. *The Oxford History of the Classical World* (Oxford University Press, 1986).**
3. **Coogan, Michael, ed. *The Oxford History of the Biblical World* (Oxford University Press, 2001).**
4. **Edwards, I., ed. *Cambridge Ancient History,* 2d ed., 14 vols. (Cambridge University Press, 1970–). Only three volumes left to appear.**
5. **Hoerth, Alfred. *Archaeology and the Old Testament* (Baker, 1998).**
6. **Matthews, Victor. *Manners and Customs in the Bible,* rev. ed. (Hendrickson, 1991).**
7. **Walton, John. *Chronological and Background Charts of the OT,* rev. ed. (Zondervan, 1994).**
8. **Walton, John, Victor Matthews, and Mark Chavalas. *The IVP Bible Background Commentary: Old Testament* (IVP, 2000).**

Ancient Near East Parallels

1. **Arnold, Bill, and Bryan Beyer. *Readings from the Ancient Near East* (Baker, 2001).** Companion to their *Encountering the OT.*

2. **Block, Daniel. *The Gods of the Nations,* 2d ed. (Baker, 2000).**
3. **Hallo, William, and Lawson Younger, eds. *The Context of Scripture,* 3 vols. (Brill, 1997–2002).**
4. Lichtheim, Miriam. *Ancient Egyptian Literature,* 3 vols. (University of California, 1973–1980).
5. Matthews, Victor, and Don Benjamin. *Old Testament Parallels,* 2d ed. (Paulist, 1997).
6. McCarthy, Dennis. *Treaty and Covenant,* 2d ed. (Pontifical Biblical Institute, 1981). Vassal treaty/covenant.
7. Parker, Simon. *Stories in Scripture and Inscriptions* (Oxford University Press, 1997). Northwest Semitic inscriptions as closest parallel.
8. Pritchard, James. *Ancient Near East Texts Relating to the Old Testament,* 3d ed. (Princeton University Press, 1969).
9. **Walton, John. *Ancient Israelite Literature in Its Cultural Context* (Zondervan, 1989).**

History of Israel Textbooks*

1. **Ahlström, Gösta. *The History of Ancient Palestine* (Fortress, 1993).** Moderate.
2. Albertz, Rainier. *History of Israelite Religion in the Old Testament,* 2 vols. (Westminster John Knox, 1994–95). Critical.
3. **Bright, John. *A History of Israel,* 4th ed. (Westminster John Knox, 2000).** Moderate.
4. de Vaux, Roland. *Ancient Israel,* 2 vols. (McGraw-Hill, 1961).
5. Hayes, John, and Maxwell Miller, eds. *Israelite and Judean History* (Trinity Press International, 1990).
6. **Hayes, John, and Sara Mandell. *The Jewish People in Classical Antiquity: From Alexander to Bar Kochba* (Westminster John Knox, 1998).** Moderate.
7. **Kaiser, Walter. *A History of Israel* (Broadman & Holman, 1998).** Includes brief intertestamental history.
8. Merrill, Eugene. *Kingdom of Priests* (Baker, 1987).

---

* Forthcoming: V. Philips Long, Tremper Longman, and Iain Provan (Westminster John Knox).

9. Miller, Maxwell, and John Hayes. *A History of Ancient Israel and Judah,* rev. ed. (SCM, 1999). Moderate critical.
10. Shanks, Hershel, ed. *Ancient Israel,* rev. ed. and expanded (BAS, 2000). 2000 B.C.–A.D. 70.
11. Soggin, Alberto. *An Introduction to the History of Israel and Judah,* 3d ed. (Trinity Press International, 1999). Critical synthesis of Continental scholarship.
    ———. *Israel in the Biblical Period* (T & T Clark, 2001). Brief.

Other Historical References and Helps

1. Amit, Yairah. *History and Ideology* (Sheffield Academic Press, 1999). Historiography.
2. **Anderson, Robert, and Terry Giles. *The Keepers* (Hendrickson, 2002).** Samaritan history.
3. **Begg, Christopher. *Josephus' Story of the Later Monarchy* (Peeters, 2000).**
4. **Bruce, F. F., and David Payne. *Israel and the Nations,* 2d ed. (IVP, 1999).**
5. Campbell, Antony, and Mark O'Brien. *Unfolding the Deuteronomistic History* (Fortress, 2000).
6. Coote, Robert. *Early Israel* (Fortress, 1990).
7. Davies, Philip. *In Search of "Ancient Israel"* (JSOT Press, 1992).
8. Dever, William. *What Did the Bible Writers Know and When Did They Know It?* (Eerdmans, 2001).
9. **Fritz, Volkmar. *The City in Ancient Israel* (Sheffield Academic Press, 1995).**
10. Fritz, Volkmar, and Philip Davies, eds. *The Origins of the Ancient Israelite States* (Sheffield Academic Press, 1996).
11. Gilbert, Martin. *Israel* (William Morrow, 1999).
12. Grabbe, Lester. *Can a "History of Israel" Be Written?* (Sheffield Academic Press, 1997).
13. Hester, H. *The Heart of Hebrew History* (Broadman & Holman, 1998).
14. Hinson, D. *Old Testament Introduction,* vol. 1: *History of Israel,* rev. ed. (SPCK, 1990).

15. **Hoffmeier, James. *Israel in Egypt* (Oxford University Press, 1997).** Exodus validation.
16. **Isserlin, B. *The Israelites* (Fortress, 2001).** Thirteenth century–586 B.C.
17. Jagersma, Henk. *A History of Israel in the Old Testament Period* (Fortress, 1983).
    ———. *A History of Israel from Alexander to Bar Kochba* (Fortress, 1986).
18. **Knoppers, Gary, and Gordon McConville, eds. *Reconsidering Israel and Judah* (Eisenbrauns, 2000).**
19. Lemche, Niels. *Ancient Israel* (Sheffield Academic Press, 1988).
    ———. *Early Israel* (Brill, 1985). Evaluates three premonarchical establishment of Israel theories.
    ———. *Prelude to Israel's Past* (Hendrickson, 1998).
    ———. *The Israelites in History and Tradition* (Westminster John Knox, 1998).
20. **Long, V. Philips. *The Art of Biblical History* (Zondervan, 1994).**
    ———. *Israel's Past in Present Research* (Eisenbrauns, 1999).
21. **Long, V. Philips, David Baker, and Gordon Wenham, eds. *Windows into Old Testament History* (Eerdmans, 2002).**
22. McDermott, John. *What Are They Saying About the Formation of Ancient Israel?* (Paulist, 1999).
23. Millard, A. R., James Hoffmeier, and David Baker, eds. *Faith, Tradition, and History* (Eisenbrauns, 1994). Old Testament historiography.
24. Miller, Maxwell. *The History of Israel* (Abingdon, 1999). Expanded NIB entry.
25. Schultz, Samuel. *The Old Testament Speaks*, 5th ed. (HarperCollins, 2000).
26. Thiele, Edwin. *The Mysterious Numbers of the Hebrew Kings*, 3d ed. (Kregel, 1994). Chronology.
27. Thompson, Thomas. *Early History of the Israelite People* (Brill, 1992).
28. Van Seters, John. *In Search of History* (Eisenbrauns, 1997). Historiography.

29. Wesselius, Jan-Wim. *The Origin of the History of Israel* (Sheffield Academic Press, 2002). Unity of Genesis–2 Kings from 440–420 B.C.E. modeled on Herodotus.
30. Wood, Leon. *A Survey of Israel's History*, rev. ed. (Zondervan, 1986).

Principal Archaeological Resources

1. Aharoni, Yohanan. *The Archaeology of the Land of Israel* (Westminster, 1982).
2. **Ben-Tor, Amnon, ed. *The Archaeology of Ancient Israel* (Yale University Press, 1992).**
3. Lance, H. Darrell. *The Old Testament and the Archaeologist* (Fortress, 1981). Introduction.
4. Mazar, Amihai. *Archaeology of the Land of the Bible 10,000–586 b.c.e.,* vol. 1, ABRL (Doubleday, 1990).
5. **Meyers, Eric, ed. *The Oxford Encyclopedia of Archaeology in the Near East,* 5 vols. (Oxford University Press, 1997).**
6. Millard, Alan. *Treasures from Bible Times* (Lion, 1985).
7. Moorey, P. R. S. *A Century of Biblical Archaeology* (Westminster John Knox, 1991).

   ———, ed. *The Bible and Recent Archaeology* (John Knox, 1987).
8. Rast, Walter. *Through the Ages in Palestinian Archaeology* (Trinity Press International, 1992).
9. **Stern, Ephraim, ed. *The New Encyclopedia of Archaeological Excavations in the Holy Land,* 4 vols. (Simon and Schuster, 1993).**
10. **Stern, Ephraim. *Archaeology of the Land of the Bible,* vol. 2, ABRL (Doubleday, 2001).** 737–530 B.C.

Other Archaeological Resources

1. Auld Graeme, and Margaret Steiner. *Cities of the Biblical World: Jerusalem,* vol. 1 (Mercer, 1996).
2. Bahn, Paul, ed. *The Atlas of World Archaeology* (Checkmark Books, 2000).
3. ***Biblical Archaeological Society Slide Sets* (BAS, 1981–).**

Mesopotamia, Egypt, Sinai and Negev, Biblical Archaeology, and Jerusalem (*see* NT Archaeology).

***The Biblical World on CD-ROM* (BAS, 2002).** Same categories as above at fraction of cost. More than a thousand images with NT.

4. **Bolen, Todd. *Pictorial Library of Bible Lands* (Maranatha Media, 2002).** Eight CDs—Galilee, Judah, Jerusalem, Samaria, Jordan, Greece and Rome, Egypt, and Turkey. PowerPoint. Ideal for classroom.
5. Coogan, Michael, Cheryl Exum, and Lawrence Stager, eds. *Scripture and Other Artifacts* (Westminster John Knox, 1995).
6. Currid, John. *Doing Archaeology in the Land of the Bible* (Baker, 1999).
7. Finkelstein, Israel. *The Archaeology of the Israelite Settlement* (IES, 1988).
8. Finkelstein, Israel, and Nadav Na'aman, eds. *From Nomadism to Monarchy* (IES, 1994).
9. Fritz, Volkmar. *An Introduction to Biblical Archaeology* (Sheffield Academic Press, 1993).
10. Greenberg, Raphael. *Early Urbanizations in the Levant* (Sheffield Academic Press, 2002). Principally based on evidence from fourth to second millennium B.C. Tels Dan and Hazor.
11. **Harris, Roberta. *The World of the Bible* (Thames and Hudson, 1995).**
12. **King, Philip. *Amos, Hosea, Micah: An Archaeological Commentary* (Westminster, 1988).**

    ———. *Jeremiah* (Westminster John Knox, 1993).
13. **Levy, Thomas, ed. *The Archaeology of Society in the Holy Land* (Sheffield/Continuum, 1998).**
14. Negev, Abraham, ed. (revised by Shimon Gibson). *The Archaeological Encyclopedia of the Holy Land,* 3d ed. (Continuum, 2001).
15. ***Ritmeyer Archaeological Slides* (Kregel, 1999).** From Sinai to Sakhra, Alex Garrad's Model of the Second Temple (thirty-six slides each), and The Archaeology of Herod's Temple Mount (sixty slides).

16. Schoville, Keith. *Biblical Archaeology in Focus* (Baker, 1978).
17. Shanks, Hershel, and Dan Cole, eds. *Archaeology and the Bible: The Best of Biblical Archaeological Review* (BAS, 1990).
18. ***Zondervan Image Archives* (Zondervan).** Five thousand photos of the Holy Land, Egypt, and Greece on CD.

General Manners and Customs References

1. Barton, John. *The Biblical World* (Routledge, 2002).
2. **Deist, Ferdinand. *The Material Culture of the Bible* (Sheffield Academic Press, 2000).**
3. Gower, Ralph. *The New Manners and Customs of Bible Times* (Moody, 1987).
4. **King, Philip, and Lawrence Stager. *Life in Biblical Israel* (Westminster John Knox, 2001).** An enormously attractive, glossy, and erudite survey of archaeological history as it relates to the common man in ancient Israel, replete with photographs, illustrations, and maps. Highly recommended.
5. Vos, Howard. *Nelson's New Illustrated Bible Manners and Customs* (Thomas Nelson, 1999). Excellent bibliography.
6. *See* Old Testament Background: Primary References.

Social Background

1. **Berquist, Jon. *Judaism in Persia's Shadow* (Fortress, 1995).**
2. Campbell, Ken, ed. *Marriage and Family in the Ancient World* (IVP, 2002).
3. **Carroll R., M. Daniel, ed. *Rethinking Contexts, Reading Texts* (Sheffield Academic Press, 2000).**
4. Carter, Charles, and Carol Meyers, eds. *Community, Identity, and Ideology* (Eisenbrauns, 1996).
5. Chalcraft, David, ed. *Social-Scientific Old Testament Criticism* (Sheffield Academic Press, 1997). JSOT compendium.
6. **Clements, Ronald. *The World of Ancient Israel* (Cambridge University Press, 1989).**
7. **Crenshaw, James. *Education in Ancient Israel,* ABRL (Doubleday, 1998).**

8. **Cross, Frank. *From Epic to Canon* (John Hopkins University Press, 1998).**
9. Gottwald, Norman. *The Hebrew Bible* (Fortress, 1985).
10. ———. *The Politics of Ancient Israel* (Westminster John Knox, 1998).
11. **Hugenberger, Gordon. *Marriage as Covenant* (Baker, 1998).** Especially Malachi 2.
12. Matthews, Victor. *Social World of the Hebrew Prophets* (Hendrickson, 2001).
13. **Matthews, Victor, and Don Benjamin. *Social World of Ancient Israel, 1250–587 bce* (Hendrickson, 1993).**
14. **Meyers, Carol. *Women in Scripture* (Eerdmans, 2001).**
15. McNutt, Paula. *Reconstructing the Society of Ancient Israel* (Westminster John Knox, 1999).
16. **Overholt, Thomas. *Cultural Anthropology and the Old Testament* (Fortress, 1996).** Application to prophets.
17. **Perdue, Leo, et al. *Families in Ancient Israel* (Westminster John Knox, 1997).**
18. Pleins, David. *The Social Visions of the Hebrew Bible* (Westminster John Knox, 2000).
19. Roaf, Michael. *Cultural Atlas of Mesopotamia and the Ancient Near East* (Facts on File, 1990).
20. **Rogerson, John. *Anthropology and the Old Testament* (Sheffield Academic Press, 1984).**
21. Weinfeld, Moshe. *Social Justice in Ancient Israel and in the Ancient Near East* (Fortress, 1995).
22. Wright, Christopher. *God's People in God's Land* (Eerdmans, 1990).

Religious Background[1]

1. Blenkinsopp, Joseph. *Sage, Priest, Prophet* (Westminster John Knox, 1995).

1. I am indebted to the "Annotated Old Testament Bibliography" of Drs. M. Daniel Carroll R. and Richard Hess (*Denver Journal* 5, no. 0101 [2002]) for several of the suggestions here.

2. Dearman, Andrew. *Religion and Culture in Ancient Israel* (Hendrickson, 1992).
3. de Moor, Jacobus. *The Rise of Yahwism* (Peeters, 1990). Important monotheistic perspective.
4. Edelman, Diana. *The Triumph of Elohim* (Eerdmans, 1995).
5. Gnuse, Robert. *No Other Gods* (Sheffield Academic Press, 1997).
6. Grabbe, Lester. *Priests, Prophets, Diviners, Sages* (Trinity Press International, 1995).
7. Henshaw, Richard. *Female and Male: The Cultic Personnel* (Pickwick, 1994).
8. **Keel, Othmar, and Christoph Uehlinger. *Gods, Goddesses, and Images of God in Ancient Israel* (Fortress, 1998).** Archaeological evidence.
9. Mettinger, Tryggve. *No Graven Image?* (Almqvist and Wiksell, 1995). ANE aniconism.
10. Miller, Patrick. *The Religion of Ancient Israel* (Westminster John Knox, 2000).
11. Niditch, Susan. *Ancient Israelite Religion* (Oxford University Press, 1997).
12. Schmidt, Brian. *Israel's Benificent Dead* (Eisenbrauns, 1995).
13. Smith, Mark. *The Origins of Biblical Monotheism* (Oxford University Press, 2001).
   ———. *The Early History of God,* 2d ed. (Eerdmans, 2002). Convergence of deities.
14. Tigay, Jeffrey. *You Shall Have No Other Gods* (Scholars, 1987). Monotheism present throughout monarchy.
15. van der Toorn, Karel. *The Image and the Book* (Peeters, 1997).
   ———. *Family Religion in Babylonia, Syria and Israel* (Brill, 1996). Ancestor worship versus monotheism.
   ———, et al., eds. *Dictionary of Deities and Demons in the Bible,* 2d ed. (Brill, 1998).
16. **Zevit, Ziony. *The Religions of Ancient Israel* (Continuum, 2001).** 1200–586 B.C.

6

ANCIENT NEAR EASTERN HISTORY

General References

1. **Bienkowski, Piotr, and Alan Millard, eds. *Dictionary of the Ancient Near East* (University of Pennsylvania, 2000).** Ancient–539 B.C.
2. Bosworth, A. *Conquest and Empire: The Reign of Alexander the Great* (Cambridge University Press, 1988).
3. Daviau, Michèle, et al., eds. *The World of the Arameans,* 2 vols. (Sheffield Academic Press, 2001).
4. Finley, Moses. *Economy and Society in Ancient Greece* (Penguin, 1983).
5. Frankfort, Henri. *The Art and Architecture of the Ancient Orient,* 5th ed. (Yale University Press, 1996).
6. Gordon, Cyrus, and Gary Rendsburg. *The Bible and the Ancient Near East,* 4th ed. (Norton, 1997).
7. **Hallo, William, and William Simpson. *The Ancient Near East,* 2d ed. (Harcourt Brace, 1998).**
8. **Hillard, T., et al., eds. *Ancient History in a Modern University,* vol. 1 (Eerdmans, 1997).**
9. **Hoerth, Alfred, Gerald Mattingly, and Edwin Yamauchi, eds. *Peoples of the Old Testament World* (Baker, 1994).**
10. Kuhrt, Amelie. *The Ancient Near East: 3000–300 b.c.,* 2 vols. (Routledge, 1995).
11. Lipinski, Edward. *The Arameans* (Peeters, 2000).
12. Pitard, Wayne. *Ancient Damascus* (Eisenbrauns, 1987).

13. **Sasson, Jack, ed. *Civilizations of the Ancient Near East,* 4 vols. (Hendrickson, 2001).**
14. Snell, Daniel. *Life in the Ancient Near East* (Yale University Press, 1997).
15. **von Soden, Wolfram. *The Ancient Orient* (Eerdmans, 1994).**
16. **Wiseman, Donald, ed. *People of Old Testament Times* (Oxford University Press, 1973).**

Babylon, Mesopotamia, and Sumeria

1. **Bottero, Jean. *Mesopotamia* (The University of Chicago Press, 1992).**
2. **Chavalas, Mark, and Lawson Younger, eds. *Mesopotamia and the Bible* (Baker, 2002).**
3. Crawford, Harriet. *Sumer and the Sumerians (*Cambridge University Press, 1991).
4. Dalley, Stephanie, ed. *The Legacy of Mesopotamia* (Oxford University Press, 1997). Spread of culture through literature to Palestine, Egypt, and Greece.
5. Gurney, O. *The Hittites* (Penguin, 1990).
6. Kramer, Samuel. *The Sumerians* (The University of Chicago Press, 1963).
7. Michalowski, P. *Letters from Early Mesopotamia* (Scholars, 1993).
8. **Nemet-Nejat, Karen. *Daily Life in Ancient Mesopotamia* (Hendrickson, 2002).**
9. **Oates, Joan. *Babylon,* rev. ed. (Thames and Hudson, 1986).**
10. **Oppenheim, Leo. *Ancient Mesopotamia,* rev. ed. (The University of Chicago Press, 1977).**
11. Postgate, J. *Early Mesopotamia* (Routledge, 1992).
12. Pollock, S. *Ancient Mesopotamia* (Cambridge University Press, 1999). Introductory.
13. Roux, George. *Ancient Iraq,* 3d ed. (Penguin, 1992).
14. **Saggs, H. *The Greatness That Was Babylon,* rev. ed. (St. Martin's, 1988).**

    ———. *The Might That Was Assyria* (St. Martin's, 1990).

15. **Wiseman, Donald. *Nebuchadnezzar and Babylon* (Oxford University Press, 1985).**
16. Van DeMieroop, Marc. *The Ancient Mesopotamian City* (Oxford University Press, 1998).

Egypt

1. **Aldred, Cyril. *The Egyptians,* 3d ed. (Thames and Hudson, 1998).**
2. **Aling, Charles. *Egypt and Bible History: From Earliest Times to 1000 b.c.* (Baker, 1981).**
3. Baines, John, and Jaromir Malek. *Cultural Atlas of Ancient Egypt,* rev. ed. (Checkmark Books, 2000).
4. Bierbrier, Morris. *Historical Dictionary of Ancient Egypt* (Scarecrow, 1999).
5. Bowman, A. *Egypt after the Ptolemies* (University of California, 1986). 332 B.C.–A.D. 642.
6. **Currid, John. *Ancient Egypt and the Old Testament* (Baker, 1997).**
7. Davies, Gordon. *Israel in Egypt* (Sheffield Academic Press, 1992).
8. Emery, Walter. *Archaic Egypt* (Penguin, 1987).
9. Fagan, Brian. *The Rape of the Nile* (Moyer Bell, 1992).
10. Grimal, Nicolas. *A History of Ancient Egypt* (Blackwell, 1992).
11. **Kemp, Barry. *Ancient Egypt,* 2d ed. (Routledge, 1992).**
12. Kitchen, Kenneth. *Pharaoh Triumphant* (Aris and Phillips, 1982). Rameses II.
13. Manley, Bill, ed. *The Penguin Historical Atlas of Ancient Egypt* (Penguin, 1996).
14. Murnane, W. *The Penguin Guide to Ancient Egypt,* 2d ed. (Penguin, 1996).
15. **Rainey, A., ed. *Egypt, Israel, Sinai* (Tel Aviv University Press, 1987).**
16. **Redford, Donald. *Egypt, Canaan, and Israel in Ancient Times* (Princeton University Press, 1992).**

    ———, ed. *The Oxford Encyclopedia of Ancient Egypt,* 3 vols. (Oxford University Press, 2000).

17. Robins, Gay. *Women in Ancient Egypt* (Harvard University Press, 1993).
18. Shafer, Byron, ed. *Religion in Ancient Egypt* (Cornell University Press, 1991).
19. Hoffmeier, James. *Israel in Egypt* (Oxford University Press, 1997).

Persia

1. **Briant, Pierre. *From Cyrus to Alexander,* E. T. (Eisenbrauns, 2002).**
2. Cook, John. *The Persian Empire* (Schocken, 1983).
3. Wieserhofer, A. *Ancient Persia from 550 b.c. to a.d. 650* (St. Martin's, 1998).
4. **Yamauchi, Edwin. *Persia and the Bible* (Baker, 1990).**

Philistines

1. **Bierling, Neal. *Giving Goliath His Due* (Baker, 1992).**
2. **Dothan, Trude, and Moshe Dothan. *People of the Sea* (Macmillan, 1992).**
3. Ehrlich, C. *The Philistines in Tradition* (Brill, 1996).
4. Gitin, Seymour, Amihai Mazar, and Ephraim Stern, eds. *Mediterranean Peoples in Transition* (IES, 1998).
5. Margalith, O. *The Sea Peoples in the Bible* (Harrassowitz, 1994).
6. **Sanders, N. *The Sea Peoples* (Thames and Hudson, 1978).**

Ugaritic Studies

1. **Smith, Mark. *Untold Stories* (Hendrickson, 2001).** Ugaritic studies.
2. Watson, W., and Nicolas Wyatt. *Handbook of Ugaritic Studies* (Brill, 1999). Study of archaeology, socioreligious background, and texts.
3. Yon, M. *The City of Ugarit at Tell Ras Shamra* (Eisenbrauns, 1999).

7 NEW TESTAMENT INTRODUCTION, SURVEY, AND THEOLOGY

New Testament Introduction*

1. Carson, D. A., Douglas Moo, and Leon Morris. *An Introduction to the New Testament* (Zondervan, 1992).
2. **Guthrie, Donald. *New Testament Introduction*, 4th ed. (IVP, 1990).**
3. **McDonald, Lee, and Stanley Porter. *Early Christianity and Its Sacred Literature* (Hendrickson, 2000).**[1]

New Testament Survey

1. Achtemeier, Paul, Joel Green, and Marianne Meye Thompson. *Introducing the New Testament* (Eerdmans, 2001).

---

* Forthcoming: Carson, Moo, and Morris (revision).

1. Porter and McDonald manage to engage the scope of issues pertaining to authorship, date, basic characteristics, and message, etc., with admirable clarity and an irenic manner. It begins with sections on critical approaches to NT interpretation; the Jewish and Greco-Roman background of early Christianity; an extended (175 pages) treatment of the historical Jesus (Porter); a section on the emergence of the church; the introduction proper; and final sections on language, text, transmission, and canon. Throughout the introduction proper, in particular, Porter, calling on his expertise in rhetoric and discourse analysis, does significant justice to literary questions. McDonald firmly establishes the original history of the NT as a collection of documents. If I have any reservations, McDonald and Porter's treatment really doesn't enter the arena of biblical theology, which it never promised to do in the first place.

2. **Elwell, Walter, and Robert Yarbrough. *Encountering the New Testament* (Baker, 1998).** Includes multimedia, interactive CD-ROM (for companion reader, *see* Primary Sources).
3. Gundry, Robert. *A Survey of the New Testament,* 3d ed. (Zondervan, 1994).
4. Lea, Thomas. *The New Testament* (Broadman & Holman, 1996).

Advanced Survey

1. **Blomberg, Craig. *Jesus and the Gospels* (Broadman & Holman, 1997).**
2. Charles, Daryl, Kendall Easley, and Terry Wilder, *Introduction to Hebrews, the General Epistles, and Revelation* (Broadman & Holman, 2002).
3. **Marshall, I. Howard, Stephen Travis, and Ian Paul. *Exploring the New Testament,* vol. 2 (IVP, 2002).** Paul's epistles through Revelation.
4. **Polhill, John. *Paul and His Letters* (Broadman & Holman, 1999).**
5. Smith, Colin. *Unfolding the Bible Story,* vols. 3–4 (Moody, 2002).[2]
6. Wenham, David, and Steve Walton. *Exploring the New Testament,* vol. 1 (IVP, 2001). Gospels and Acts.

Critical Introduction

1. **Brown, Raymond E. *Introduction to the New Testament,* ABRL (Doubleday, 1997).** Massive.
2. Brown, Schuyler. *The Origins of Christianity: A Historical Introduction to the New Testament,* rev. ed. (Oxford University Press, 1993).
3. Childs, Brevard. *The New Testament as Canon: An Introduction,* rev. ed. (Trinity Press International, 1994). History of research.

2. The first two volumes of this set cover the OT.

4. Drane, John. *Introducing the New Testament,* rev. ed. (Fortress, 2001). Survey.
5. **Ehrman, Bart. *The New Testament: A Historical Introduction to the Early Christian Writings,* 2d ed. (Oxford University Press, 1999).** Advanced college level (for companion reader *see* Primary Sources).
6. **Johnson, Luke. *The Writings of the New Testament: An Interpretation,* rev. ed. (Fortress, 1999).** With CD-ROM.
7. Kee, Howard. *Understanding the New Testament,* 5th ed. (Prentice-Hall, 1993). Especially gospels, socioliterary context.
8. Koester, Helmut. *Introduction to the New Testament,* 2d ed., 2 vols. (de Gruyter, 1995–2000). Especially Hellenistic background.
9. Kümmel, W. *Introduction to the New Testament,* rev. and enl. (Abingdon, 1986).
10. Perkins, Pheme. *Reading the New Testament: An Introduction,* rev. ed. (Paulist, 1988).
11. Powell, Mark. *Fortress Introduction to the Gospels* (Fortress, 1997).
12. Reddish, Mitchell. *An Introduction to the Gospels* (Abingdon, 1997). College level, including noncanonical writings, historical Jesus.
13. Schnelle, Udo. *The History and Theology of New Testament Writings* (Fortress, 1998). Kümmel replacement.

New Testament Theology

1. Adam, A. *Making Sense of New Testament Theology* (Mercer University Press, 1995).
2. Balla, Peter. *Challenges to New Testament Theology* (Mohr, 1997; Hendrickson, 1998).
3. Caird, G. B. *New Testament Theology* (Oxford University Press, 1996).
4. **Goppelt, Leonard. *Theology of the New Testament,* 2 vols. (Eerdmans, 1981–83).** Salvation history.
5. **Guthrie, Donald. *New Testament Theology* (IVP, 1981).**

6. **Ladd, George. *A Theology of the New Testament,* 2d ed. (Eerdmans, 1993).**
7. Räisänen, Heikki. *Beyond New Testament Theology,* 2d ed. (SCM, 2000).
8. Schlatter, Adolf. *New Testament Theology,* 2 vols. (Baker, 1999).
9. *See* OT Introduction, Survey, and Theology: Biblical Theologies of Both Testaments.
10. Strecker, Georg. *Theology of the New Testament* (Westminster John Knox, 2001). From German (1994).
11. **Wright, N. T. *Christian Origins and the Question of God,* 5 vols. (Fortress, 1992–).**

Pauline Theology

1. **Barrett, C. K. *Paul* (Westminster John Knox, 1994).** Introduction.
2. Bassler, Jouette, David Hay, and Elizabeth Johnson, eds. *Pauline Theology,* 3 vols. (Fortress, 1991–95). Critical.
3. **Bruce, F. F. *Paul* (Eerdmans, 1977).**
4. Carter, T. *Paul and the Power of Sin* (Cambridge University Press, 2002).
5. **Dunn, James. *The Theology of Paul the Apostle* (Eerdmans, 1998).**
6. **Fitzmyer, Joseph. *According to Paul* (Paulist, 1993).**
7. **Gathercole, Simon. *Where Is Boasting?* (Eerdmans, 2002).** Romans 1–5.
8. Hubbard, Moyer. *New Creation of Paul's Letters and Thought* (Cambridge University Press, 2002).
9. Lovering, Eugene, and Jerry Sumney, eds. *Theology and Ethics in Paul and His Interpreters* (Abingdon, 1996).
10. Martyn, J. Louis. *Theological Issues in the Letters of Paul* (Abingdon, 1997).
11. Pate, Marvin. *The End of the Age Has Come* (Zondervan, 1995).
12. Reymond, Robert. *Paul* (Christian Focus, 2000).
13. **Ridderbos, Herman. *Paul* (Eerdmans, 1997).**
14. **Schreiner, Thomas. *Paul, Apostle of God's Glory in Christ* (IVP, 2001).**

15. Strom, Mark. *Reframing Paul* (IVP, 2000).
16. White, John. *Apostle of God* (Hendrickson, 1999).
17. Wiles, Virginia. *Making Sense of Paul* (Hendrickson, 2000). Introduction.

Paul and the Law

1. Bell, Richard. *No One Seeks for God* (Mohr, 1998).
2. Boers, Hendrikus. *The Justification of the Gentiles* (Hendrickson, 1994). Galatians and Romans, discourse analysis, semiotics.
3. **Carson, D. A., Peter O'Brien, and Mark Seifrid, eds. *Justification and Variegated Nomism,* 2 vols. (Mohr/Baker, 2001–02).** Response to Sanders.
4. **Cummins, Stephen. *Paul and the Crucified Christ in Antioch* (Cambridge University Press, 2001).** Both Judaizers and Paul influenced by ideals of Maccabean martyrdom.
5. Das, Andrew. *Paul, the Law, and the Covenant* (Hendrickson, 2001).
6. Donaldson, Terence. *Paul and the Gentiles* (Fortress, 1997).
7. Dunn, James. *Jesus, Paul, and the Law: Studies in Mark and Galatians* (Westminster John Knox, 1990).
   ———, ed. *Paul and the Mosaic Law* (Eerdmans, 2001).
8. Eastman, Brad. *The Significance of Grace in the Letters of Paul* (Lang, 1999).
9. Goulder, Michael. *Paul and the Competing Mission in Corinth* (Hendrickson, 2001). Two-mission theory.
10. Kim, Seyoon. *Paul and the New Perspective* (Eerdmans, 2001). Rebuttal of Sanders.
11. Koperski, Veronica. *What Are They Saying About Paul and the Law?* (Paulist, 2001).
12. **Kruse, Colin. *Paul, the Law, and Justification* (Hendrickson, 1997).** Recent debate.
13. Laato, Timo. *Paul and Judaism* (Scholars, 1995).
14. Moore, Richard. *The Doctrine of "Justification" in Paul* (Mellen, 2002).
15. Pate, Marvin. *The Reverse of the Curse* (Mohr, 2000). Wisdom as reverse of Deuteronomic blessings and curses.

16. Rapa, Robert. *The Meaning of "Works of the Law" in Galatians and Romans* (Lang, 2001).
17. **Sanders, E. P. *Paul, the Law, and the Jewish People* (Fortress, 1983).**
    ———. *Paul and Palestinian Judaism* (Fortress, 1977). Law = covenant keeping.
18. **Schreiner, Thomas. *The Law and Its Fulfillment* (Baker, 1993).**
19. Seifrid, Mark. *Justification by Faith* (Brill, 1992).
20. Stuhlmacher, Peter. *Revisiting Paul's Doctrine of Justification* (IVP, 2001).
21. **Thielman, Frank. *Paul and the Law* (IVP, 1994).** Rebuttal of Dunn, Sanders.
    ———. *The Law and the New Testament,* CCNT (Herder and Herder, 1999). Introduction, includes Gospels and Acts.
22. Tomson, Paul. *Paul and the Jewish Law* (Van Gorcum/Fortress, 1990).
23. Westerholm, Stephen. *Israel's Law and the Church's Faith* (Eerdmans, 1988).
24. Young, Brad. *Paul the Jewish Theologian* (Hendrickson, 1997).

8

JESUS AND THE GOSPELS

Synoptics

1. Barr, Allan. *A Diagram of Synoptic Relationships* (T & T Clark, 1938).
2. **Bellinzoni, Arthur, ed. *The Two-Source Hypothesis* (Mercer University Press, 1985).**
3. **Black, David, and David Beck, eds. *Rethinking the Synoptic Problem* (Baker, 2001).** McKnight, Farmer, Osborne, Blomberg, and Bock (Q).
4. Davies, Margaret, and E.P. Sanders, eds. *Studying the Synoptic Gospels* (Trinity Press International, 1989).
5. Fleddermann, H. *Mark and Q* (Leuven University Press, 1995).
6. **Goodacre, Mark. *The Synoptic Problem* (Sheffield Academic Press, 2001).**

   ———. *Goulder and the Gospels* (Sheffield Academic Press, 1996).
7. Head, Peter. *Christology and the Synoptic Problem* (Cambridge University Press, 1997).
8. Johnson, Sherman. *The Griesbach Hypothesis and Redaction Criticism* (Scholars, 1991).
9. Knight, George W. *A Simplified Harmony of the Gospels* (Holman Bible Publishers, 2001). Sequential HCSB.
10. **Koester, Helmut. *Ancient Christian Gospels* (Trinity Press International, 1990).** Including Q.
11. Linnemann, Eta. *Is There a Synoptic Problem?* (Baker, 1992).

12. **McKnight, Scot. *Interpreting the Synoptic Gospels* (Baker, 1988).**
13. **Neville, David. *Arguments from Order in Synoptic Source Criticism* (Mercer University Press, 1994).**
    ———. *Mark's Gospel Prior or Posterior?* (Sheffield Academic Press, 2002).
14. New, David. *Old Testament Quotations in the Synoptic Gospels and the Two-Document Hypothesis* (Scholars, 1993).
15. Orton, David, ed. *The Synoptic Problem and Q* (Brill, 1999).
16. Paffenroth, Kim. *The Story of Jesus According to L* (Sheffield Academic Press, 1997).
17. **Stein, Robert. *Studying the Synoptic Gospels,* 2d ed. (Baker, 2001).**
18. Theissen, Gerd. *The Gospels in Context* (Fortress, 1991).
19. **Thomas, Robert, ed. *Three Views on the Origins of the Synoptic Gospels* (Kregel, 2002).**
20. **Tuckett, Christopher. *The Revival of the Griesbach Hypothesis* (Cambridge University Press, 1983).**

Synoptic Problem
(Matthean Priority)

1. **Black, David. *Why Four Gospels?* (Kregel, 2001).** Provides alternative to Oxford-Griesbach debate.
2. Dungan, David. *A History of the Synoptic Problem,* ABRL (Doubleday, 1999). Assumes anti-Semitism in Markan priority and NA text.
3. Farmer, William. *The Gospel of Jesus* (Westminster John Knox, 1994).
4. McNicol, Allan. *Jesus' Direction for the Future* (Mercer University Press, 1996). Examination of Paul/Jesus eschatological tradition.
5. **McNicol, Allen, David Dungan, and David Peabody, eds. *Beyond the Q Impasse* (Trinity Press International, 1996).**
6. Neirynck, Frans. *The Minor Agreements of Matthew and Luke Against Mark with a Cumulative List* (Leuven University Press, 1974).

7. Neirynck, Frans, and J. Verhayden. *The Gospel of Matthew and Sayings Source Q: A Cumulative Bibliography,* 2 vols. (Leuven University Press, 1998).
8. Orchard, Bernard, and Harold Riley. *The Order of the Synoptics* (Mercer University Press, 1987). Especially patristic evidence.
9. Peabody, David, ed. *One Gospel from Two: Mark's Use of Matthew and Luke*(Trinity Press International, 2001).
10. Wenham, John. *Redating Matthew, Mark, and Luke* (IVP, 1992). Suggests essential independence with Matthew as earliest gospel based on patristic evidence.

Source Q

1. Allison, Dale. *The Jesus Tradition in Q* (Trinity Press International, 1997).
———. *The Intertextual Jesus* (Trinity Press International, 2000).
2. Borg, Marcus, ed. *The Lost Gospel Q* (Ulysses, 1996).
3. Catchpole, David. *The Quest for Q* (T & T Clark, 1993).
4. Goodacre, Mark. *The Case Against Q* (Trinity Press International, 2001). Advocates Markan priority and the lack of necessity for Q.
5. Horsley, Richard, and Jonathan Draper. *Whoever Hears You Hears Me* (Trinity Press International, 1999).
6. Jacobson, A. *The First Gospel* (Polebridge, 1992).
7. Kloppenborg, John. *Q Parallels* (Polebridge, 1988).
———. *The Formation of Q* (Fortress, 1987).
———, ed. *The Shape of Q* (Fortress, 1994).
———, ed. *Conflict and Invention* (Trinity Press International, 1995).
———. *Excavating Q* (Fortress, 2000).
8. Mack, Burton. *The Lost Gospel: The Book of Q & Christian Origins* (HarperSanFrancisco, 1993). Jesus as Cynic sage.
9. Meadors, Edward. *Jesus the Messianic Herald of Salvation* (Hendrickson, 1997). Q rebuttal.

10. **Piper, R., ed. *The Gospel Behind the Gospels* (Brill, 1995).**
11. **Robinson, James, John Kloppenborg, and Paul Hoffman. *Critical Edition of Q,* Hermeneia (Fortress, 2000).** Synopsis, including Mark, Luke, and Thomas.
12. **Tuckett, Christopher. *Q and the History of Earliest Christianity* (Hendrickson, 1996).** Wisdom sayings, Cynic influence.
13. Vaage, Leif. *Galilean Upstarts* (Trinity Press International, 1994). Q as Cynic document.

Conservative Historical Jesus

1. Barnett, Paul. *Jesus and the Logic of History* (Eerdmans, 1998).
2. **Bock, Darrell. *Studying The Historical Jesus* (Baker, 2002).** Introduction.[1]

   ———. *Jesus According to Scripture* (Baker, 2002).
3. **Bockmuehl, Markus. *This Jesus: Martyr, Lord, Messiah* (IVP, 1996).**

   ———, ed. *The Cambridge Companion to Jesus* (Cambridge University Press, 2001).
4. Boice, J. M., and Philip Ryken. *Jesus on Trial* (Crossway, 2002).
5. Bryan, Steven. *Jesus and Israel's Tradition of Judgment and Restoration* (Cambridge University Press, 2002).
6. Burridge, Richard. *Four Gospels, One Jesus?* (Eerdmans, 1994).
7. Chilton, David, and Craig Evans. *Jesus in Context* (Brill, 1997).

---

1. Darrell Bock's *Studying the Historical Jesus* is divided into two parts, the first part providing the historical and cultural background to Jesus and the second part delving into the various criticisms. *Jesus According to Scripture* (Baker, 2002), an attempt to lay out the scriptural portrait of Jesus, is divided into three parts. The first part interacts with the portrait of Jesus as portrayed in the Synoptic Gospels (following the argument as would a synopsis). The second part describes the portrait of Jesus that emerges in the gospel of John. The third part, the principal focus of the book, addresses the major theological themes that continue to appear throughout the Gospels.

8. Copan, Paul, ed. *Will the Real Jesus Please Stand Up?* (Baker, 1998). Debate between Craig and Crossan.
9. Copan, Paul, and Ronald Tacelli, eds. *Jesus' Resurrection* (IVP, 2000). Craig versus Lüdemann debate.
10. Evans, Craig. *The Historical Christ and the Jesus of Faith* (Clarendon, 1996).
———. *Jesus and His Contemporaries* (Brill, 1995).
11. Evans, Craig, and Stanley Porter, eds. *The Historical Jesus* (Sheffield Academic Press, 1995). Annotated bibliography.
12. Green, Joel, and Max Turner, eds. *Jesus of Nazareth* (Eerdmans, 1994).
13. McKnight, Scot. *A New Vision for Israel* (Eerdmans, 1999).
14. Stein, Robert. *Jesus The Messiah* (IVP, 1996).
15. Thomas, Robert. *Charts of the Life of Christ* (Zondervan, 2000).
16. Twelftree, Graham. *Jesus the Exorcist* (Hendrickson, 1995).
———. *Jesus the Miracle Worker* (IVP, 1999).
17. Van Voorst, Robert. *Jesus Outside the New Testament* (Eerdmans, 2000).
18. Witherington, Ben. *Jesus the Sage* (Fortress, 1994).
———. *The Many Faces of the Christ,* CCNT (Crossroad, 1998).
———. *Jesus the Seer* (Hendrickson, 1999).
19. Wright, N. T. *Who Was Jesus?* (Eerdmans, 1993).
———. *The Original Jesus* (Eerdmans, 1996).
———. *The Challenge of Jesus* (IVP, 1999).
———. *The Contemporary Quest for Jesus* (Fortress, 2002). Booklet.

Critical Historical Jesus

1. Allison, Dale. *Jesus of Nazareth* (Fortress, 1998).
2. Bellinger, William, and William Farmer, eds. *Jesus and the Suffering Servant* (Trinity Press International, 1998). Isaiah 53 influence.
3. Charlesworth, James, ed. *The Messiah* (Fortress, 1992).
4. Dawes, Gregory, ed. *The Historical Jesus Question* (Westminster John Knox, 2001).

———, ed. *The Historical Jesus Quest* (Westminster John Knox, 2000).

5. denHeyer, Christian. *Jesus Matters: 150 Years of Research* (Trinity Press International, 1997).
6. Ehrman, Bart. *Jesus, Apocalyptic Prophet of the New Millennium* (Oxford University Press, 1999). Believes that Jesus was convinced that a new kingdom would be created on earth.
7. **Freyne, Sean. *Galilee, Jesus, and the Gospels* (Fortress, 1998).**
8. **Gnilka, Joachim. *Jesus of Nazareth* (Hendrickson, 1997).**
9. Hengel, Martin. *Studies in Early Christology* (T & T Clark, 1995).
10. Horsley, Richard. *Sociology and the Jesus Movement,* rev. ed. (Continuum, 1993).
11. Horsley, Richard, and Neil Silberman. *The Message and the Kingdom* (Grossett/Putnam, 1997). Jesus and Paul.
12. Keck, Leander. *Who Is Jesus?* (University of South Carolina, 2000; Fortress, 2001).
13. **Loader, William. *Jesus' Attitude Towards the Law* (Eerdmans, 2002).** Gospel study.
14. **Meier, John. *A Marginal Jew,* 3 vols. (Doubleday, 1991, 1994, 2001).**
15. **Meyer, Ben. *The Aims of Jesus* (SCM, 1979).**
16. Patterson, Stephen. *The God of Jesus* (Trinity Press International, 1998).
17. Powell, Mark. *Jesus as a Figure in History* (Westminster John Knox, 1998).
18. Powell, Mark, and David Bauer, eds. *Who Do You Say That I Am?* (Westminster John Knox, 1999).
19. Reed, Jonathan. *Archaeology and the Galilean Jesus* (Trinity Press International, 2002).
20. **Sanders, E. P. *Jesus and Judaism* (Fortress, 1985).**
21. Schnackenburg, Rudolf. *Jesus in the Gospels* (Westminster John Knox, 1995).
22. **Stanton, Graham. *Gospel Truth?* (Trinity Press International, 1995).** Rebuttal to Thiede.

———. *The Gospels and Jesus,* 2d ed. (Oxford University Press, 2001).

23. Theissen, Gerd, and Annette Merz. *The Historical Jesus* (Fortress, 1998).
24. **Vermes, Geza. *Jesus the Jew* (Fortress, 1973).**
    ———. *The Changing Faces of Jesus,* 1st American ed. (Viking Compass, 2001).
25. **Weaver, Walter. *The Historical Jesus in the Twentieth Century,* 3 vols. (Trinity Press International, 1999–).**

Jesus Seminar

1. Armstrong, Donald, ed. *The Truth About Jesus* (Eerdmans, 1998).
2. Borg, Marcus. *Jesus in Contemporary Scholarship* (Trinity Press International, 1994).
   ———. *Conflict, Holiness, and Politics in the Teachings of Jesus,* rev. ed. (Trinity Press International, 1998).
3. **Borg, Marcus, and N. T. Wright. *The Meaning of Jesus* (HarperSanFrancisco, 1999).**
4. Boyd, Gregory. *Cynic Sage or Son of God?* (Baker, 1995). Response to Jesus Seminar.
5. Chilton, David, and Craig Evans, eds. *Studying the Historic Jesus* (Brill, 1994).
6. Crossan, John. *The Historical Jesus* (HarperCollins, 1991).
   ———. *After the Crucifixion* (HarperSanFrancisco, 1996).
   ———. *Who Killed Jesus?* (HarperSanFrancisco, 1995). Popular response to Raymond Brown's *Death of the Messiah.*
   ———. *Excavating Jesus* (HarperSanFrancisco, 2002).
7. Downing, Gerald. *Christ and the Cynics* (Sheffield Academic Press, 1988).
8. Funk, Robert, and Roy Hoover. *The Five Gospels* (Macmillan, 1993).
9. Horsley, Richard, and John Hanson. *Bandits, Prophets, and Messiahs* (Winston, 1987).
10. Jenkins, Philip. *Hidden Gospels* (Oxford University Press, 2001). Extracanonicals written late.

11. **Johnson, Luke. *The Real Jesus* (HarperSanFrancisco, 1996).** Seminar critique.
12. Mack, Burton. *Who Wrote the New Testament?* (Harper-SanFrancisco, 1995).
13. Newman, Carey, ed. *Jesus and the Restoration of Israel* (IVP, 1999). Assessment of Wright (see below).
14. Radner, Ephraim, and George Sumner, eds. *The Rule of Faith* (Morehouse, 1997).
15. Sanders, E. P. *The Historical Figure of Jesus* (Penguin, 1993). Popular alternative view to Jesus Seminar.
16. **Strimple, Robert. *The Modern Search for the Real Jesus* (Presbyterian & Reformed, 1995).** Evangelical response to the Jesus Seminar.
17. Thomas, Robert, and David Farnell, eds. *The Jesus Crisis* (Kregel, 1998).
18. **Wilkins, Michael, and James Moreland, eds. *Jesus Under Fire* (Zondervan, 1995).** Response to Jesus Seminar.
19. **Witherington, Ben. *The Jesus Quest,* 2d ed. (IVP, 1997).**
20. **Wright, N. T. *Christian Origins and the Question of God* (Fortress, 1997).**
21. **Wright, N. T. *Jesus and the Victory of God* (Fortress, 1997).**

9 NEW TESTAMENT COMMENTARIES

Matthew*

Technical, Semitechnical

L/Cr 1. Boring, Eugene. NIB, vol. 8 (Abingdon, 1995). Dates between A.D. 80–100.

E 2. Carson, D. A. EBC, vol. 8 (Zondervan, 1984).

C/M 3. Davies, W. D., and Dale Allison. ICC, 3 vols. (T & T Clark, 1988–97). Jewish, extrabiblical background.

C/M 4. Gundry, Robert. *Matthew,* 2d ed. (Eerdmans, 1994). Redactional, literary background.

E/Cr 5. Hagner, Donald. WBC, 2 vols. (Word, 1993–95).

L/Cr 6. Harrington, Daniel. Sacra Pagina (Liturgical, 1991). Jewish background.

L/Cr 7. Hill, David. NCBC (Eerdmans, 1981).

E 8. Keener, Craig. *A Commentary on the Gospel of Matthew* (Eerdmans, 1999). Sociohistorical context. More than ten thousand references to primary sources and more than two thousand to secondary literature in a volume with 720 pages of commentary, 150 pages of bibliography, and almost 170 pages of indices.

---

* Forthcoming: John Nolland, NIGTC (Eerdmans); Richard France, NICNT (Eerdmans); David Turner, BECNT (Baker); Jack Kingsbury, ECC; Clifton Black, NTL (Westminster John Knox); and Michael Wilkins, NIVAC (Zondervan). If Nolland's Greek commentary is like his three-volume work on Luke, it will provide a thoroughgoing display of interpretative options, which tends to obscure his own judgments. Perhaps his Matthew will rectify this tendency. France and Turner should prove compelling alternatives to Hagner and Keener.

L/Cr 9. Luz, Ulrich. Hermeneia, 3 vols. (Fortress, 1992–). Volume 1 under revision, redaction critical, history of interpretation.

E/Cr 10. Schnackenburg, Rudolf. *The Gospel of Matthew* (Eerdmans, 2002). Brief.

Exposition

E 1. Blomberg, Craig. NAC (Broadman & Holman, 1992).

E/Cr 2. France, Richard. TOTC (Eerdmans, 1988).

E 3. Green, Michael. BST (IVP, 2001).

E 4. Keener, Craig. IVPNTC (IVP, 1997).

E 5. Morris, Leon. Pillar (Eerdmans, 1992).

E 6. Mounce, Robert. NIBCNT (Hendrickson, 1991).

L/Cr 7. Overman, Andrew. *Church and Community in Crisis,* NTC (Trinity Press International, 1996).

L/Cr 8. Senior, Donald. ANTC (Abingdon, 1998).

Sermon on the Mount

C/M 1. Allison, Dale. CCNT (Crossroad, 1999). Introduction.
———. *The Jesus Tradition in Q* (Trinity Press International, 1997). Includes critique of Betz.

L/Cr 2. Betz, Hans. *The Sermon on the Mount,* Hermeneia (Fortress, 1995). Especially Hellenistic Jewish, Greco-Roman background.

L/Cr 3. Carter, Warren. *What Are They Saying About Matthew's Sermon on the Mount?* (Paulist, 1994).

E/Cr 4. Guelich, Robert. *The Sermon on the Mount* (Word, 1982).

E 5. Hughes, R. Kent. *The Sermon on the Mount* (Crossway, 2001).

L/Cr 6. Patte, Daniel. *Discipleship According to the Sermon on the Mount* (Trinity Press International, 1996). Strecker, Kingsbury (historical), Edwards (narrative), Luz, Davies, and Allison (figurative) and Patte (thematic).
———. *The Challenge of Discipleship* (Trinity Press International, 1999).

E 7. Stott, John. *The Message of the Sermon on the Mount,* BST (IVP, 1978).

L/Cr 8. Strecker, Georg. *The Sermon on the Mount* (Abingdon, 1988).

L/Cr 9. Worth, Roland. *The Sermon on the Mount* (Paulist, 1997). Law validation.

Matthew as Story

E 1. Bauer, David. *The Structure of Matthew's Gospel* (Almond, 1988).

E-L/Cr 2. Bauer, David, and Mark Powell, eds. *Treasures New and Old* (Scholars, 1996).

L/Cr 3. Carter, Warren. *Matthew* (Hendrickson, 1996). Reader-response, narrative-critical counterpart to France.

E/Cr 4. France, Richard. *Matthew: Evangelist and Teacher* (Zondervan, 1990; IVP, 1998).

E 5. Garland, David. *Reading Matthew* (Crossroad, 1993). Literary, theological commentary.

L/Cr 6. Howell, David. *Matthew's Inclusive Story* (Sheffield Academic Press, 1990).

L/Cr 7. Kingsbury, Jack. *Matthew as Story,* 2d ed. (Fortress, 1988).

Special Studies

L/Cr 1. Aune, David, ed. *The Gospel of Matthew in Current Study* (Eerdmans, 2000).

L/Cr 2. Balch, David, ed. *Social History of the Matthean Community* (Fortress, 1991).

L/Cr 3. Brown, Raymond E. *Death of the Messiah,* ABRL, 2 vols. (Doubleday, 1994). Passion narratives.[1]

———. *Birth of the Messiah,* ABRL, rev. ed. (Doubleday, 1993). Nativities.

1. The now-deceased Catholic scholar Raymond E. Brown is to be distinguished from the conservative Raymond Brown (author of BST entries on Numbers, Deuteronomy, Nehemiah, and Hebrews).

E 4. Gibbs, Jeffery. *Jerusalem and Parousia* (Concordia Academic Press, 2000). Eschatological Discourse.

L/Cr 5. Luz, Ulrich. NTT (Cambridge University Press, 1995).
———. *Matthew in History* (Fortress, 1994).

L/Cr 6. Saldarini, Anthony. *Matthew's Christian-Jewish Community* (The University of Chicago Press, 1994).

L/Cr 7. Senior, Donald. IBT (Abingdon, 1997). Survey of modern scholarship.
———. *What Are They Saying About Matthew?* (Paulist, 1996).

C/M 8. Sim, David. *Apocalyptic Eschatology in the Gospel of Matthew* (Cambridge University Press, 1996).
———. *The Gospel of Matthew and Christian Judaism* (T & T Clark, 1998).

C/M 9. Stanton, Graham. *A Gospel for a New People* (Westminster John Knox, 1993).
———, ed. *The Interpretation of Matthew,* 2d ed. (T & T Clark, 1995).

E 10. Wilkins, Michael. *Discipleship in the Ancient World and Matthew's Gospel,* 2d ed. (Baker, 1995).

Mark*

Technical, Semitechnical

C/M 1. Cranfield, C. E. B. *The Gospel According to St. Mark* (Cambridge University Press, 1959).

L/Cr 2. Donahue, John, and Daniel Harrington. Sacra Pagina (Liturgical, 2002).

E/Cr 3. Evans, Craig. *Mark 8:27–16:20,* WBC (Thomas Nelson, 2001).

E/Cr 4. France, R. T. NIGTC (Eerdmans, 2002).

E/Cr 5. Guelich, Robert. *Mark 1:1–8:26,* WBC (Word, 1989).

* Forthcoming: Robert Stein, BECNT (Baker); Richard Horsley, NTC (Trinity); Donald Juel, NTL (Westminster John Knox); and Ron Kernaghan, IVPNTC (IVP). Purchase the three new commentaries by France and Edwards (Eerdmans) and Evans on 9–16 (Thomas Nelson). You might want to wait for Stein instead of Edwards.

E 6. **Gundry, Robert. *Mark* (Eerdmans, 1992).**

E/Cr 7. **Lane, William. NICNT (Eerdmans, 1974).**

L/Cr 8. Mann, C. AB (Doubleday, 1986). Griesbach Hypothesis.

L/Cr 9. Marcus, Joel. AB. (Doubleday, 2000). Liturgical drama.[2]

L/Cr 10. Perkins, Pheme. NIB, vol. 8 (Abingdon, 1995). Dates Mark around A.D. 70.

E 11. Witherington, Ben. *The Gospel of Mark* (Eerdmans, 2001). Sociorhetorical.

Exposition

L/Cr 1. Anderson, Hugh. NCBC (Eerdmans, 1981). Redactional, history of critical interpretation.

E 2. Brooks, James. NAC (Broadman & Holman, 1991).

E 3. Cole, R. Alan. TNTC (Eerdmans, 1989).

E/Cr 4. Edwards, James. Pillar (Eerdmans, 2001). Posits multiple, sandwiched textual interpolations (e.g., the cursing of the fig tree and the cleansing of the temple).

E 5. Garland, David. NIVAC (Zondervan, 1996).

E 6. Geddert, Timothy. BCBC (Herald, 2002).

L/Cr 7. Hare, Douglas. WBComp (Westminster John Knox, 1996). Study guide.

C/M 8. Hooker, Morna. BNTC (Hendrickson, 1993). Especially Jewish background.

E/Cr 9. Hurtado, Larry. NIBCNT (Hendrickson, 1989).

Mark as Story

L/Cr 1. Anderson, Janice, and Stephen Moore, eds. *Mark and Method* (Fortress, 1992). Five criticisms exemplified.

C/M 2. Best, Ernest. *Mark: The Gospel of Story* (T & T Clark, 1983).

---

2. You might also consider Marcus on 1–8, although he believes that John Mark *might* have written the gospel, and he tends to be skeptical about the historical Jesus. However, his commentary includes three brief appendices: "The Scribes and the Pharisees," "The Messianic Secret Motif," and "The Son of Man." The latter is particularly valuable because it traces the Son of Man development back to Daniel.

L/Cr 3. Dowd, Sharon. *Reading Mark* (Smyth and Helwys, 2000).

L/Cr 4. Fowler, Robert. *Let the Reader Understand* (Trinity Press International, 2001).

L/Cr 5. Horsley, Richard. *Hearing the Whole Story* (Westminster John Knox, 2001).

L/Cr 6. Juel, Donald. IBT (Abingdon, 1999).

L/Cr 7. Rhoads, David, J. Dewey, and Donald Michie. *Mark as Story,* 2d ed. (Fortress, 1999).

L/Cr 8. Robbins, Vernon. *Jesus the Teacher* (Fortress, 1992).

C/M 9. Telford, William, ed. *The Interpretation of Mark,* 2d ed. (T & T Clark, 1995).

L/Cr 10. Tolbert, Mary Ann. *Sowing the Gospel* (Fortress, 1989).

Special Studies

E 1. Beasley-Murray, George. *Jesus and the Last Days* (Hendrickson, 1993). Mark 13: Olivet discourse.

L/Cr 2. Black, Clifton. *Mark: Images of an Apostolic Interpreter* (Fortress, 2001).

E 3. Bock, Darrell. *Blasphemy and Exaltation in Judaism* (Baker, 2000). Mark 14:53–65.

L/Cr 4. Garrett, Susan. *The Temptations of Jesus in Mark's Gospel* (Eerdmans, 1998).

E 5. Geddert, Timothy. *Watchwords* (JSOT, 1989). Mark 13.

C/M 6. Hengel, Martin. *Studies in the Gospel of Mark* (SCM/Fortress, 1985).

L/Cr 7. Marcus, Joel. *The Way of the Lord* (Westminster John Knox, 1992). Old Testament usage.

L/Cr 8. Myers, Ched. *Binding the Strong Man* (Orbis, 1988). Liberation perspective commentary.

C/M 9. Oden, Thomas, and Christopher Hall, eds. ACCS (IVP, 1998). Patristic commentary.

L/Cr 10. Thurston, Bonnie. *Preaching Mark* (Fortress, 2002). Very informative.

E 11. Watts, Rikki. *Isaiah's New Exodus in Mark* (Mohr, 1997; Baker, 2000).

E 12. Williams, Joel. *Other Followers of Jesus: Minor Characters as Major Figures in Mark's Gospel* (Sheffield Academic Press, 1994).

Luke*

Technical, Semitechnical

E 1. Bock, Darrell. BECNT, 2 vols. (Baker, 1994–96). Reviews debated points.

L/Cr 2. Bovon, François. *Luke 1,* Hermeneia (Fortress, 2002). Luke 1:1–9:50 from 1989 German edition. Two volumes to follow through 19:27 (German editions, 1996, 2001).

C/M 3. Danker, Frederick. *Jesus and the New Age,* 2d ed. (Fortress, 1988). Especially Greco-Roman context.

L/Cr 4. Evans, C. F. NTC (Trinity Press International, 1990). Cites obscurities, difficulties.

L/Cr 5. Fitzmyer, Joseph. AB, 2 vols. (Doubleday, 1981, 1985). Especially Aramaic, tradition critical.

E/Cr 6. Green, Joel. NICNT (Eerdmans, 1997). Needs to be complemented by a standard commentary.

C/M 7. Johnson, Luke. Sacra Pagina (Liturgical, 1991). Literary background.

E/Cr 8. Marshall, Howard. NIGTC (Eerdmans, 1978). Historicity, issues concerning redaction criticism. Dense.

C/M 9. Nolland, John. WBC, 3 vols. (Word, 1989–1993).

---

* Forthcoming: François Bovon, Hermeneia, 2 vols. (Fortress); John Carroll, NTL (Westminster John Knox); and Peter Head, Pillar (Eerdmans). I would keep Bock (2 vols.) and wait for Peter Head. Bock is especially strong on historical-grammatical matters and somewhat sparse in addressing Luke as literature. Of course, this is the principal focus of Green's commentary at the expense of historical background (i.e., the relationship between Luke and the synoptics). D. A. Carson believes that Bovon is as deep exegetically and more seminal theologically than any other commentary on Luke (*New Testament Commentary Survey,* 5th ed. [Baker, 2001], 54). However, Bovon holds that Luke represents a specific form of the Pauline school in the third generation of churches, thus dating it rather late.

L/Cr 10. Tannehill, Robert. ANTC (Abingdon, 1996). Socioliterary, canonical approach.

Exposition

E 1. Bock, Darrell. NIVAC (Zondervan, 1996). Essentially an abridgement of the author's BECNT volumes.
———. IVPNTC (IVP, 1994).

C/M 2. Culpepper, R. Alan. NIB, vol. 9 (Abingdon, 1995). Dates in the mid-80's.

E/Cr 3. Ellis, E. Earle. NCBC (Eerdmans, 1974). Especially introduction, but dated.

E/Cr 4. Evans, Craig. NIBCNT (Hendrickson, 1990). Old Testament background.

E 5. Liefeld, Walter. EBC, vol. 8 (Zondervan, 1984).

E 6. Morris, Leon. TNTC (Eerdmans, 1988).

E 7. Pate, C. Marvin. *The Gospel of Luke* (Moody, 1995).

E 8. Stein, Robert. NAC (Broadman & Holman, 1993). Composition critical.

L/Cr 9. Tiede, David. ACNT (Augsburg, 1988). Especially biblical theology.

E 10. Wilcock, Michael. BST (IVP, 1984).

Theology of Luke–Acts*

E 1. Crump, David. *Jesus the Intercessor* (Baker, 1999). Prayer.

E 2. Cunningham, Scott. *Through Many Tribulations* (Sheffield Academic Press, 1997).

E/Cr 3. Doble, P. *The Paradox of Salvation* (Cambridge University Press, 1996).

L/Cr 4. Fitzmyer, Joseph. *Luke the Theologian* (Paulist, 1989).

L/Cr 5. Gillman, J. *Possessions and the Life of Faith* (Liturgical, 1991).

* Forthcoming: Beverly Gaventa, IBT (Abingdon).

E/Cr 6. Green, Joel. NTT (Cambridge University Press, 1995). Greco-Roman influence.

L/Cr 7. Moessner, David, ed. *Jesus and the Heritage of Israel* (Trinity Press International, 1999).

C/M 8. Nielsen, Aalders. *Until It Is Fulfilled* (Mohr, 2000). Rhetorical, eschatological study of Luke 22; Acts 20.

CM 9. Squires, John. *The Plan of God in Luke–Acts* (Cambridge University Press, 1993).

E 10. Strauss, Mark. *The Davidic Messiah in Luke–Acts* (Sheffield Academic Press, 1995).

L/Cr 11. Tyson, Joseph, ed. *Luke–Acts and the Jewish People* (Augsburg, 1988).

The Holy Spirit in Luke–Acts

E/Cr 1. Dunn, James. *Jesus and the Spirit* (Eerdmans, 1997).
———. *The Christ and the Spirit,* vol. 2: *Pneumatology* (Eerdmans, 1998).
———. *Baptism in the Holy Spirit* (Westminster, 1970). Rebuts baptism of the Spirit subsequent to salvation.

E 2. Ervin, Howard. *Conversion-Initiation in the Baptism in the Holy Spirit* (Hendrickson, 1984). Contra Dunn.

E 3. Pettegrew, Larry. *The New Testament Ministry of the Holy Spirit,* 2d ed. (Kregel, 2001). Cessationist.

E 4. Menzies, Robert. *Empowered for Witness* (Sheffield Academic Press, 1994).
———. *The Development of Early Christian Pneumatology with Special Reference to Luke–Acts* (Sheffield Academic Press, 1991). Gift of Spirit as prophetic endowment for special insight, inspired speech.

E 5. Shelton, James. *Mighty in Word and Deed* (Hendrickson, 1991; Wipf & Stock, 1999). Charismatic.

E/Cr 6. Shepherd, William. *The Narrative Function of the Holy Spirit as a Character in Luke–Acts* (Scholars, 1994).

E 7. Stott, John. *Baptism and Fullness,* rev. ed. (IVP, 1999).

E 8. Stronstad, Roger. *The Charismatic Theology of St. Luke* (Hendrickson, 1984).

E/Cr 9. Turner, Max. *Power from On High* (Sheffield Academic Press, 1996). Charismatic.

10. *See* Systematic Theology: The Holy Spirit and Spiritual Gifts (both Traditional and Pentecostal and Charismatic).

Special Studies

C/M 1. Alexander, Loveday. *The Preface to Luke's Gospel* (Cambridge University Press, 1993). Also Acts 1:1.

L/Cr 2. Arlandson, James. *Women, Class, and Society in Early Christianity* (Hendrickson, 1997).

L/Cr 3. Darr, John. *On Character Building* (Westminster John Knox, 1992).

L/Cr 4. Esler, Philip. *Community and Gospel in Luke–Acts* (Cambridge University Press, 1987).

E-L/Cr 5. Evans, Craig, and J. A. Sanders, eds. *Luke and Scripture* (Fortress, 1993).

E 6. Forbes, Greg. *The God of Old* (Sheffield Academic Press, 2000). Role of Lukan Parables.

L/Cr 7. Goulder, Michael. *Luke: A New Paradigm,* 2 vols. (Sheffield Academic Press, 1989).

E/Cr 8. Green, Joel, and Michael McKeever, eds. *Luke–Acts and New Testament Historiography,* IBR (Baker, 1994). Bibliography.

E 9. Ireland, Dennis. *Stewardship and the Kingdom of God* (Brill, 1992). Luke 16:1–13.

L/Cr 10. Kurz, William. *Reading Luke–Acts* (Westminster John Knox, 1993).

C/M 11. Maddox, Robert. *The Purpose of Luke–Acts* (T & T Clark, 1982).

E/Cr 12. Marshall, Howard. *Luke,* 2d ed. (Zondervan, 1989; IVP, 1998).

L/Cr 13. Moessner, David. *Lord of the Banquet* (Trinity Press International, 1998). Travel Narrative.

L/Cr 14. Powell, Mark. *What Are They Saying About Luke?* (Paulist, 1989). Introduction.

L/Cr 15. Sterling, G. *Historiography and Self Definition* (Brill, 1992).

L/Cr 16. Talbert, Charles. *Reading Luke* (Crossroad, 1987). Literary, theological commentary.

L/Cr 17. Tannehill, Robert. *The Narrative Unity of Luke–Acts*, 2 vols. (Fortress, 1986–90).

E-L/Cr 18. Thompson, Richard, and Thomas Phillips, eds. *Literary Studies in Luke–Acts* (Mercer University Press, 1998).

L/Cr 19. Verheyden, Jozef, ed. *The Unity of Luke–Acts* (Peeters, 1999).

20. *See* New Testament Background: Social Background.

John*

Technical, Semitechnical

C/M 1. Barrett, C. K. *The Gospel According to St. John* (Westminster, 1978).

E 2. Beasley-Murray, George. WBC, rev. ed. (Thomas Nelson, 1999).

L/Cr 3. Brown, Raymond E. AB, 2 vols. (Doubleday, 1966, 1970). Sacramental.

C/M 4. Lindars, Barnabas. NCBC (Eerdmans, 1972).

L/Cr 5. Moloney, Francis. Sacra Pagina (Liturgical, 1998). Chapter 21 later addition.

E 6. Morris, Leon. NICNT, rev. ed. (Eerdmans, 1994). Updated bibliography, footnotes.

L/Cr 7. O'Day, Gail. NIB, vol. 9 (Abingdon, 1995). Dates between 80–100.

E 8. Ridderbos, Herman. *The Gospel of John: A Theological Commentary* (Eerdmans, 1997). Dutch original: 1987, 1992.

* Forthcoming: Craig Keener, 3 vols. (Hendrickson); Richard Bauckham, NIGTC (Eerdmans); Ramsey Michaels, NICNT (Eerdmans) as a replacement for Morris; Marianne Meye Thompson, NTL (Westminster John Knox); and Andreas Köstenberger, BECNT (Baker). Wait for Bauckham and Keener and use them with Carson or Blomberg.

L/Cr **9. Schnackenburg, Rudolf. *The Gospel According to St. John,* 3 vols. (Seabury/Crossroad, 1968–82).**

Exposition

E **1. Blomberg, Craig. *The Historical Reliability of John's Gospel* (IVP, 2002).**

E 2. Borchert, Gerald. NAC, 2 vols. (Broadman & Holman, 1996, 2002).

E/Cr 3. Bruce, F. F. *The Gospel of John* (Eerdmans, 1983).

E 4. Burge, Gary. NIVAC (Zondervan, 2000).

E 5. Carson, D. A. Pillar (Eerdmans, 1991).

E 6. Milne, Bruce. BST (IVP, 1993).

E 7. Morris, Leon. *Expository Reflections on the Gospel of John* (Hendrickson, 2000).

E 8. Pryor, John. *John* (IVP, 1992). Thematic treatment of Christ and covenant.

L/Cr 9. Smith, D. Moody. ANTC (Abingdon, 1999). Product of Johannine community in three or four stages. No interaction with Motyer or Bauckham below, and limited interaction with others.

E 10. Whitacre, Rodney. IVPNTC (IVP, 1999). Especially theological message.

E 11. Witherington, Ben. *John's Wisdom* (Westminster John Knox, 1995).

John as Story

L/Cr **1. Ashton, John. *Studying John* (Oxford University Press, 1995).**

———. *Understanding the Fourth Gospel* (Oxford University Press, 1991). Introduction.

———, ed. *The Interpretation of John,* rev. and expanded (T & T Clark, 1997).

C/M 2. Culpepper, R. Alan. IBT (Abingdon, 1996). Gospels and Letters.

———, ed. *Critical Readings of John 6* (Brill, 1997).

L/Cr 3. Moloney, Francis. *Belief in the Word: Reading John 1–4* (Fortress, 1993).
———. *Signs and Wonders: Reading John 5–12* (Fortress, 1996).
———. *Glory Not Dishonor: Reading John 13–21* (Fortress, 1998).

E **4. Pryor, John. *John: Evangelist of the Covenant People* (IVP, 1992).** Linkage of Jesus' new covenant community with OT antecedents.

C/M 5. Smalley, Stephen. *John: Evangelist and Interpreter*, 2d ed. (IVP, 1998).

E 6. Stibbe, Mark. *John as Storyteller* (Cambridge University Press, 1992). John 18–19.

L/Cr 7. Talbert, Charles. *Reading John* (Crossroad, 1992). Literary-theological commentary; includes Epistles.

Special Studies

E-C/M 1. Bauckham, Richard, ed. *The Gospel for All Christians* (Eerdmans, 1997). Refutation of "Johannine community" concept.

E 2. Beasley-Murray, George. *Gospel of Life* (Hendrickson, 1991).

E 3. Burge, Gary. *Interpreting the Fourth Gospel* (Baker, 1992).

L/Cr 4. Casey, Maurice. *Is John's Gospel True?* (Routledge, 1996).

L/Cr 5. Charlesworth, James. *The Beloved Disciple* (Trinity Press International, 1996). Thomas, "the one whom Jesus loved."

C/M 6. Culpepper, Alan. *John, the Son of Zebedee* (Fortress, 2000).

C/M-L/Cr 7. Culpepper, Alan, and Clifton Black, eds. *Exploring the Gospel of John* (Westminster, 1995).

E 8. Ensor, Peter. *Jesus and His Works* (Mohr, 1996).

L/Cr 9. Fortna, Robert, and T. Thatcher, eds. *Jesus in Johannine Tradition* (Westminster John Knox, 2001).

C/M 10. Hengel, Martin. *The Johannine Question* (Trinity Press International, 1994).

E 11. Köstenberger, Andreas. *Encountering the Book of John* (Baker, 1999).

E/Cr 12. Lincoln, Andrew. *Truth on Trial* (Hendrickson, 2000). Lawsuit motif.

E/Cr 13. Motyer, Stephen. *Your Father the Devil?* (Paternoster, 1997). John 8:31–59.

E 14. Morris, Leon. *Jesus Is the Christ* (Eerdmans, 1989).

L/Cr 15. Schneiders, Sandra. *Written That You May Believe* (Herder and Herder, 1999). Introduction.

L/Cr 16. Smith, D. Moody. NTT (Cambridge University Press, 1995).

E/Cr 17. Thompson, Marianne Meye. *The God of the Gospel of John* (Eerdmans, 2001).

L/Cr 18. van Tilborg, Sjef. *Reading John in Ephesus* (Brill, 1996). Historical setting.

L/Cr 19. Westermann, Claus. *The Gospel of John in Light of the Old Testament* (Hendrickson, 1998).

Acts*

Technical, Semitechnical

C/M 1. Barrett, C. K. ICC, 2 vols. (T & T Clark, 1994, 1999). Non-Lukan, introduction in volume 2.

E/Cr 2. Bruce, F. F. NICNT, rev. ed. (Eerdmans, 1988). Historical background.

---

* Forthcoming: Steve Walton, WBC, 2 vols. (Thomas Nelson); Joel Green, NICNT (Eerdmans); Stanley Porter, NIGTC (Eerdmans); Carl Holladay, NTL (Westminster John Knox); Darrell Bock, BECNT (Baker); and David Peterson, Pillar (Eerdmans), especially for its theology. With Witherington or Barrett's shorter commentary, one should wait for Bock and Porter. Porter will be particularly valuable for his perspective on the function of the aorist. Bock, however, might be a longer wait than you care for (at least until 2008). The two-volume commentary by Barrett is outstanding, but is much too obtuse for practical pastoral use, and his view of non-Lukan authorship sometimes colors his interpretation. The expositional field is well-populated with several outstanding middle-level commentaries.

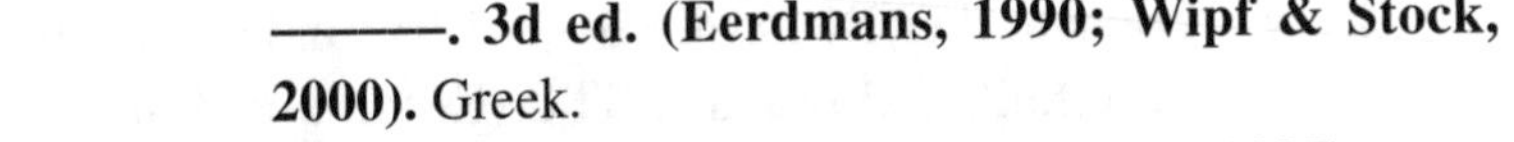

———. 3d ed. (Eerdmans, 1990; Wipf & Stock, 2000). Greek.

L/Cr 3. Conzelmann, Hans. Hermeneia (Fortress, 1987).

L/Cr 4. Fitzmyer, Joseph. AB (Doubleday, 1999). Especially OT in New, table of passages comparing Paul and Acts.

L/Cr 5. Haenchen, Ernst (Westminster, 1971). Early church, interpretation history.

C/M 6. Johnson, Luke. Sacra Pagina (Liturgical, 1992). Extrabiblical parallels, as apologetic history.

Sociorhetorical Studies and Commentaries

E/Cr 1. Dunn, James. *Acts of the Apostles* (Trinity Press International, 1996).

L/Cr 2. Gaventa, Beverly. ANTC (Abingdon, 2003).

L/Cr 3. Kee, Howard. *To Every Nation Under Heaven,* NTC (Trinity Press International, 1998). Especially social context, excellent historicity appendix.

L/Cr 4. Pervo, Richard. *Profit with Delight* (Fortress, 1987).

C/M 5. Soards, Marion. *The Speeches in Acts* (Westminster John Knox, 1994).

E/Cr 6. Spencer, Scott. *Acts* (Sheffield Academic Press, 1997).

L/Cr 7. Talbert, Charles. *Reading Acts* (Crossroad, 1997). Literary-theological.

E/Cr 8. Wall, Robert. NIB, vol. 10 (Abingdon, 2002).

E 9. Witherington, Ben. *The Acts of the Apostles* (Eerdmans, 1997). Acts like Thucyclides, Polybius, Jewish historiography.

———, ed. *History, Literature and Society in the Book of Acts* (Cambridge University Press, 1996).

Exposition

C/M 1. Barrett, C. K. *Acts: A Shorter Commentary* (T & T Clark, 2002). Abridgement of above minus technical notes, foreign-language material, and excursuses

E 2. Fernando, Ajith. NIVAC (Zondervan, 1998).

E 3. Larkin, William. IVPNTC (IVP, 1995).

E **4. Longenecker, Richard. EBC, vol. 9 (Zondervan, 1981).**

E/Cr **5. Marshall, I. Howard. TNTC (Eerdmans, 1980).**

E **6. Polhill, John. NAC (Broadman & Holman, 1992).**

E **7. Stott, John. BST (IVP, 1990).**

C/M 8. Williams, David. NIBCNT (Hendrickson, 1990). Especially background.

Special Studies

E 1. Arrington, French. *The Acts of the Apostles* (Hendrickson, 1988). Pentecostal commentary.

L/Cr 2. Ascough, Richard. *What Are They Saying About the Formation of the Pauline Churches?* (Paulist, 1998).

L/Cr 3. Cassidy, Richard. *Society and Politics in the Acts of the Apostles* (Orbis, 1987).

E **4. Gasque, W. Ward. *A History of the Interpretation of the Acts of the Apostles* (Hendrickson, 1989).**

E **5. Hemer, Colin. *The Book of Acts in the Setting of Hellenistic History* (Mohr, 1989).**

L/Cr 6. Jervell, Jacob. NTT (Cambridge University Press, 1996).

E **7. Johnson, Dennis. *The Message of Acts in the History of Redemption* (Presbyterian & Reformed, 1997).**

C/M 8. Keathley, N., ed. *With Steadfast Purpose* (Baylor University Press, 1990).

E 9. Liefeld, Walter. *Interpreting the Book of Acts* (Baker, 1995).

L/Cr 10. Lüdemann, Gerd. *Early Christianity According to the Traditions in Acts* (Fortress, 1989).

E/Cr **11. Marshall, I. Howard, and David Peterson, eds. *Witness to the Gospel* (Eerdmans, 1998).**

E **12. Pao, David. *Acts and the Isianic New Exodus* (Baker, 2002).**[3]

3. David Pao, assistant professor of New Testament at Trinity Evangelical Divinity School, has reworked his 1998 Harvard dissertation into a monograph of excellence. His thesis concerns the thematic influence of Isaiah's new exodus (especially chap. 40) on Luke's theology of the restoration of the people of God; similar to Rikki Watts's less-successful study of Mark. Incidentally, J. Ross

E/Cr 13. Porter, Stanley. *Paul of Acts* (Hendrickson, 2001).

E 14. Smith, David. *The Canonical Function of Acts* (Liturgical, 2002).

E/Cr 15. Spencer, Scott. *The Portrait of Philip in Acts* (Sheffield Academic Press, 1992).

E/Cr 16. Walton, Steve. *Leadership and Lifestyle* (Cambridge University Press, 2000). Paul in Miletus speech–1 Thessalonians.

17. *See* Luke: Theology of Luke–Acts, The Holy Spirit in Luke–Acts, and Special Studies.

Romans*

Technical, Semitechnical

C/M 1. Cranfield, C. E. B. ICC, 2 vols. (T & T Clark, 1975).

E/Cr 2. Dunn, James. WBC, 2 vols. (Word, 1988). Influenced by Sanders.

L/Cr 3. Fitzmyer, Joseph. AB (Doubleday, 1993). Introduction plus extensive (entire) church history bibliography constitutes two-thirds of the book. Especially Targumic, apocalyptic, DSS parallels.

L/Cr 4. Kasemann Ernst. *Commentary on Romans* (Eerdmans, 1980).

E 5. Moo, Douglas. NICNT (Eerdmans, 1996). Especially synthetic flow.

E 6. Murray, John. NICNT (Eerdmans, 1959–65).

L/Cr 7. Nygren, Anders *Commentary on Romans* (Fortress, 1944).

E 8. Schreiner, Thomas. BECNT (Baker, 1998).

Wagner, following up on his own 1999 Duke dissertation, follows a similar tack in suggesting the influence of the "preaching of good news" (especially Isa. 52:13–53:6) on Paul's thought (*see* Romans: Special Studies).

* Forthcoming: Richard Longenecker, NIGTC (Eerdmans); Beverly Gaventa, NTL (Westminster John Knox); and Robert Jewett, Hermeneia (Fortress). Wait for Longenecker and use it with Moo and Schreiner. Although Schreiner is semitechnical, it is extraordinarily lucid.

C/M 9. Stuhlmacher, Peter. *Paul's Letter to the Romans* (Westminster John Knox, 1994). Paul and the Old Testament/Jewish tradition, fifteen excursuses.

L/Cr 10. Ziesler, John. NTC (Trinity Press International, 1989).

Exposition

C/M 1. Barrett. C. K. BNTC, rev. ed. (Hendrickson, 1993). Completed in 1988.

E/Cr 2. Bruce, F. F. TNTC (Eerdmans, 1985).

E/Cr 3. Edwards, James. NIBCNT (Hendrickson, 1992). Influenced by Sanders.

E 4. Johnson, Alan. EvBC (Moody, 2000). Ideal popular treatment.

L/Cr 5. Keck, Leander. ANTC (Abingdon, 2002).

E 6. Moo, Douglas. NIVAC (Zondervan, 2000).

E 7. Morris, Leon. Pillar (Eerdmans, 1988). Somewhat semitechnical, does not interact with Sanders.

E 8. Mounce, Robert. NAC (Broadman & Holman, 1995). Especially synthetic flow.

E 9. Stott, John. BST (IVP, 1995).

E/Cr 10. Wright, N. T. NIB, vol. 10 (Abingdon, 2002). Interesting perspective on baptism.

Special Studies

C/M 1. Bell, Richard. *No One Seeks for God* (Mohr, 1998). Romans 1:18–3:20.

E 2. Bray, Gerald, ed. ACCS (IVP, 1998).

C/M 3. Bryan, Christopher. *A Preface to Romans* (Oxford University Press, 2000).

C/M 4. Cranfield, C. E. B. *On Romans and Other New Testament Essays* (T & T Clark, 1998).

L/Cr 5. Donfried, Karl, ed. *The Romans Debate,* rev. ed. (Hendrickson, 1991).

L/Cr 6. Goulder, Michael. *Early Christians in Conflict* (Hendrickson, 2001).

L/Cr 7. Grenholm, Cristina, and Daniel Patte, eds. *Reading Is-*

rael in Romans (Trinity Press International, 2000). Romans 4; 9–11.

C/M 8. Johnson, Luke. *Reading Romans* (Crossroad, 1997).

E 9. Moo, Douglas. *Encountering the Book of Romans* (Baker, 2002).

L/Cr 10. Morgan, Robert. NTG (Sheffield Academic Press, 1995).

E 11. Piper, John. *The Justification of God,* 2d ed. (Baker, 1993). Romans 9:1–23.

E 12. Seifrid, Mark, and Randall Tan. *The Pauline Writings,* IBR (Baker, 2002).

E/Cr 13. Soderlund, Sven, and N. T. Wright, eds. *Romans and the People of God* (Eerdmans, 1999).

L/Cr 14. Stowers, Stanley. *A Rereading of Romans* (Yale University Press, 1994).

E 15. Thomas, Robert, ed. *The Master's Perspective on Difficult Passages* (Kregel, 1998). Romans 11:2–6, 25–27.

L/Cr 16. Wagner, Gunter. *An Exegetical Bibliography of the New Testament: Romans and Galatians* (Mercer University Press, 1996).

C/M 17. Wagner, J. Ross. *Heralds of Good News* (Brill, 2002).

18. *See* New Testament Introduction, Survey and Theology: Pauline Theology, Paul and the Law, and New Testament Background: Pauline Background.

1 Corinthians*

Technical, Semitechnical

L/Cr 1. Collins, Raymond. Sacra Pagina (Liturgical, 1999).

L/Cr 2. Conzelmann, Hans. Hermeneia (Fortress, 1975).

---

* Forthcoming: David Garland, BECNT (Baker); Linda Belleville, WBC (Thomas Nelson); Earle Ellis, ICC (T & T Clark); Brian Rosner, Pillar (Eerdmans); Alan Johnson, IVPNTC (IVP); Alexandra Brown, NTL (Westminster John Knox); and Trevor Burke and Keith Elliott, eds., *The Corinthian Correspondence* (Cambridge University Press). Use Thiselton with Garland and Fee. This is a tough call to make because Ellis promises to be his meticulous self in a meticulous series. Belleville, whose middle-level commentary on 2 Corinthians is outstanding in a crowded field, also promises much. Of course, Barrett is still quite outstanding, but Rosner would meet an expository need as well.

E/Cr	**3. Fee, Gordon. NICNT (Eerdmans, 1987).** Charismatic.
E	4. Robertson, Archibald, and Alfred Plummer. ICC, 2d ed. (T & T Clark, 1914).
E/Cr	**5. Thiselton, Anthony. NIGTC (Eerdmans, 2000).**[4]

Exposition

C/M	**1. Barrett, C. K. BNTC (Hendrickson, 1987).**
E	**2. Blomberg, Craig. NIVAC (Zondervan, 1995).**
E/Cr	3. Bruce, F. F. NCBC (Eerdmans, 1981). 1–2 Corinthians.
C/M	**4. Hays, Richard. IBC (Westminster John Knox, 1997).** Especially Paul's use of the Old Testament and ethics.
E	5. Kistemaker, Simon. *1 Corinthians* (Baker, 1994).
E	6. Morris, Leon. TNTC (Eerdmans, 1983).
L/Cr	7. Murphy-O'Connor, Jerome. DBC (Doubleday, 1998).
E	8. Prior, David. BST (IVP, 1985).
C/M	**9. Soards, Marion. NIBCNT (Hendrickson, 1999).**

Sociorhetorical Studies and Commentaries

C/M	1. Eriksson, Anders. *Traditions and Rhetorical Proof* (Almqvist and Wiksell, 1998). 1 Corinthians 8:10–16.
L/Cr	2. Horsley, Richard. ANTC (Abingdon, 1998).
E	**3. Litfin, Duane. *St. Paul's Theology of Proclamation* (Cambridge University Press, 1994).** 1 Corinthians 1–4.
L/Cr	4. Mitchell, Margaret. *Paul and the Rhetoric of Reconciliation* (Westminster John Knox, 1992).
L/Cr	5. Murphy-O'Connor, Jerome. *St. Paul's Corinth,* rev. ed. (Liturgical, 2002).
E	**6. Peterson, Brian. *Eloquence and the Proclamation of the Gospel in Corinth* (Scholars, 1998).** 1 Corinthians 1–4; 2 Corinthians 10–13.

4. Thiselton is an absolute necessity, although not necessarily for the Greek-trained pastor only. Its distinguishing features are its combination of linguistic and hermeneutic theory, its sociohistorical emphasis, and its selective interaction with the Greek in a Greek series.

E/Cr **7. Pogoloff, S. *Logos and Sophia* (Scholars, 1992).** 1 Corinthians 1–4.

L/Cr 8. Talbert, Charles. *Reading Corinthians* (Crossroad, 1987). 1–2 Corinthians.

C/M 9. Welborn, Larry. *Politics and Rhetoric in the Corinthian Epistles* (Mercer University Press, 1997). Especially 2 Corinthians 1–2:13 and 7:1–40, also 1 Corinthians 1–4.

E 10. Williams, Drake. *The Wisdom of the Wise* (Brill, 2001). 1 Corinthians 1:18–3:23.

E 11. Winter, Bruce. *Philo and Paul Among the Sophists* (Cambridge University Press, 1997).

E 12. Witherington, Ben. *Conflict and Community in Corinth* (Eerdmans, 1995). Commentary, includes 2 Corinthians.

Special Studies

E 1. Bray, Gerald, ed. ACCS (IVP, 1999). Includes 2 Corinthians.

E 2. Carson, D. A. *Showing the Spirit* (Baker, 1987). 1 Corinthians 12–14.

E/Cr 3. Cheung, Alex. *Idol Food in Corinth* (Sheffield Academic Press, 1999). 1 Corinthians 8–10.

E 4. Clarke, Andrew. *Secular and Christian Leadership in Corinth* (Brill, 1993). 1 Corinthians 1–6.

L/Cr 5. Furnish, Victor. NTT (Cambridge University Press, 1999).

E/Cr 6. Gardner, Paul. *The Gifts of God and the Authentification of a Christian* (University Press of America, 1994). 1 Corinthians 8–11:1.

L/Cr 7. Grant, Robert. *Paul in the Roman World* (Westminster John Knox, 2001).

E/Cr 8. Rosner, Brian. *Paul, Scripture, and Ethics* (Brill, 1994). 1 Corinthians 5–7.

E 9. Thomas, Robert. *Understanding Spiritual Gifts*, rev. ed. (Kregel, 1999). 1 Corinthians 12–14.

———, ed. *The Master's Perspective on Difficult Passages* (Kregel, 1998). 1 Corinthians 3:12; 5:5; 6:9; 13:11.

2 Corinthians*

Technical, Semitechnical

E **1. Barnett, Paul. NICNT (Eerdmans, 1997).** Especially biblical theology, historical, social background.

L/Cr **2. Furnish, Victor. AB (Doubleday, 1984).** Greco-Roman background.

E 3. Hughes, Philip. NICNT (Eerdmans, 1962). Annihilationist.

E/Cr **4. Martin, Ralph. WBC (Word, 1986).** Especially history of interpretation.

C/M 5. Thrall, Margaret. ICC, 2 vols. (T & T Clark, 1994). Three letters in one.

E **6. Witherington, Ben. *Chaos and Community in Corinth* (Eerdmans, 1995).** Sociorhetorical, includes 1 Corinthians.

Exposition

E 1. Barnett, Paul. BST (IVP, 1988).

C/M **2. Barrett, C. K. BNTC (Harper, 1973; Hendrickson, 1993).**

E/Cr **3. Belleville, Linda. IVPNTC (IVP, 1995).**

L/Cr 4. Fitzgerald, John. ANTC (Abingdon, 2002).

E **5. Garland, David. NAC (Broadman & Holman, 1999).**

E **6. Hafemann, Scott. NIVAC (Zondervan, 2000).**

E **7. Harris, Murray. EBC, vol. 10 (Zondervan, 1976).**

E 8. Kistemaker, Simon. *2 Corinthians* (Baker, 1997).

E **9. Kruse, Colin. TNTC (Eerdmans, 1987).**

---

* Forthcoming: George Guthrie, BECNT (Baker); Murray Harris, NIGTC (Eerdmans); Frank Matera, NTL (Westminster John Knox); and Mark Seifrid, Pillar (Eerdmans). One could hardly do better than to wait for these commentaries, although Barrett (outstanding for 365 pp.), Garland (for his theology), and Hafemann's present volume (for exegesis and application) can scarcely be ignored. If you already have one of these, wait for Harris and Guthrie.

E/Cr 10. Scott, James. NIBCNT (Hendrickson, 1998). Especially Jewish background.

C/M 11. Watson, Nigel. Epworth (Epworth, 1993). Available through Trinity Press International.

Special Studies

E 1. Carson, D. A. *From Triumphalism to Maturity* (Baker, 1986). 2 Corinthians 10–13.

E 2. Hafemann, Scott. *Suffering and Ministry in the Spirit* (Eerdmans, 1990). 2 Corinthians 2:14–3:3.

———. *Paul, Moses, and the History of Israel* (Mohr, 1995; Hendrickson, 1996). 2 Corinthians 3.

E 3. Hubbard, Moyer. *New Creation* (Cambridge University Press, 2003). New creation in 2 Corinthians and Galatians.

L/Cr 4. Murphy-O'Connor, Jerome. NTT (Cambridge University Press, 1991).

E/Cr 5. Savage, Timothy. *Power Through Weakness* (Cambridge University Press, 1995). 2 Corinthians 3–4.

E/Cr 6. Winter, Bruce. *After Paul Left Corinth* (Eerdmans, 2000). Greco-Roman background.

Galatians*

Technical, Semitechnical

L/Cr 1. Betz, Hans. Hermeneia (Fortress, 1979). Rhetorical analysis, Greco-Roman parallels.

E/Cr 2. Bruce, F. F. NIGTC (Eerdmans, 1982).

C/M 3. Burton, E. ICC (T & T Clark, 1921). Vocabulary index.

E 4. Fung, Ronald. NICNT (Eerdmans, 1988).

E 5. Longenecker, Richard. WBC (Word, 1990). Rhetorical analysis, surveys disputed points.

---

* Forthcoming: D. A. Carson, Pillar (Eerdmans); Graham Stanton, ICC (T & T Clark); Martinus de Boer, NTL (Westminster John Knox); and Gerald Borchert (Tyndale). I'd keep Longenecker and Bruce and wait for Carson. This is one of four projected commentaries from Carson. He is also slated to comment on Hebrews (BECNT), 1–3 John (NIGTC), and Revelation (also Pillar).

L/Cr 6. Martyn, J. Louis. AB (Doubleday, 1997). North Galatian, reproclamation of apocalyptic gospel.

L/Cr 7. Matera, Frank. Sacra Pagina (Liturgical, 1992). New perspective on Paul.

Sociorhetorical Studies and Commentaries

E/Cr 1. Kern, Philip. *Rhetoric and Galatians* (Cambridge University Press, 1998).

L/Cr 2. Perkins, Pheme. *Abraham's Divided Children,* NTC (Trinity Press International, 2001).

L/Cr 3. Williams, Sam. ANTC (Abingdon, 1997).

E 4. Witherington, Ben. *Grace in Galatia* (Eerdmans, 1998).

Exposition

L/Cr 1. Cousar, Charles. IBC (John Knox, 1982).

E/Cr 2. Dunn, James. BNTC (Hendrickson, 1993). New perspective, parallels from ancient Jewish texts.

E 3. George, Timothy. NAC (Broadman & Holman, 1994). Theology, history of interpretation, rebuttal of new perspective.

E 4. Guthrie, Donald. NCBC (Eerdmans, 1981).

E/Cr 5. Hansen, Walter. IVPNTC (IVP, 1994).

C/M 6. Hays, Richard. NIB, vol. 11 (Abingdon, 2000).

E/Cr 7. Jervis, Ann. NIBC (Hendrickson, 1999). New perspective.

E/Cr 8. McKnight, Scot. NIVAC (Zondervan, 1995). New perspective.

E 9. Morris, Leon. *Galatians* (IVP, 1996).

E 10. Stott, John. BST (IVP, 1986).

L/Cr 11. Ziesler, John. Epworth (Epworth, 1992). Available through Trinity Press International.

Special Studies

E/Cr 1. Barclay, John. *Obeying the Truth* (T & T Clark, 1988).

E/Cr 2. Dunn, James. NTT (Cambridge University Press, 1993). New perspective.

E 3. Edwards, Mark, ed. ACCS (IVP, 1999). Includes Ephesians and Philippians.

E/Cr 4. Hansen, Walter. *Abraham in Galatians* (JSOT, 1989).

C/M 5. Hays, Richard. *The Faith of Jesus Christ,* 2d ed. (Eerdmans, 2002). Galatians 3:1–4:11.

C/M 6. Longenecker, Bruce. *The Triumph of Abraham's God* (Abingdon/T & T Clark, 1998).

L/Cr 7. Martyn, Louis. *Theological Issues in the Letters of Paul* (T & T Clark, 1997). Mostly Galatians. Available through Abingdon.

L/Cr 8. Nanos, Mark. *The Irony of Galatians* (Fortress, 2001). Dubious theory of Jewish-Christian relations. Wealth of background, however.

E 9. Silva, Moisés. *Interpreting Galatians,* 2d ed. (Baker, 2001). New appendix on 3:6–14.

Ephesians*

Technical, Semitechnical

L/Cr 1. Abbott, T. ICC (T & T Clark, 1897). With Colossians.

C/M 2. Barth, Markus. AB, 2 vols. (Doubleday, 1974). Pauline, extensive theology.

C/M 3. Best, Ernest. ICC (T & T Clark, 1998). Ephesians mutually dependent on Colossians, separate authors.

* Forthcoming: Frank Thielman, BECNT (Baker); David Dockery, NAC (Broadman & Holman); William Klein, New Expositor's Bible Commentary (Zondervan); Stephen Fowl, NTL (Westminster John Knox); and Max Turner, NIGTC (Eerdmans). The sturdy BCBC series has contributed Tom Neufeld (Herald, 2001), but I have not yet seen it. This is a very difficult field to evaluate, as O'Brien, Hoehner, Best, and Lincoln are more than adequate, but Thielman and Turner should be eagerly anticipated. Thielman, who is an expert on the law-versus-grace issue, should well illumine the believer's new position in Christ. Turner, whose expertise lies in the function of the Holy Spirit, could well develop this position even further. Hoehner's encyclopedic nine hundred-page work (of which one hundred pages defends Pauline authorship), published as a standalone volume by Baker, covers every imaginable issue. Although O'Brien retains preeminence, Hoehner, along with Best, must be consulted for exegetical papers.

E/Cr 4. Bruce, F. F. NICNT (Eerdmans, 1984). With Colossians/ Philemon.

E 5. Hoehner, Harold. *Ephesians* (Baker, 2002).

E/Cr 6. Lincoln, Andrew. WBC (Word, 1990). Non-Pauline authorship, influence of rhetoric.

L/Cr 7. MacDonald, Margaret. Sacra Pagina (Liturgical, 2000). With Colossians, occasional forced comparisons of epistles.

C/M 8. Mitton, C. NCBC (Eerdmans, 1982). Non-Pauline.

C/M 9. Muddiman, John. BNTC (Continuum, 2001).[5]

E 10. O'Brien, Peter. Pillar (Eerdmans, 1999).

E 11. Robinson, J. Armitage. *St. Paul's Epistle to the Ephesians,* 2d ed. (Kregel, 1979).

C/M 12. Schnackenburg, Rudolf. *Ephesians* (T & T Clark, 2001). Non-Pauline, logical flow and theology.

Exposition

E/Cr 1. Kreitzer, Larry. Epworth (Epworth, 1997). Pseudonymous. Available through Trinity Press International,

E 2. Liefeld, Walter. IVPNTC (IVP, 1997).

E 3. Morris, Leon. *Expository Reflections on the Letter to the Ephesians* (Baker, 1994).

L/Cr 4. Perkins, Pheme. ANTC (Abingdon, 1997). Especially church fathers, Essene parallels, pseudonymous.
———. NIB, vol. 11 (Abingdon, 2000).

E/Cr 5. Snodgrass, Klyne. NIVAC (Zondervan, 1996).

5. The Black's New Testament Commentaries series, henceforth appropriated by Continuum (the older titles are still available from Hendrickson) and available in both hardback and paperback (although the hardback cost is more than three times what Hendrickson charges), usually runs the divide between semitechnical and expositional. Unlike the others, I've included Muddiman's commentary in the Technical, Semitechnical category because it is more technical than its counterparts. Muddiman, who thoroughly engages the secondary literature, believes that Ephesians is the "lost" Laodicean letter plus interpolations that account for more than half the reconstructed letter authored forty years after the fact. The difficulties with such an approach (i.e., the relative innocuousness of the supposed, original Laodicean letter) should not obscure the value of this commentary for its numerous, pertinent insights.

E 6. Stott, John. BST (IVP, 1979).

Special Studies

E 1. Arnold, Clinton. *Ephesians, Power and Magic* (Baker, 1992).

C/M 2. Best, Ernest. NTG (Sheffield Academic Press, 1993). ———. *Essays on Ephesians* (T & T Clark, 1998). Expanded introduction to above.

E 3. Caragounis, Chrys. *The Ephesian Mysterion* (Gleerup, 1977).

L/Cr 4. Dahl, Nils. *Studies in Ephesians* (Mohr, 2000).

E/Cr 5. Dawes, Gregory. *The Body in Question* (Brill, 1998). Ephesians 5:21–33.

E 6. Harris, Hall. *The Descent of Christ* (Brill, 1996; Baker, 1998). Ephesians 4:7–11.

E 7. Klein, William. *The Book of Ephesians: An Annotated Bibliography* (Garland, 1996).

E/Cr 8. Lincoln, Andrew, and Arthur Wedderburn. *The Theology of the Later Pauline Epistles,* NTT (Cambridge University Press, 1993).

E/Cr 9. Moritz, Thorsten. *A Profound Mystery: The Use of the Old Testament in Ephesians* (Brill, 1996).

E/Cr 10. Neufeld, Thomas. *"Put On the Armor of God"* (Sheffield Academic Press, 1997). Divine warrior motif.

Philippians*

Technical, Semitechnical

E 1. Fee, Gordon. NICNT (Eerdmans, 1995).

E/Cr 2. Hawthorne, Gerald. WBC (Word, 1983).

E 3. O'Brien, Peter. NIGTC (Eerdmans, 1991).

---

* Forthcoming: John Reumann, AB (Doubleday); D. Whitely, ICC (T & T Clark); Moisés Silva, BECNT, rev. ed. (Baker); Charles Cousar, NTL (Westminster John Knox); and Walter Hansen, Pillar (Eerdmans). Look for Hansen and Silva, but Philippians is already well represented by Fee, O'Brien, and Bockmuehl. The production of exposition commentaries on Philippians is a virtual cottage industry with only Bockmuehl and Thielman standing ahead of the pack.

E/Cr	4.	Reed, Jeffrey. *Philippians* (Sheffield Academic Press, 1997). Highly technical discourse analysis.
E	**5.**	**Silva, Moisés. BECNT (Baker, 1992).** Formerly WEC (Moody, 1988).
E	6.	Witherington, Ben. *Friendship and Finances in Philippi*, NTC (Trinity Press International, 1995). Sociorhetorical.

Exposition

L/Cr	1.	Beare, Francis. HNTC, 3d ed. (Harper, 1973).
E	**2.**	**Bockmuehl, Markus. BNTC (Hendrickson, 1998).** Socioliterary, theological background. A masterpiece of concise erudition.
E/Cr	3.	Bruce, F. F. NIBCNT, 2d ed. (Hendrickson, 1989).
E	4.	Fee, Gordon. IVPNTC (IVP, 1999). Somewhat thin condensation of above.
C/M	5.	Hooker, Morna. NIB, vol. 11 (Abingdon, 2000).
E/Cr	6.	Marshall, Howard. Epworth (Epworth, 1991).
E/Cr	7.	Martin, Ralph. NCBC (Eerdmans, 1980). Influenced by Käsemann's "odyssey of Christ."
		———. TNTC (Eerdmans, 1987). 1959 edition preferred for the same reasons as given above.
E	8.	Motyer, J. Alec. BST (IVP, 1984).
L/Cr	9.	Osiek, Carolyn. ANTC (Abingdon, 2000). With Philemon, sociorhetorical.
E	**10.**	**Thielman, Frank. NIVAC (Zondervan, 1995).**

Special Studies

C/M-L/Cr	1.	Bakirtzis, C., and Helmut Koester, eds. *Philippi at the Time of Paul and After His Death* (Trinity Press International, 1999).
E/Cr	2.	Bloomquist, Gregory. *The Function of Suffering in Philippians* (Sheffield Academic Press, 1993). Rhetorical analysis.
E/Cr	**3.**	**Martin, Ralph. *A Hymn of Christ* (IVP, 1997).** Philippians 2:5–11, *Carmen Cristi* with updated preface, technical.

E/Cr-L/Cr 4. Martin, Ralph, and Brian Dodd, eds. *Where Christology Began* (Westminster John Knox, 1998). Philippians 2.

E 5. Oakes, Peter. *Philippians* (Cambridge University Press, 2000). Greco-Roman background.

E/Cr 6. Peterlin, Davorin. *Paul's Letter to the Philippians in Light of Disunity in the Church* (Brill, 1995).

E 7. Peterman, Gerald. *Paul's Gift from Philippi* (Cambridge University Press, 1997). Philippians 4:10–20.

Colossians/Philemon*

Technical, Semitechnical

C/M 1. Barth, Markus, and Helmut Blanke. ECC (Eerdmans, 2000). Philemon only, bibliography to 1994, exhaustive study of slavery, ancient world, less than half is exegesis.[6]

———. AB (Doubleday, 1995). Colossians only, bibliography to 1986.

E/Cr 2. Bruce, F. F. NICNT (Eerdmans, 1984). Especially Philemon, with Ephesians and Colossians.

E/Cr 3. Dunn, James. NIGTC (Eerdmans, 1996).[7]

* Forthcoming: Gregory Beale, BECNT (Baker); S. Wilson, ICC (T & T Clark); Jerry Sumney, NTL (Westminster John Knox); and Gerald Hawthorne, Pillar (Eerdmans). Keep O'Brien and Garland, and wait for Beale.

6. Needless to say, scholars will welcome the 255 pages of exegesis on the twenty-five verses in Barth and Blanke's Philemon. Of these, Blanke wrote the last seventy-five pages from Barth's notes, which include sixty-four pages of commentary on Philemon 16 alone! This is in addition to 240 pages of introduction. Fitzmyer is comparatively thin with ninety-two pages of exegesis matched by thirty-six pages of bibliography. Hopefully, the forthcoming commentaries by Beale and Hawthorne will find the middle ground and bring forth the latest scholarship on the practice of slavery in the Greco-Roman world. O'Brien, Dunn, and Garland provide adequate coverage of fifty to eighty pages on Philemon and fuller treatments on Colossians.

7. In Colossians, Dunn believes that Timothy reworked Pauline material just before or after Paul's death, and that the opponents are from the synagogue rather than representatives of a Christian heresy. This necessarily puts a spin on his interpretation.

L/Cr 4. Fitzmyer, Joseph. AB (Doubleday, 2000). Philemon only.

C/M 5. Lohse, Eduard. Hermeneia (Fortress, 1971). Non-Pauline authorship. Gnostic and syncretistic opponents.

L/Cr 6. Moule, C. F. D. *The Epistle to Colossians and to Philemon* (Cambridge University Press, 1957).

E 7. O'Brien, Peter. WBC (Word, 1982).

L/Cr 8. Schweizer, Eduard. *The Letter to the Colossians* (Augsburg, 1982).

Exposition

E 1. Garland, David. NIVAC (Zondervan, 1998).

L/Cr 2. Hay, David. ANTC (Abingdon, 2000). Colossians only.

E/Cr 3. Lincoln, Andrew. NIB, vol. 11 (Abingdon, 2000). Colossians only.

E 4. Lucas, Raymond. BST (IVP, 1980).

E 5. Martin, Ernest. BCBC (Herald, 1993).

E/Cr 6. Martin, Ralph. NCBC (Eerdmans, 1981). Written from Ephesus.

L/Cr 7. Osiek, Carolyn. ANTC (Abingdon, 2000). Philemon and Philippians, sociorhetorical.

E/Cr 8. Wall, Robert. IVPNTC (IVP, 1993).

E 9. Wright, N. T. TNTC (Eerdmans, 1987).

Special Studies

E 1. Arnold, Clinton. *The Colossian Syncretism* (Mohr, 1995; Baker, 1997). Paul combats Christianity/folk belief syncretism.

C/M 2. Barclay, John. *Colossians and Philemon* (Sheffield Academic Press, 1997).

L/Cr 3. Cannon, G. *The Use of Traditional Materials in Colossians* (Mercer University Press, 1983).

L/Cr 4. DeMaris, Richard. *The Colossian Controversy* (Sheffield Academic Press, 1994). Author versus Jewish, Christian, Middle Platonic elements.

E 5. Harris, Murray. EGGNT (Eerdmans, 1991). Grammatical guide.

E 6. **Martin, Troy. *By Philosophy and Empty Deceit* (Sheffield Academic Press, 1996).** Response to philosophical cynics.

L/Cr 7. Peterson, Norman. *Rediscovering Paul* (Fortress, 1985).

C/M 8. Sappington, Thomas. *Revelation and Redemption at Colossae* (Sheffield Academic Press, 1991). Colossians seen through ascetic, mystical piety of Jewish apocalyptic.

L/Cr 10 Wilson, Walter. *The Hope of Glory* (Brill, 1997). As philosophic moral exhortation.

1 and 2 Thessalonians*

Technical, Semitechnical

E 1. **Bruce, F. F. WBC (Word, 1982).** Believers receive resurrection body at death, Antichrist excursus.

E 2. **Green, Gene. Pillar (Eerdmans, 2002).**[8]

C/M 3. **Malherbe, Abraham. AB (Doubleday, 2000).**[9]

E 4. Morris, Leon. NICNT, rev. ed. (Eerdmans, 1991).

L/Cr 5. Richard, Earl. Sacra Pagina (Liturgical, 1995). 2 Thessalonians non-Pauline, lexical, grammatical, literary background.

---

* Forthcoming: Jeffrey Weima, BECNT (Baker); Karl Donfried, ICC (T & T Clark); Holland Hendrix, NTC (Trinity); Helmut Koester, Hermeneia (Fortress); Elizabeth Johnson, NTL (Westminster John Knox); and Gregory Beale, IVPNTC (IVP). First and Second Thessalonians is already well served by Wanamaker, Green, Malherbe, Bruce, Best, Stott, Holmes, and Marshall, but I would wait to see how Weima and Beale are received. Newer isn't always better, but it usually is. After all, you're drawing on all of the wealth that came before you, including what used to be new! It just costs more.

8. Although Green's commentary is pastor sensitive with an eye toward application, it's semitechnical enough to warrant inclusion here.

9. Many people might be surprised to discover that Malherbe supports the Pauline authorship of *both* letters around A.D. 50. In response to criticism of his earlier monograph, he also delves much deeper into unpacking Paul's eschatology. Readers should turn to a more conventional explanation of the parousia before wading into Malherbe's rather technical exegesis. The strengths of this commentary are the frequent allusions to Greco-Roman background literature, particularly that of the Epicureans.

E	**6.**	**Wanamaker, Charles. NIGTC (Eerdmans, 1990).** Rhetorical analysis.

Exposition

C/M	**1.**	**Best, Ernest. BNTC (Harper, 1972; Hendrickson, 1987).** Semitechnical.
E	2.	Elias, Jacob. BCBC (Herald, 1995).
L/Cr	**3.**	**Furnish, Victor. ANTC (Abingdon, 2002).**
L/Cr	4.	Gaventa, Beverly. IBC (Westminster John Knox, 1998). Maternal imagery, persistence of evil.
E	5.	Hiebert, D. Edmond. *1 and 2 Thessalonians,* rev. ed. (Moody, 1992). Pretribulational, dispensational.
E	**6.**	**Holmes, Michael. NIVAC (Zondervan, 1998).** Posttribulational.
E	7.	Jackman, David. *1 and 2 Thessalonians* (Christian Focus, 1998).
E/Cr	**8.**	**Marshall, I. Howard. NCBC (Eerdmans, 1983).** Semitechnical.
E	9.	Martin, Michael. NAC (Broadman & Holman, 1995). Semitechnical, rhetorical analysis, posttribulational.
E	**10.**	**Stott, John. BST (IVP, 1992).**
E	11.	Thomas, Robert. EBC, vol. 11 (Zondervan, 1978). Dispensational.
C/M	12.	Williams, David. NIBCNT (Hendrickson, 1992).

Special Studies

L/Cr	1.	Collins, Raymond, ed. *The Thessalonian Correspondence* (Peeters, 1990).
C/M	**2.**	**Donfried, Karl. *Paul, Thessalonica, and Early Christianity* (Eerdmans, 2002).**
C/M	**3.**	**Donfried, Karl, and Johannes Beutler, eds. *The Thessalonians Debate* (Eerdmans, 2000).** First Thessalonians 2:1–12.
E/Cr-C/M	4.	Donfried, Karl, and I. Howard Marshall. *The Theology of the Shorter Pauline Letters,* NTT (Cambridge University Press, 1993).

C/M 5. Malherbe, Abraham. *Paul and the Thessalonians* (Fortress, 1987).

E-E/Cr 6. Weima, Jeffrey, and Stanley Porter. *An Annotated Bibliography of 1 and 2 Thessalonians* (Brill, 1998).

1 and 2 Timothy, Titus*

Technical, Semitechnical[10]

L/Cr 1. Collins, Raymond, NTL (Westminster John Knox, 2003). Noticeable paucity of footnotes.

C/M 2. Johnson, Luke. AB (Doubleday, 2001).[11]

E 3. Knight, George W. III. NIGTC (Eerdmans, 1992). Complementarian.

E/Cr 4. Marshall, I. Howard. ICC (T & T Clark, 2000). Egalitarian.

---

* Forthcoming: Philip Towner, NICNT (Eerdmans); Reggie Kidd, BECNT (Baker); Abraham Malherbe, Hermeneia (Fortress); Terry Wilder, Mentor (Christian Focus); Robert Yarbrough, Pillar (Eerdmans); and Andreas Köstenberger, New Expositor's Bible Commentary (Zondervan). Once, conservative pastors had to depend upon liberal commentators if they were to continue in utilizing the Greek and Hebrew skills they acquired in seminary. Now that has changed. Nowhere is that more evident than in the Pastoral Letters, where fourteen commentaries in the past thirteen years (of sixteen mentioned) and eight commentaries in the last five years have taken their place on the bookshelf.

10. With the recent, excellent commentaries by Marshall (with Towner's help), Mounce, and Quinn/Wacker, together with the already excellent Knight and Johnson, these letters are well covered (see comment). If you're starting from scratch, purchase Marshall and either Knight or Mounce. Marshall is very dense but magnificent and is further embellished by eleven excursuses dealing with significant theological matters. However, his approach is non-Pauline and egalitarian as opposed to Mounce and Knight's traditional views. Then there's the matter of Luke Johnson's recent commentary on 1–2 Timothy (see comment) in the Anchor series (Jerome Quinn having previously covered Titus before his death). Of course, this commentary shares the same deficit as the other three, recent, technical commentaries mentioned (Marshall, Mounce, and Quinn/Wacker). Their nearly simultaneous release disqualified each from interacting with one another. If either Towner or Kidd takes advantage of what certainly is the ultimate research base anyone could imagine, then *that* commentary should take pride of place.

11. In his lengthy introduction, Johnson covers thoroughly the history of interpretation. He also defends Pauline authorship. Finally, he downplays the hierarchical relationship of men to women, another surprising twist from a Catholic.

E	**5.**	**Mounce, William. WBC (Thomas Nelson, 2000).** Complementarian.
C/M	**6.**	**Quinn, Jerome, and William Wacker. ECC (Eerdmans, 1999).** Especially philology, 1–2 Timothy post-Pauline (A.D. 80–85), like AB series with application.
C/M	**7.**	**Quinn, Jerome. AB (Doubleday, 1990).** Only Titus, non-Pauline.

Exposition[12]

L/Cr	1.	Donelson, Lewis. WBComp (Westminster John Knox, 1996).
E/Cr	2.	Dunn, James. NIB, vol. 11 (Abingdon, 2000). Egalitarian.
E	**3.**	**Fee, Gordon. NIBCNT (Hendrickson, 1988).** Egalitarian.
L/Cr	4.	Hanson, A. NCBC (Eerdmans, 1982). Post-Pauline.
C/M	**5.**	**Johnson, Luke. *Letters to Paul's Delegates,* NTC (Trinity Press International, 1996).**
C/M	**6.**	**Kelly, J. N. D. BNTC (Harper, 1963; Hendrickson, 1993).** Especially patristic background.
E	**7.**	**Liefeld, Walter. NIVAC (Zondervan, 1999).**
C/M	**8.**	**Oden, Thomas. IBC (Westminster/John Knox, 1989).**
E	9.	Stott, John. BST (IVP, 1973). 2 Timothy only.
E	10.	Stott, John. *Guard the Truth,* BST (IVP 1997). 1 Timothy and Titus only.
E/Cr	**11.**	**Towner, Philip. IVPNTC (IVP, 1994).** Egalitarian.

Special Studies

L/Cr	1.	Collins, J. N. *DIAKONIA* (Oxford University Press, 1990).
L/Cr	**2.**	**Donelson, Lewis. *Pseudepigraphy and Ethical Argument in the Pastoral Epistles* (Mohr, 1986).**
E	3.	Grudem, Wayne, ed. *Biblical Foundations for Manhood and Womanhood* (Crossway, 2002).

12. If you obtain Marshall, Knight, or Mounce for technical coverage, then obtain either Johnson or Towner (exposition) or watch for Yarbrough (when it is released). If you already have Kelly, Oden, Liefeld, or Fee, that will do.

L/Cr 4. Harding, Mark. *What Are They Saying About the Pastoral Epistles?* (Paulist, 2001).

E 5. Köstenberger, Andreas, Thomas Schreiner, and Scott Baldwin, eds. *Women in the Church* (Baker, 1995). 1 Timothy 2:9–15.

E 6. Lau, Andrew. *Manifest in Flesh: The Epiphany Christology of the Pastoral Epistles* (Mohr, 1996).

E/Cr 7. Miller, J. *The Pastoral Letters as Composite Documents* (Cambridge University Press, 1997).

E 8. Piper, John, and Wayne Grudem, eds. *Recovering Biblical Manhood and Womanhood* (Crossway, 1991).

E/Cr 9. Prior, Michael. *Paul the Letter-Writer and the Second Letter to Timothy* (Sheffield Academic Press, 1989). Defends Pauline authorship.

L/Cr 10. Richard, Earl. *The Secretary in the Letters of Paul* (Mohr, 1991).

C/M 11. Young, Frances. NTT (Cambridge University Press, 1994). Egalitarian and non-Pauline, especially Patristic theology.

Hebrews*

Technical, Semitechnical

L/Cr 1. Attridge, Harold. Hermeneia (Fortress, 1989). Primary sources.

E/Cr 2. Bruce, F. F. NICNT, rev. ed. (Eerdmans, 1990). Little change from 1964 edition.

* Forthcoming: D. A. Carson, BECNT (Baker); Luke Timothy Johnson, NTL (Westminster John Knox); and Peter O'Brien, Pillar (Eerdmans). Once again we are faced with a bibliophilic conundrum. For those who have *both* Bruce and Hughes, these will do. However, you should obtain George Guthrie's NIVAC entry for its sensitivity to the overall structure of Hebrews. The same goes for those that possess Attridge, Lane, or Ellingworth. However, in a perfect world, a combination of Lane, Ellingworth, Koester, deSilva, and Guthrie would cover the theology, grammar, rhetorical features, social setting, and overall structure quite nicely. Of these, Lane does the best job in addressing each facet of Hebrews. Enter Carson and O'Brien. Use with Lane.

E **3. deSilva, David. *Perseverance in Gratitude* (Eerdmans, 2000).** Sociorhetorical.[13]

E **4. Ellingworth, Paul. NIGTC (Eerdmans, 1993).** Especially grammar, textual criticism.

E/Cr 5. Hughes Philip. *A Commentary on the Epistle to the Hebrews* (Eerdmans, 1977). Especially history of interpretation.

C/M 6. Koester, Craig. AB (Doubleday, 2001). Especially rhetoric (sees as sermon), history of interpretation, concept of suffering.

E/Cr 7. Lane, William. WBC, 2 vols. (Word, 1991). Especially theological flow.

L/Cr 8. Wilson, Robert. NCBC (Eerdmans, 1987).

Exposition

E 1. Brown, Raymond. BST (IVP, 1988).

L/Cr 2. Craddock, Fred. NIB, vol. 12 (Abingdon, 1998). *See* "Reflections" for applications.

E 3. Ellingworth, Paul. Epworth (Epworth, 1992).

E 4. Guthrie, Donald. TNTC (Eerdmans, 1983).

E 5. Guthrie, George. NIVAC (Zondervan, 1998). Especially discourse analysis.

E 6. Hagner, Donald. NIBCNT (Hendrickson, 1990).

E/Cr 7. Lane, William. *Call to Commitment* (Hendrickson, 1988).

L/Cr 8. Pfitzner, Victor. ANTC (Abingdon, 1997). Theological.

Special Studies

E 1. Bateman, Herbert. *Early Jewish Hermeneutics and Hebrews 1:5–13* (Lang, 1997).

C/M 2. Croy, Clayton. *Endurance in Suffering* (Cambridge University Press, 1998). Hebrews 12:1–3.

---

13. I hesitate to recommend specialized commentaries (the other exceptions being Witherington's sociorhetorical commentary on Acts, and Blomberg's historical commentary on John), but deSilva's commentary builds on his much-noticed dissertation *Despising Shame.*

E 3. deSilva, David. *Despising Shame* (Scholars, 1995). Honor-shame rhetoric.

E 4. Guthrie, George. *The Structure of Hebrews* (Brill, 1994; Baker, 1998).

E 5. Hagner, Donald. *Encountering the Epistle to the Hebrews* (Baker, 2002).

L/Cr 6. Hurst, L. D. *The Epistle to the Hebrews* (Cambridge University Press, 1990).

E 7. Laansma, Jon. *"I Will Give You Rest"* (Mohr, 1997). Matthew 11 and Hebrews 3–4.

C/M 8. Lindars, Barnabas. NTT (Cambridge University Press, 1991).

E 9. Peterson, David. *Hebrews and Perfection* (Cambridge University Press, 1982).

E 10. Rhee, Victor. *Faith in Hebrews* (Lang, 2001). Theological study.

E 11. Trotter, Andrew. *Interpreting the Epistle to the Hebrews* (Baker, 1996).

James*

Technical, Semitechnical

E/Cr 1. Davids, Peter. NIGTC (Eerdmans, 1982).

L/Cr 2. Dibelius, Martin, and Hans Greeven. Hermeneia (Fortress, 1975).

C/M 3. Johnson, Luke. AB (Doubleday, 1995). Extensive 162-page introduction, history of interpretation.[14]

---

* Forthcoming: John Kloppenborg, Hermeneia (Fortress); Dan McCartney, BECNT (Baker); Joel Green, NTL (Westminster John Knox); and Donald Verseput, NICNT (Eerdmans). I'm not familiar enough with McCartney or Verseput to anticipate the quality of their forthcoming commentaries, but if you have Johnson, Davids, Martin, or Moo, you are already pretty well off. If not, obtain Johnson and Moo, Pillar, (Eerdmans), and wait for the verdict on Verseput or McCartney. I am also encouraged by the spate of special studies that have appeared in the last six years, particularly those that affirm James as the brother of Jesus.

14. Luke Johnson's moderate commentary, which he holds to be authored by James, the brother of Jesus, is the best commentary available. It is particularly noteworthy on matters of introduction. He devotes forty pages to the history of its interpretation and an even longer section on the relationship of James to the rest

E/Cr **4. Martin, Ralph. WBC (Word, 1989).**
E/Cr 5. Mayor, Joseph. *The Epistle of James,* 3d ed. (Macmillan, 1913; Kregel, 1990).
L/Cr 6. Mitton, C. *The Epistle of James* (Eerdmans, 1966).

Exposition

E/Cr 1. Davids, Peter. NIBCNT (Hendrickson, 1989).
E 2. Hiebert, D. Edmond. *The Epistle of James,* rev. ed. (Moody, 1992).
C/M 3. Johnson, Luke. NIB, vol. 12 (Abingdon, 1998).
L/Cr **4. Laws, Sophie. BNTC (Harper, 1980; Hendrickson, 1987).** Roman origin.
E **5. Moo, Douglas. Pillar (Eerdmans, 2000).**
———. TNTC (Eerdmans, 1986).
E 6. Motyer, Alec. BST (IVP, 1985).
E 7. Nystrom, David. NIVAC (Zondervan, 1997).
E 8. Stulac, George. IVPNTC (IVP, 1993). Appendix: identity of the rich.
E/Cr 9. Wall, Robert. NTC (Trinity Press International, 1997). Socioliterary context, canonical criticism appendix.

Special Studies

E 1. Adamson, James. *James* (Eerdmans, 1989).
E 2. Baker, William. *Personal Speech-Ethics in the Epistle of James* (Mohr, 1995).
C/M 3. Bauckham, Richard. *James* (Routledge, 1999).
L/Cr 4. Bernheim, Pierre. *James, Brother of Jesus* (SCM, 1997). Includes Gospels of Thomas and Hebrews.
E 5. Bratcher, Robert. UBS Helps for Translators (UBS, 1983).
L/Cr 6. Cargal, T. *Restoring the Diaspora* (Scholars, 1993).

---

of the New Testament (especially Paul). In this regard, Johnson believes that James and Paul have a lot more in common than is usually recognized. More than four hundred years later, who would have thought that a Catholic would correct Luther in this regard?

E/Cr 7. Chester, A., and Ralph Martin. *The Theology of the Letters of James, Peter, and Jude,* NTT (Cambridge University Press, 1994).

E/Cr-L/Cr 8. Chilton, Bruce, and Craig Evans, eds. *James the Just and Simon Peter* (Brill, 2002).

———, eds. *James the Just and Christian Origins* (Brill, 1999).

L/Cr 9. Chilton, Bruce, and Jacob Neusner, eds. *The Brother of Jesus* (Westminster John Knox, 2001).

E 10. Deppe, Dean. *The Sayings of Jesus in James* (Bookcrafters, 1989).

C/M 11. Edgar, David. Has God Not Chosen the Poor? (Sheffield Academic Press, 2001).

L/Cr 12. Eisenman, Robert. *James the Brother of Jesus* (Penguin, 1997).

L/Cr 13. Maynard-Reid, Pedrito. Poverty and Wealth in James (Orbis, 1987). Sociological.

E/Cr-L/Cr 14. Neusner, Jacob, and Bruce Chilton, eds. *The Judaism of James the Brother of Jesus* (Westminster John Knox, 2002).

L/Cr 15. Painter, John. *Just James* (Fortress, 1999).

C/M 16. Penner, Todd. *The Epistle of James and Eschatology* (Sheffield Academic Press, 1996). Continuity with early Christian and Jewish texts on ethics and eschatology.

1 Peter*

Technical, Semitechnical[15]

C/M 1. Achtemeier, Paul. Hermeneia (Fortress, 1996). Pseudepigraphic.

L/Cr 2. Beare, Francis. *The First Epistle of Peter,* 3d ed. (Basil Blackwell, 1970). Non-Petrine.

* Forthcoming: Troy Martin, NIGTC (Eerdmans); Scott Hafemann, Pillar (Eerdmans); Karen Jobes, BECNT (Baker); Daniel Harrington, Sacra Pagina (Liturgical); Lewis Donelson, NTL (Westminster John Knox); and Earl Richard,

E/Cr	**3.**	**Davids, Peter. NICNT (Eerdmans, 1990).** Silvanus by Petrine commission.
L/Cr	**4.**	**Elliott, John. AB (Doubleday, 2001).** Pseudepigraphic, especially cultural background.
C/M	**5.**	**Goppelt, Leonard. *A Commentary on 1 Peter* (Eerdmans, 1993).** Sociological background, extracanonical material, links to DSS and OT.
E/Cr	**6.**	**Michaels, Ramsey. WBC (Word, 1988).** Essentially Petrine, written by approved disciple.
E	**7.**	**Schreiner, Thomas. NAC (Broadman, 2003).**
E/Cr	8.	Selwyn, Edward. *The First Epistle of St. Peter,* 2d ed. (Macmillan, 1947). Petrine through Silvanus.

Exposition

C/M	1.	Bartlett, David. NIB, vol. 12 (Abingdon, 1998). Pseudepigraphic.
L/Cr	2.	Boring, Eugene. ANTC (Abingdon, 1999). Pseudepigraphic, "Narrative World of Peter" appendix.
E	3.	Clowney, Edmund. BST (IVP, 1989).
L/Cr	4.	Craddock, Fred. WBComp (Westminster John Knox, 1995). 1–2 Peter/Jude.

Peter, Jude and 2 Peter (Smyth and Helwys). If you already have Achtemeier, Michaels, Davids, or Goppelt plus an expositional commentary such as Marshall or Grudem, you are well supplied. The best currently available commentary on 1 Peter is a toss-up between Michaels and Achtemeier (when used with some discretion). Troy Martin's forthcoming commentary should be very good on the Greek, and Hafemann should be well worth anticipating. He's also been assigned 2 Peter/Jude (NIGTC). Elliott can be useful when used with some discretion, especially when he overstates his sociological model for Peter's audience.

15. The fact that only relatively few moderate-liberal commentaries (about 30 of 180, or 17 percent) are recommended as primary choices thus far demonstrates how highly regarded Achtemeier's moderate commentary on 1 Peter is considered. This fact represents a huge improvement from twenty years ago, when the best available commentaries were almost half moderate-liberal. Evangelical scholarship has come a long way. Commentaries such as Daniel Block's two-volume work on Ezekiel often garnish universal praise. The vast majority of technical/semitechnical commentaries that will come out in the next five years are evangelical. A glance at what is projected for 1–2 Peter/Jude demonstrates this fact.

E 5. Grudem, Wayne. TNTC (Eerdmans, 1988). Petrine, 1 Peter 3:19–20 appendix.

E 6. Hillyer, Norman. NIBCNT (Hendrickson, 1992). 1–2 Peter/Jude.

C/M 7. Kelly, J. N. D. BNTC (Hendrickson, 1993). 1 Peter by Silvanus, denies authenticity of 2 Peter, also includes Jude.

E/Cr 8. Marshall, Howard. IVPNTC (IVP, 1992).

E/Cr 9. McKnight, Scot. NIVAC (Zondervan, 1996).

E 10. Waltner, E., and J. Daryl Charles. BCBC (Herald, 1999). 1–2 Peter/Jude.

Special Studies

E/Cr 1. Campbell, B. *Honor, Shame, and the Rhetoric of 1 Peter* (Scholars, 1998).

L/Cr 2. Dalton, W. *Christ's Proclamation to the Spirits,* 2d ed. (Pontifical Biblical Institute, 1989). 1 Peter 3:18–4:6.

E 3. Dubis, Mark. *Messianic Woes in First Peter* (Lang, 2002). 1 Peter 4:12–19.

L/Cr 4. Elliott, John. *A Home for the Homeless,* 2d ed. (Fortress, 1990). Analysis of "aliens and strangers" in 1 Peter.

L/Cr 5. Perkins, Pheme. *Peter* (Fortress, 2000).

C/M 6. Thurén, Lauri. *Argument and Theology in 1 Peter* (Sheffield Academic Press, 1995).

E/Cr 7. *See* Chester and Martin under James: Special Studies.

2 Peter/Jude*

C/M 1. Bauckham, Richard. WBC (Word, 1983). Pseudepigraphic, rich extrabiblical material, Jewish background.

---

* Forthcoming: Peter Davids, Pillar (Eerdmans); Scott Hafemann, NIGTC (Eerdmans); Robert Webb, NICNT (Eerdmans); Lewis Donelson, NTL (Westminster John Knox); Gene Green, BECNT (Baker); and Robert Harvey, IVPNTC (IVP). So many promising commentaries on 1–2 Peter/Jude are coming out that I am tempted to invoke my twenty-year statute of limitations on

E/Cr 2. Mayor James. *The Epistle of St. Jude and the Second Epistle of St. Peter* (Baker, 1979). Non-Petrine.

L/Cr 3. Neyrey, Jerome. AB (Doubleday, 1993). Socioliterary background, pseudepigraphic.

E 4. Schreiner, Thomas. NAC (Broadman, 2003).

5. *See* Kelly above.

Exposition

E 1. Green, Michael. TNTC, rev. ed. (Eerdmans, 1987). Annihilationist, solid author defense.

E 2. Hiebert, D. Edmond. *2 Peter and Jude* (Unusual, 1989).

L/Cr 3. Kraftchick, Stephen. ANTC (Abingdon, 2002).

E 4. Lucas, Dick, and Christopher Green. BST (IVP, 1995). Semitechnical, authorship appendix.

E 5. Moo, Douglas. NIVAC (Zondervan, 1996).

L/Cr 6. Watson, Duane. NIB, vol. 12 (Abingdon, 1998).

Special Studies

C/M 1. Bauckham, Richard. Jude and the Relatives of Jesus in the Early Church (T & T Clark, 1990).

E 2. Charles, Daryl. *Literary Strategy in the Epistle of Jude* (University of Scranton, 1993).

———. *Virtue Amidst Vice* (Sheffield Academic Press, 1997). Posits Christianization of Stoicism in 2 Peter 1 as elsewhere in NT. Centrist-Arminian position.

C/M 3. Landon, Charles. *A Text-Critical Study of the Epistle of Jude* (Sheffield Academic Press, 1996).

E 4. Lyle, Kenneth. *Ethical Admonition in the Epistle of Jude* (Lang, 1998).

C/M 5. Watson, Duane. *Invention, Arrangement, and Style* (Scholars, 1988). 2 Peter/Jude.

Bauckham, but his commentary is brilliant and will continue to be used. Green recently offered an excellent commentary on 1–2 Thessalonians. Hafemann is slated for a semitechnical effort on 1 Peter. Davids's NICNT entry on 1 Peter was most serviceable. Therefore, I would recommend Hafemann, Bauckham, Davids, and Green on 2 Peter/Jude.

1–3 John*

Technical, Semitechnical

L/Cr	**1.**	**Brown, Raymond. AB (Doubleday, 1982).** Sacramental.
L/Cr	2.	Grayston, Kenneth. NCBC (Eerdmans, 1984).
✓**E/Cr**	**3.**	**Marshall, I. Howard. NICNT (Eerdmans, 1978).**
✓C/M	4.	Schnackenburg, Rudolf. *The Johannine Epistles,* 7th ed. (Crossroad, 1992). Theological.
C/M	**5.**	**Smalley, Stephen. WBC (Word, 1984).**
L/Cr	6.	Strecker, Georg. Hermeneia (Fortress, 1996). Presbyter John author of 2–3 John, 1 John non-Johannine, contra Brown on order of authorship.

Exposition

E	**1.**	**Akin, Daniel. NAC (Broadman & Holman, 2001).**
L/Cr	2.	Black, Clifton. NIB, vol. 12 (Abingdon, 1998).
E	3.	Burdick, Donald. *The Letters of John the Apostle* (Moody, 1985).
E	4.	Burge, Gary. NIVAC (Zondervan, 1996).
E/Cr	5.	Johnson, Thomas. NIBCNT (Hendrickson, 1993).
E	**6.**	**Kruse, Colin. Pillar (Eerdmans, 2000).** Extensive use of the early church fathers to establish setting.
E/Cr	7.	Meye Thompson, Marianne. IVPNTC (IVP, 1992).
L/Cr	8.	Painter, John. Sacra Pagina (Liturgical, 2002).
L/Cr	9.	Rensberger, David. ANTC (Abingdon, 1997).

---

* Forthcoming: D. A. Carson, NIGTC (Eerdmans); Robert Yarbrough, BECNT (Baker); Judith Lieu, NTL (Westminster John Knox); and Elizabeth Schüssler Fiorenza, WBComp (Westminster John Knox). I would keep Marshall because it is an admirable recapitulation of previous scholarship and very useful for the pastor, but Brown, Smalley, and Schnackenburg are almost dated. The recent expositions by Daniel Akin and Colin Kruse lean toward the semitechnical and are both very good, but it is time for another more technical commentary. That void will soon be remedied by D. A. Carson and Robert Yarbrough. Carson has already provided an outstanding, semitechnical commentary on the gospel of John (also Eerdmans). Yarbrough's commentary promises to pay close attention to the relationship of the OT and Jesus' teaching to 1–3 John. Frequent allusions will be made to Jewish, Greco-Roman, and patristic authors.

——. WBComp (Westminster John Knox, 2001).

L/Cr 10. Sloyan, Gerard. NTC (Trinity Press International, 1998). Social context commentary.

E 11. Stott, John. TNTC, rev. ed. (Eerdmans, 1988).

Special Studies

E 1. Burge, Gary. *The Anointed Community* (Eerdmans, 1987).

C/M 2. Lieu, Judith. *The Second and Third Letters of John* (T & T Clark, 1986).

——. NTT (Cambridge University Press, 1991).

C/M 3. Smalley, Stephen. *John,* 2d ed. (IVP, 1998). Especially literary features.

4. *See* John: John as Story, Special Studies.

Revelation*

Technical, Semitechnical

C/M 1. Aune, David. WBC, 3 vols. (Thomas Nelson, 1997–98). Especially grammatical, text-critical analysis, source/composition critical, extensive introduction, proposes early/late editions, top heavy in extrabiblical citations of Greco-Roman, Jewish parallels, limited use to pastors.

E 2. Beale, Gregory. NIGTC (Eerdmans, 1999). Especially OT, Jewish parallels, historical, idealist, amillennial, later date more probable.

L/Cr 3. Harrington, Wilfred. Sacra Pagina (Liturgical, 1994).

---

* Forthcoming: Elizabeth Schüssler Fiorenza, Hermeneia (Fortress); Josephine Ford, AB, rev. ed. (Doubleday); Brian Blount, NTL (Westminster John Knox); Paige Patterson, NAC, 2 vols. (Broadman & Holman); and D. A. Carson, Pillar (Eerdmans). At present, Revelation is already well served. I am tempted to say that one could hardly do better than Beale and Mounce for technical/semitechnical commentaries, but, ultimately, I think that one can. Particularly, I think that Osborne and Carson supplement Beale quite well. Elizabeth Schüssler Fiorenza has argued previously that Revelation is a collection of traditions unified by a single author.

E 4. **Mounce, Robert. NICNT, rev. ed. (Eerdmans, 1997).** Posttribulational.

E 5. **Osborne, Grant. BECNT (Baker, 2002).**

L/Cr 6. Roloff, Jürgen. Continental (Fortress, 1993). Amillennial.

E 7. Thomas, Robert. *Revelation,* 2 vols. (Moody, 1992, 95). Dispensational.

Exposition[16]

E 1. **Beasley-Murray, George. NCBC, rev. ed. (Eerdmans, 1978).** Premillennial.

L/Cr 2. Boring, Eugene. IBC (John Knox, 1989).

C/M 3. **Caird, George. BNTC (Hendrickson, 1993).**

E 4. Hendriksen, William. *More Than Conquerors* (Baker, 1939).

E 5. Johnson, Alan. EBC, vol. 12 (Zondervan, 1983). Semi-technical, premillennial.

E 6. **Johnson Dennis. *Triumph of the Lamb* (Presbyterian & Reformed, 2001).** Amillennial.[17]

E 7. **Keener, Craig. NIVAC (Zondervan, 2000).** Premillennial.

E 8. **Kistemaker, Simon. *Exposition of the Book of Revelation* (Baker, 2001).** Premillennial.

E 9. **Ladd, George. *A Commentary on the Revelation of John* (Eerdmans, 1972).** Premillennial.

E/Cr 10. Michaels, J. Ramsey. IVPNTC (IVP, 1997).

E 11. Morris, Leon. TNTC, rev. ed. (Eerdmans, 1987). Amillennial.

L/Cr 12. Rowland, Christopher. Epworth (Epworth, 1993).

---

16. Keener's commentary weighs on the semitechnical side but comes closer to an exposition than Carson's probably will. I would hate to give Keener short schrift, but go with Johnson (see the following comment if you must).

17. Dennis Johnson's *Triumph of the Lamb* is as masterful as Keener but is much more layman friendly. Johnson, an amillennialist, is to be especially commended for the irenic manner in which he countenances contrary opinions, notably those of dispensationalists. This commentary is one of the surest indicators that the rapprochement broached vis-à-vis progressive dispensationalism is putting behind a conflict that once mirrored the argument expressed in the text.

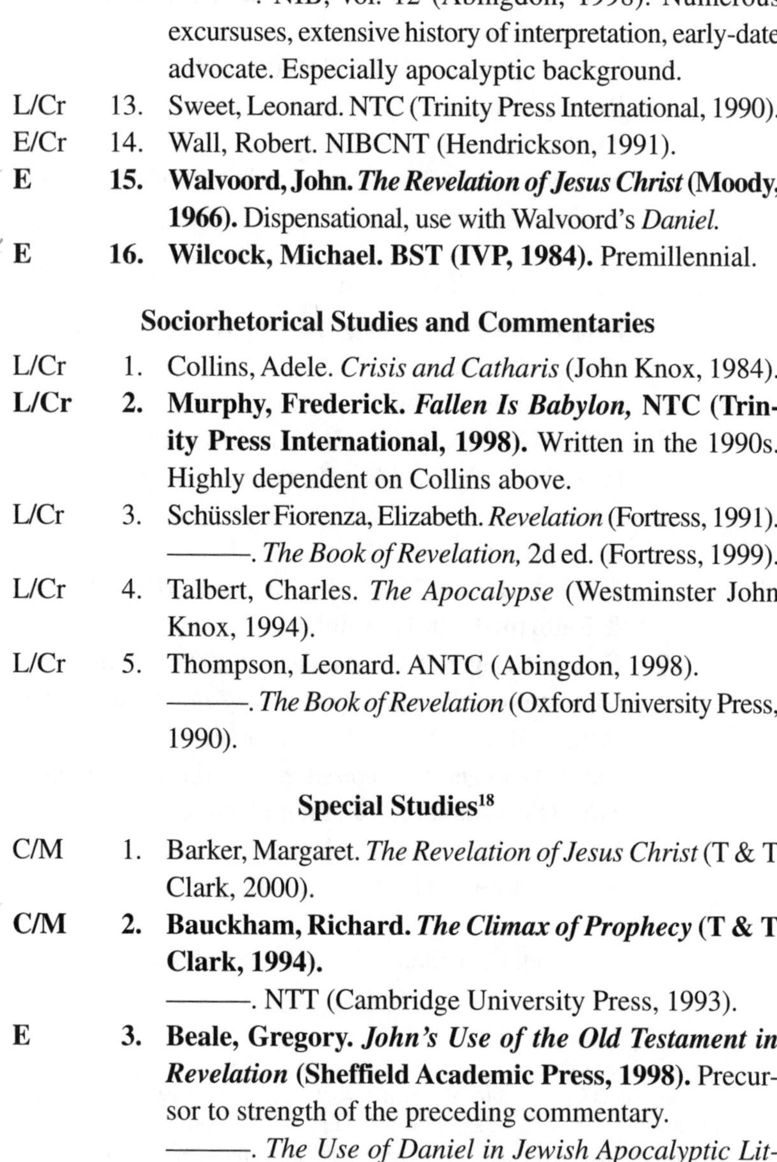

———. NIB, vol. 12 (Abingdon, 1998). Numerous excursuses, extensive history of interpretation, early-date advocate. Especially apocalyptic background.

L/Cr 13. Sweet, Leonard. NTC (Trinity Press International, 1990).

E/Cr 14. Wall, Robert. NIBCNT (Hendrickson, 1991).

E 15. Walvoord, John. *The Revelation of Jesus Christ* (Moody, 1966). Dispensational, use with Walvoord's *Daniel.*

E 16. Wilcock, Michael. BST (IVP, 1984). Premillennial.

Sociorhetorical Studies and Commentaries

L/Cr 1. Collins, Adele. *Crisis and Catharis* (John Knox, 1984).

L/Cr 2. Murphy, Frederick. *Fallen Is Babylon,* NTC (Trinity Press International, 1998). Written in the 1990s. Highly dependent on Collins above.

L/Cr 3. Schüssler Fiorenza, Elizabeth. *Revelation* (Fortress, 1991).
———. *The Book of Revelation,* 2d ed. (Fortress, 1999).

L/Cr 4. Talbert, Charles. *The Apocalypse* (Westminster John Knox, 1994).

L/Cr 5. Thompson, Leonard. ANTC (Abingdon, 1998).
———. *The Book of Revelation* (Oxford University Press, 1990).

Special Studies[18]

C/M 1. Barker, Margaret. *The Revelation of Jesus Christ* (T & T Clark, 2000).

C/M 2. Bauckham, Richard. *The Climax of Prophecy* (T & T Clark, 1994).
———. NTT (Cambridge University Press, 1993).

E **3. Beale, Gregory. *John's Use of the Old Testament in Revelation* (Sheffield Academic Press, 1998).** Precursor to strength of the preceding commentary.
———. *The Use of Daniel in Jewish Apocalyptic Literature and the Revelation of St. John* (University Press

18. Dave Mathewson, *The Meaning and Function of the Old Testament in Revelation 21:1–22:5* (Sheffield Academic Press, forthcoming).

of America, 1984). Links Daniel 7 to Revelation 1:4–20 and Revelation 4–5.

E 4. Bock, Darrell, ed. *Three Views on the Millennium and Beyond* (Zondervan, 1999).

E 5. Davis, R. *The Heaven in Court Judgment of Revelation 4–5* (University Press of America, 1992).

E 6. Gentry, Kenneth. *Before Jerusalem Fell* (Institute for Christian Economics, 1989). Thorough early-date study.

E 7. Gregg, Steve, ed. *Revelation: Four Views—A Parallel Commentary* (Thomas Nelson, 1997). Preterist, historicist, futurist, idealist. Numerous excerpts from Chilton, Hendriksen, Ladd, Mounce, Russell, Ryrie, Swete, Walvoord, Wilcock, etc.

E 8. Hemer, Colin. *The Letters to the Seven Churches of Asia in Their Local Setting* (JSOT, 1986; Eerdmans, 2001). Revelation 2–3.

C/M 9. Koester, Craig. *Revelation and the End of All Things* (Eerdmans, 2001).

E/Cr 10. Kraybill, Nelson. *Imperial Cult and Commerce in John's Apocalypse* (Sheffield Academic Press, 1996). Socio-economic perspective culled from archaeological and epigraphical evidence.

L/Cr 11. Malina, Bruce, and John Pilch. *Social-Scientific Commentary on the Book of Revelation* (Fortress, 2000).

E/Cr 12. Michaels, Ramsey. *Interpreting the Book of Revelation* (Baker, 1992).

C/M 13. Moyise, Steve. *The Old Testament in the Book of Revelation* (Sheffield Academic Press, 1995).

E 14. Pate, Marvin, ed. *Four Views on the Book of Revelation* (Zondervan, 1998). Preterist, idealist, dispensationalist, progressive dispensational.

C/M 15. Stevenson, Gregory. *Power and Place* (de Gruyter, 2001). The temple in Revelation.

L/Cr 16. Wainwright, Arthur. *Mysterious Apocalypse* (Abingdon, 1993; Wipf & Stock, 2001). History of interpretation.

L/Cr 17. Worth, Roland. *The Seven Cities of the Apocalypse,* vol. 2 (Paulist, 1999). Revelation 2–3.

18. *See* Systematic Theology: The Last Days.

Scholarly One-Volume Commentaries*

1. **Barton, John, and John Muddiman, eds. *The Oxford Bible Commentary* (Oxford University Press, 2001). Moderate-liberal.**[19]
2. **Brown, Raymond E., Joseph Fitzmyer, and Roland Murphy, eds. *New Jerome Bible Commentary,* 2d ed. (Prentice-Hall, 1999).** Catholic, liberal.
3. Bruce, F.F, ed. *New International Bible Commentary* (Zondervan, 1986).
4. Dockery, David, ed. *Holman Bible Handbook* (Broadman & Holman, 1993).
5. Kroeger, Catherine, and Mary Evans, eds. *The IVP Women's Bible Commentary* (IVP, 2002).
6. **Mays, James, ed. *HarperCollins Bible Commentary,* rev. ed. (HarperSanFrancisco, 2000).** Moderate-liberal.
7. Mills, Watson, and Richard Wilson, eds. *Mercer Commentary on the Bible* (Mercer University Press, 1995).
8. **Wenham, Gordon, et al., eds. *New Bible Commentary: Twenty-First Century Edition* (IVP, 1994).**

---

* Forthcoming: James Dunn and John Rogerson, eds., *Eerdmans Commentary on the Bible.* The former promises to be an exciting contribution and will be the leading work on the Old Testament in the New.

19. Certainly the most stunning volume (1,400 pages) is the recent *Oxford Bible Commentary.* It is authored by eighty-three moderate-liberal, international scholars (many prominent) of Catholic, Jewish Orthodox, and Protestant persuasion. This number is relatively few given the size of this project (an average of 170 pages per author). It has a fifteen-page bibliographical guide that refers to conservative works on top of the often voluminous references appended to each article (two full pages of eight-point font at the end of Isaiah and Jeremiah, for instance), and the highest-quality collection of maps (eleven plates) I have ever seen in a reference. Also worth mentioning is its highly attractive typeset. Finally, it is accompanied by a Logos-compatible CD that replicates the contents (demo unlockable for $60.00), enabling a search of its 1.5 million words. Of course, when you are dealing with a project of this magnitude, the result is that most of the individual commentaries are five to ten years old.

10 NEW TESTAMENT BACKGROUND

Primary References

1. Arnold, Clinton, ed. *The Zondervan Illustrated Bible Background Commentary: New Testament,* 4 vols. (Zondervan, 2002).[1]
2. **Evans, Craig, and Stanley Porter, eds. *Dictionary of New Testament Background* (IVP, 2000).** Greco-Roman influences, etc. This is not only the best but also the most technical of the IVP dictionaries (*see* 3, 4, and 7 below).
3. **Green, Joel, Scot McKnight, and I. Howard Marshall, eds. *Dictionary of Jesus and the Gospels* (IVP, 1992).**
4. **Hawthorne, Gerald, Ralph Martin, and Daniel Reid, eds. *Dictionary of Paul and His Letters* (IVP, 1993).**
5. House, Wayne. *Chronological and Background Charts of the New Testament* (Zondervan, 1981).
6. **Keener, Craig. *The IVP Bible Background Commentary: New Testament* (IVP, 1994).**

---

1. Although this study supercedes Keener in length and documentation of its sources, its popular format (though written by scholars) makes it prohibitively expensive for the amount of extra information it provides in contrast to Keener (with the exception of Mark Strauss on Luke, Andreas Köstenberger on John, and Clinton Arnold on Acts). Still, pastors might find that the fleshing out of information in *ZIBBC* will better fit their homiletical needs. Nevertheless, I would have to prefer Keener regardless of whether you already have it because it can be obtained from CBD at one-fifth the cost. Perhaps obtaining just volume 2 of the *ZIBBC* (John, Acts) would be advisable.

7. **Martin, Ralph, and Peter Davids, eds. *Dictionary of the Later New Testament and Its Developments* (IVP, 1997).** Up to the second-century church fathers.
8. Matthews, Victor. *Manners and Customs in the Bible,* rev. ed. (Hendrickson, 1991).

Primary Source Anthologies

1. Barrett, C. K. *New Testament Background,* 2d ed. (Harper, 1987).
2. Bettenson, Henry, and Chris Maunder, eds. *Documents of the Christian Church,* 3d ed. (Oxford University Press, 1999).
3. Boring, Eugene, Klaus Berger, and Carsten Colpe, eds. *Hellenistic Commentary to the New Testament* (Abingdon, 1995). History-of-religions approach.
4. Doepp, Siegmar, and Wilhelm Geerlings, eds. *Dictionary of Early Christian Literature* (Herder and Herder, 2000).
5. Dungan, David, and David Cartlidge, eds. *Documents for the Study of the Gospels,* rev. ed. and enl. (Fortress, 1994). With noncanonicals.
6. Ehrman, Bart. *The New Testament and Other Early Christian Writings: A Reader* (Oxford University Press, 1997). NRSV and excerpts from anthologies.

   ———. *After the New Testament* (Oxford University Press, 1998).
7. Elliott, J. K., ed. *The Apocryphal New Testament* (Oxford University Press, 1993).
8. Elwell, Walter, and Robert Yarbrough. *Readings from the First Century World* (Baker, 1998). Companion volume for their *Encountering the NT.*
9. Kee, Howard. *The Origins of Christianity,* 2d ed. (Prentice-Hall, 1973).
10. Mason, Steve, and Thomas Robinson. *Early Christian Reader* (Hendrickson, 2002). NRSV, NT, Ignatius, 1 Clement, Didache, and Gospel of Thomas.
11. Schneemelcher, Wilhelm. *New Testament Apocrypha,* 2d ed., 2 vols. (Westminster John Knox, 1990–92).

Principal Early Church References

1. **Barnett, Paul. *Jesus and the Rise of Early Christianity* (IVP, 1999).**
2. Blasi, Anthony, Jean Duhaime, and Paul-Andre Turcotte, eds. *The Handbook of Early Christianity* (AltaMira, 2002).
3. Bowersock, G. W., Peter Brown, and Oleg Grabar, eds. *Late Antiquity* (Harvard University Press, 1999).
4. **Brown, Peter. *The Rise of Western Christendom,* 2d ed. (Blackwell, 2002).**
5. Brox, Norbert. *A History of the Early Church* (SCM, 1994). Available through Trinity Press International, introductory.
6. Bruce, F. F. *New Testament History* (Doubleday, 1971).
7. **Chadwick, Henry. *The Church in Ancient Society* (Oxford University Press, 2002).** First six centuries.[2]
8. **Di Berardino, Angelo, ed. *Encyclopedia of The Early Church,* 2 vols. (Oxford University Press, 1992).**
9. **Di Berardino, Angelo, and Basil Studer, eds. *History of Theology: The Patristic Period* (Liturgical, 1997).**
10. Doepp, Siegmar, and Wilhelm Geerlings, eds. *Dictionary of Early Christian Literature* (Herder and Herder, 1999).
11. Doran, Robert. *Birth of a Worldview* (Rowman and Littlefield, 1999). Author of commentary on 1–2 Maccabees.
12. **Ferguson, Everett. *Backgrounds of Early Christianity,* 2d ed. (Eerdmans, 1993).** Cultural, political, religious background guide.

    ———, ed. *Encyclopedia of Early Christianity,* 2d ed. (Garland, 1997).
13. **Grant, Robert. *Augustus to Constantine,* rev. ed. (Harper, 1990).**
14. Lampe, Peter. *From Paul to Valentinus* (Fortress, 1999).
15. Malherbe, Abraham, et al., eds. *The Early Church in Its Context* (Brill, 1998).

2. As a documentary source for early Christianity, this reference has no rivals, especially in its citation of German and French in addition to English references, but it is virtually colorless in composition.

16. **McKechnie, Paul. *The First Christian Centuries* (IVP, 2002).** First three centuries.
17. Novak, Ralph. *Christianity and the Roman Empire: Background Texts* (Trinity Press International, 2001). The first four centuries.
18. **Patzia, Arthur. *The Emergence of the Church* (IVP, 2001).**
19. Reicke, Bo. *The New Testament Era* (Fortress, 1968). 500 B.C.–A.D. 100.
20. **Stark, Rodney. *The Rise of Christianity* (Princeton University Press, 1996).**
21. Sullivan, Francis. *From Apostles to Bishops* (Newman, 2002). Available through Paulist.
22. **Trocmé, Etienne. *The Childhood of Christianity* (SCM, 1997).** Brief, engaging, moderate history.
23. Winter, Bruce, ed. *The Book of Acts in Its First-Century Setting,* 6 vols. (Eerdmans, 1993–).
24. **Witherington, Ben. *New Testament History* (Baker, 2001).**

Other Early Church References

1. Attridge, Harold, and Gregory Hata. *Eusebius, Christianity, and Judaism* (Wayne State University Press, 1992).
2. **Aune, David. *Prophecy in Early Christianity and the Ancient Mediterranean World* (Eerdmans, 1983).**
3. Avalos, Hector. *Health Care and the Rise of Christianity* (Hendrickson, 1999).
4. **Bauckham, Richard. *Gospel Women* (Eerdmans, 2002).**
5. Bockmuehl, Markus. *Jewish Law in Gentile Churches* (T & T Clark, 2000). Influence of halakah.
6. **Bond, Helen. *Pontius Pilate in History and Interpretation* (Cambridge University Press, 1998).**
7. Capuani, Massimo, et al. *Christian Egypt* (Liturgical, 2002).
8. Charlesworth, James. *The Old Testament Pseudepigrapha and the New Testament* (Trinity Press International, 1998).
9. **deSilva, David. *Honor, Patronage, Kinship and Purity* (IVP, 2000).**

10. Donfried, Karl, and Peter Richardson, eds. *Judaism and Christianity in First-Century Rome* (Eerdmans, 1998).

11. Evans, Craig. *Noncanonical Writings and Their Use in New Testament Interpretation* (Hendrickson, 1992).

12. Evans, Craig and Stanley Porter, eds. *New Testament Backgrounds* (Sheffield Academic Press, 1997). JSNT compendium.

13. Hoehner, Harold. *Herod Antipas* (Cambridge University Press, 1972).

14. Horbury, William. *Jewish Messianism and the Cult of Christ* (SCM, 1998).

15. Jeremias, Joachim. *Jerusalem in the Time of Jesus* (Fortress, 1969). Dated.

16. Johnson, Luke. *Religious Experience in New Testament Studies* (Fortress, 1998). Baptism, glossalalia, meals, etc.

17. Kelly, J. N. D. *Early Christian Doctrines,* 5th ed. (Continuum, 2001).

18. Klijn, A. *Jewish-Christian Gospel Tradition* (Brill, 1992). On noncanonical gospels.

19. Millard, Alan. *Reading and Writing in the Time of Jesus* (Sheffield Academic Press, 2000).

20. Nobbs, A., et al., eds. *Ancient History in a Modern University,* vol. 2: *Early Christianity and Late Antiquity* (Eerdmans, 1997).

21. Oakes, Peter, ed. *Rome in the Bible and the Early Church* (Baker, 2002).

22. Pearson, Brook, ed. *The Future of Early Christianity* (Fortress, 1991).

23. Schmithals, Walter. *The Theology of the First Christians* (Westminster John Knox, 1997).

24. Walker, Peter. *Jesus and the Holy City* (Eerdmans, 1997).

25. Wilson, Stephen. *Related Strangers* (Fortress, 1995).

26. Wright, N. T. *Christian Origins and the Question of God,* vol. 1 (Fortress, 1992).

27. Wroe, Ann. *Pontius Pilate* (Random House, 2000).

28. *See* Church History: Early Church.

Early Church Fathers

1. **Bercot, David, ed. *A Dictionary of Early Christian Beliefs* (Hendrickson, 1998).**
2. Bradshaw, Paul, Maxwell Johnson, and Edward Phillips. *The Apostolic Tradition* (Fortress, 2002). Attributed to Hippolytus (A.D. 170–235).
3. Diprose, Ronald. *Israel in the Development of Christian Thought* (Italian Biblical Institute, 2000). Claims church fathers instigated replacement theory.
4. **Hall, Christopher. *Reading Scripture with the Church Fathers* (IVP, 1998).**

   ———. *Learning Theology with the Church Fathers* (IVP, 2002).
5. **Holmes, Michael, ed. *The Apostolic Fathers*, 2d ed. (Baker, 1998).**
6. Jefford, Clayton. *Reading the Apostolic Fathers* (Hendrickson, 1996).
7. Niederwimmer, Kurt. *The Didache*. Hermeneia (Fortress, 1998).
8. **Oden, Thomas, gen. ed. ACCS, 27 vols. (IVP, 1998–).**
9. Osiek, Carolyn. *The Shepherd of Hermas,* Hermeneia (Fortress, 1998).
10. Roberts, Alexander, and James Donaldson, eds. *Ante-Nicene Fathers,* 10 vols. (Eerdmans, 1996). Tagged, cross-referenced, and indexed with introductions.
11. Simonetti, Manlio. *Biblical Interpretation in the Early Church* (T & T Clark, 1994).
12. Tugwell, Simon. *The Apostolic Fathers* (Continuum, 2002).
13. Van de Sandt, Huub, and David Flusser. *The Didache* (Fortress, 2002). Historical analysis.
14. von Campenhausen, Hans. *The Fathers of the Church* (Hendrickson, 1999).
15. Young, Frances. *Biblical Exegesis and the Formation of Christian Culture* (Cambridge University Press, 1997).

Pauline Background

1. Ashton, John. *The Religion of Paul the Apostle* (Yale University Press, 2000).
2. Banks, Robert. *Paul's Idea of Community,* rev. ed. (Hendrickson, 1994).
3. Beck, James. *The Psychology of Paul* (Kregel, 2002).
4. Bockmuehl, Markus. *Revelation and Mystery in Ancient Judaism and Pauline Christianity* (Eerdmans, 1997).
5. Dodd, Brian. *The Problem with Paul* (IVP, 1996). Gender roles, sexuality, slavery, and attitude toward Judaism.
6. Donaldson, Terence. *Paul and the Gentiles* (Fortress, 1997).
7. Engberg-Pedersen, Troels, ed. *Paul in Its Hellenistic Context* (Fortress, 1994).
   ———. *Paul and the Stoics* (Westminster John Knox, 2000).
   ———, ed. *Paul Beyond the Judaism/Hellenism Divide* (Westminster John Knox, 2001).
8. Gager, John. *Reinventing Paul* (Oxford University Press, 2000).
9. Goodwin, Mark. *Paul, Apostle of the Living God* (Trinity Press International, 2001).
10. **Hafemann, Scott. *Paul, Moses, and the History of Israel* (Hendrickson, 1996).**
11. MacDonald, Margaret. *The Pauline Churches* (Cambridge University Press, 1988).
12. Malina, Bruce, and Jerome Neyrey. *Portraits of Paul* (Westminster John Knox, 1996).
13. **McRay, John. *Paul: His Life and Teaching* (Baker, 2002).**
14. **Meggitt, Justin. *Paul, Poverty, and Survival* (T & T Clark, 1998).**
15. Picirilli, Robert. *Paul the Apostle* (Moody, 1986).
16. **Polhill, John. *Paul and His Letters* (Broadman & Holman, 1999).**
17. **Porter, Stanley. *Paul in Acts* (Hendrickson, 2001).**
18. **Roetzel, Calvin. *Paul* (University of South Carolina Press, 1998).**
    ———.*The Letters of Paul,* 4th ed. (Westminster John Knox, 1998).

19. **Rosner, Brian. *Understanding Paul's Ethics* (Eerdmans, 1995).**
20. Sampley, Paul, ed. *Paul in the Greco-Roman World* (Trinity Press International, 2001).
21. Strom, Mark. *Reframing Paul* (IVP, 2000).
22. Wallace, R., and W. Williams. *The Three Worlds of Paul of Tarsus* (Routledge, 1998).
23. Wenham, David. *Paul, Follower of Jesus or Founder of Christianity?* (Eerdmans, 1995).
   ———. *Paul and Jesus* (Eerdmans, 2002).
24. Westerholm, Stephen. *Preface to the Study of Paul* (Eerdmans, 1997).
25. Williams, David. *Paul's Metaphors* (Hendrickson, 1999).
26. **Witherington, Ben. *The Paul Quest* (IVP, 1998).**
   ———. *Paul's Narrative Thought World* (Westminster John Knox, 1994).
27. Wright, N. T. *What Paul Really Said* (Eerdmans, 1997).
28. *See* New Testament Resources: Pauline Theology, Paul and the Law.

Paul: The Early Years

1. Hengel, Martin. *The Pre-Christian Paul* (Trinity Press International, 1991).
2. **Hengel, Martin, and Ann Schwemer. *Paul Between Damascus and Antioch* (Westminster John Knox, 1997).**
3. Longenecker, Richard, ed. *The Road from Damascus* (Eerdmans, 1997).
4. **Murphy-O'Connor, Jerome. *Paul* (Oxford University Press, 1996).** Childhood, postconversion years.
5. Riesner, Rainer. *Paul's Early Period* (Eerdmans, 1997).

Paul's Imprisonment and Trial

1. **Cassidy, Richard. *Paul in Chains* (Herder and Herder, 2001).** Especially Philippians.
2. **Mauck, John. *Paul on Trial* (Thomas Nelson, 2001).** Lawyer Mauck posits Acts as a legal defense treatise. Foreword by Donald Hagner.

3. **Rapske, Brian. *Paul in Roman Custody* (Eerdmans, 1995).** Social status as measure of jail sentence.
4. **Tajra, H. *The Martyrdom of Saint Paul* (Mohr, 1994).**
   ———. *The Trial of St. Paul* (Mohr, 1989).
5. **Wansink, Craig. *Chained in Christ* (Sheffield Academic Press, 1996).**

Greco-Roman Background

1. Alston, Richard. *Aspects of Roman History: a.d. 14–117* (Routledge, 1998).
2. **Aune, David, ed. *Greco-Roman Literature and the New Testament* (Scholars, 1988).**
3. Balch, David, Everett Ferguson, and Wayne Meeks, eds. *Greeks, Romans, and Christians* (Fortress, 1990).
4. Brown, John Pairman. *Israel and Hellas* (de Gruyter, 1995).
5. Burkert, Walter. *Greek Religion* (Harvard University Press, 1985).
6. Burridge, Richard. *What Are the Gospels?* (Cambridge University Press, 1992).
7. **Christopherson, Alf, et al., eds. *Paul, Luke, and the Graeco-Roman World* (Sheffield Academic Press, 2002).**
8. **Clarke, Andrew, ed. *First-Century Christians in the Greco-Roman World,* 5 vols. (Eerdmans, 1993–96).**
9. Cook, John. *The Interpretation of the New Testament in Greco-Roman Paganism* (Mohr Siebeck, 2000).
10. **Finegan, Jack. *Myth and Mystery* (Baker, 1989).** Pagan religions.
11. Finn, Thomas. *From Death to Rebirth: Ritual and Conversion in Antiquity* (Paulist, 1997).
12. Fox, Robin Lane. *Pagans and Christians* (Harper, 1987).
13. **Frankfurter, David. *Religion in Roman Egypt* (Princeton University Press, 2001).** Confrontation between indigenous religion and early Christianity.
14. Goodman, Martin. *The Roman World 44 b.c.–a.d. 180* (Routledge, 1997).
15. Grant, Robert. *Gods and the One God,* LEC (Westminster, 1986).

16. Grant, Robert, and R. Kitzinger, eds. *Civilization of the Ancient Mediterranean: Greece and Rome,* 3 vols. (Scribners, 1988).

17. Hornblower, Simon, and Anthony Spaworth, eds. *The Oxford Classical Dictionary,* 3d ed. (Oxford University Press, 1996).
———. *The Oxford Companion to Classical Civilization* (Oxford University Press, 1999).

18. Jeffers, James. *The Greco-Roman World of the New Testament Era* (IVP, 1999). Introductory but thorough.

19. Klauck, Hans-Josef. *The Relative Context of Early Christianity* (T & T Clark, 2000).

20. Long, A. *Hellenistic Philosophy* (Duckworth, 1986).

21. MacMullen, Ramsey. *Paganism in the Roman Empire* (Yale University Press, 1981).

22. Malherbe, Abraham. *Moral Exhortation,* LEC (Westminster, 1989).

23. Millar, Fergus. *The Roman Near East, 31 b.c.–a.d. 337* (Harvard University Press, 1993).

24. Starr, C. *A History of the Ancient World,* 4th ed. (Oxford University Press, 1991). Includes Classical Greek and late Roman period.

25. Talbert, R., ed. *Barrington Atlas of the Greek and Roman World: Book and CD-ROM* (Princeton University Press, 2000).

26. Tripolitis, Antonia. *Religions of the Hellenistic-Roman Age* (Eerdmans, 2001).

27. Van der Horst, P. *Hellenism-Judaism-Christianity* (Kok Pharos, 1994).

28. Walbank, F. *The Hellenistic World,* rev. ed. (Harvard University Press, 1993).
———, et al., eds. *The Hellenistic World,* CAH, 2d ed., vol. 7.1 (Cambridge University Press,1984).
———, et al., eds. *The Rise of Rome to 220 b.c.,* CAH, 2d ed., vol. 7.2 (Cambridge University Press, 1990).

29. Worth, Roland. *The Seven Cities of the Apocalypse and Roman Culture,* 2 vols. (Paulist, 1999). Volume 2: Revelation 2–3.

The Institution of Slavery[3]

1. Bradley, K. R. *Slaves and Masters in the Roman Empire* (Oxford University Press, 1987).
   ———. *Slavery and Society at Rome* (Cambridge University Press, 1994).
2. Garnsey, Peter. *Ideas of Slavery from Aristotle to Augustine* (Cambridge University Press, 1996).
3. **Glancy, Jennifer. *Slavery in Early Christianity* (Oxford, 2002).**
4. Harrill, J. Albert. *The Manumission of Slaves in Early Christianity* (Mohr, 1995).
5. Martin, Dale. *Slavery as Salvation* (Yale University Press, 1990).

New Testament Archaeology

1. **Akurgal, Ekrem. *Ancient Civilizations and Ruins of Turkey,* 3d ed. (Istanbul, 1973).**
2. *Biblical Archaeological Society Slide Sets* (BAS, 1981–). Approximately 140 slides @ $1.20 per slide (Jerusalem, New Testament Archaeology, Galilee Archaeology, and Archaeology and Religion).
   ***The Biblical World on CD-ROM* (BAS, 2002).** Same categories as above at fraction of cost with supplemental NT Archaeology and Dead Sea Scrolls. More than one thousand images, including OT.
3. Connolly, Peter. A History of the Jewish People in the Time of Jesus (Peter Bedrick, 1987).
4. Finegan, Jack. *The Archaeology of the New Testament,* rev. ed. (Princeton University Press, 1992).
5. **Frend, W. *The Archaeology of Early Christianity* (Fortress, 1996).**

3. Although each of these sources offers valuable insights into slavery in the ancient world, occasionally they are used to eisegete select passages (i.e., texts relating to immorality when addressing membership of slaves involved in involuntary sexual servitude).

6. Koester, Helmut. *Ephesos, Metropolis of Asia* (Trinity Press International, 1995). Includes culture analysis.
   ———, ed. *Pergamon* (Trinity Press International, 1999).
7. Koester, Helmut, and Holland Hendrix, eds. *Archaeological Resources for New Testament Studies,* 2 vols. (Trinity Press International, 1995). Three hundred slides each with indexed text (Ephesus, Philippi, Corinth, Athens, Olympia, and Isthmia).
8. Magness, Jodi. *The Archaeology of Qumran and the Dead Sea Scrolls* (Eerdmans, 2002).
9. Mare, Harold. *The Archaeology of the Jerusalem Area* (Baker, 1987).
10. **McRay, John. *Archaeology and the New Testament* (Baker, 1991).**
11. Meyers, Eric, and James Strange. *Archaeology, the Rabbis and Early Christianity* (Abingdon, 1981).
12. Millard, Alan. *Discoveries from the Time of Jesus* (Lion, 1990).
13. **Murphy-O'Connor, Jerome. *St. Paul's Corinth,* rev. ed. (Liturgical, 2002).**
14. Reed, Jonathan. *Archaeology and the Galilean Jesus* (Trinity Press International, 2000).
15. *Ritmeyer Archaeological Slides* (Kregel, 1999). Jerusalem in A.D. 30 (thirty-six slides) and The Archaeology of Herod's Temple Mount (sixty slides).
16. **Rousseau, John, and Rami Arav. *Jesus and His World* (Fortress, 1995).**
17. **Stillwell, Richard, ed. *The Princeton Encyclopedia of Classical Sites* (Princeton University Press, 1976).**
18. Yamauchi, Edwin. *New Testament Cities in Western Asia Minor* (Baker, 1980).
19. White, Michael. *The Social Origins of Christian Architecture,* vol. 2 (Trinity Press International, 1996).
20. *See* Old Testament Background: Archaeology.

Social Background

1. Arnal, William. *Jesus and the Village Scribes* (Fortress, 2001).

2. **Blasi, Anthony, et al., eds. *Handbook of Early Christianity* (AltaMira, 2002).**
3. Blount, Brian. *Cultural Interpretation: Reorienting New Testament Criticism* (Fortress, 1995).
4. deSilva, David. *The Hope of Glory* (Liturgical, 1999).
5. Esler, Philip. *The First Christians in Their Social Worlds* (Routledge, 1994).
   ———, ed. *Modeling Early Christianity* (Routledge, 1995).
6. Hanson, K., and Douglas Oakman. *Palestine in the Time of Jesus* (Fortress, 2002). With multiple-link CD.
7. **Holmberg, Brent. *Sociology and the New Testament* (Fortress, 1990).** Historical overview.
8. **Horrell, David. *The Social Ethos of Corinthian Correspondence* (T & T Clark, 1996).** Comparison of Paul, 1 Clement.
   ———, ed. *Social-Scientific Approaches to New Testament Interpretation* (T & T Clark, 1999).
9. Horsley, Richard. *Galilee: History, Politics, People* (Trinity Press International, 1995).
10. **Kee, Howard. *Knowing the Truth* (Fortress, 1989).**
    ———. *Who Are the People of God?* (Yale University Press, 1993).
11. **Malherbe, Abraham. *Social Aspects of Early Christianity,* 2d ed. (Fortress, 1983).**
12. Malina, Bruce. *The Social Gospel of Jesus* (Fortress, 2001).
13. Malina, Bruce, and John Pilch. *Social-Scientific Commentary on the Book of Revelation* (Fortress, 2000).
14. Malina, Bruce, and Richard Rohrbaugh. *Social Science Commentary on the Synoptic Gospels,* 2d ed. (Fortress, 2002).
    ———. *Social Science Commentary on the Gospel of John* (Trinity Press International, 1998).
15. May, David. *Social Scientific Criticism of the New Testament: A Bibliography* (Mercer University Press, 1991).
16. **Meeks, Wayne. *The Moral World of the First Christians,* LEC (Westminster, 1986).**
    ———. *The First Urban Christians* (Yale University Press, 1983).

———. *The Origins of Christian Morality* (Yale University Press, 1993).

17. Moxnes, Halvor. *The Economy of the Kingdom* (Fortress, 1988).

    ———. *Constructing Early Christian Families* (Routledge, 1997).

18. Neyrey, Jerome, ed. *The Social World of Luke–Acts* (Hendrickson, 1991).

    ———. *Honor and Shame in the Gospel of Matthew* (Westminster John Knox, 1998).

19. Osiek, Carolyn. *What Are They Saying About the Social Setting of the New Testament?* (Paulist, 1992).

20. **Osiek, Carolyn, and David Balch. *Families in the New Testament World* (Westminster John Knox, 1997).**

21. Pilch, John, ed. *Social Scientific Models for Interpreting the Bible* (Brill, 2000).

22. **Rogerson, John. *Anthropology and the Old Testament* (John Knox, 1979).**

23. Rohrbaugh, Richard, ed. *The Social Sciences and New Testament Interpretation* (Hendrickson, 1996).

24. **Stambaugh, John, and David Balch. *The New Testament in Its Social Environment*, LEC (Westminster, 1986).** Introduction.

25. Stegemann, Wolfgang. *The Jesus Movement* (Fortress, 1999).

26. Stegemann, Wolfgang, Bruce Malina, and Gerd Theissen, eds. *The Social Setting of Jesus and the Gospels* (Fortress, 2001).

27. **Theissen, Gerd. *Social Reality and the Early Christians* (Fortress, 1992).**

28. **Tidball, Derek. *The Social Context of the New Testament* (Zondervan, 1984).**

29. **White, Michael, and Larry Yarbrough, eds. *The Social World of the First Christians* (Fortress, 1995).**

30. *See* Old Testament Background: General Manners and Customs References, Social Background, Religious Background, and New Testament Background: Primary References.

Gnosticism

1. Evans, Craig, R. Webb, and R. Wiebe. *Nag Hammadi Texts and the Bible: A Synopsis and Index* (Brill, 1993).
2. Filoramo, G. *A History of Gnosticism* (Blackwell, 1990).
3. Franzmann, Majella. *Jesus in the Nag Hammadi Writings* (T & T Clark, 1996). Simultaneous development.
4. Hedrick, Charles, and R. Hodgson. *Nag Hammadi, Gnosticism and Early Christianity* (Hendrickson, 1986).
5. King, Karen, ed. *Images of the Feminine in Gnosticism* (Trinity Press International, 2000).
6. Layton, Bernard. *The Gnostic Scriptures*, ABRL, 2d ed. (Doubleday, 1995). Translation with introduction and notes.
7. **Logan, Alistair. *Gnostic Truth and Christian Heresy* (Hendrickson/T & T Clark, 1996).** Especially the *Apocryphal Gospel of John.*
8. Logan, A. H. B., and A. J. M. Wedderburn, eds. *The New Testament and Gnosis* (T & T Clark, 1983).
9. Patterson, Stephen, and James Robinson. *The Fifth Gospel* (Trinity Press International, 1998). *Gospel of Thomas* analysis.
10. Pearson, Brook. *Gnosticism, Judaism, and Egyptian Christianity* (Fortress, 1990).
11. Perkins, Pheme. *Gnosticism and the New Testament* (Fortress, 1993). Simultaneous development.
12. Robinson, James. *The Nag Hammadi Library*, 3d ed. (Harper, 1988).
13. Roukema, R. *Gnosis and Faith in Early Christianity* (Trinity Press International, 1999).
14. Scholer, David, ed. *Gnosticism in the Early Church* (Garland, 1993).
15. Tuckett, Christopher. *Nag Hammadi and the Gospel Tradition* (T & T Clark, 1986).
16. Turner, J., and A. McGuire, eds. *The Nag Hammadi Library After Fifty Years* (Brill, 1997).
17. Uro, Risto, ed. *Thomas at the Crossroads* (T & T Clark, 1999).
18. Valantasis, Richard. *The Gospel of Thomas* (Routledge, 1997).

19. Van den Broek, R. *Studies in Gnosticism and Alexandrian Christianity* (Brill, 1996).
20. Williams, M. *Rethinking "Gnosticism"* (Princeton University Press, 1996).
21. **Yamauchi, Edwin. *Pre-Christian Gnosticism* (Eerdmans, 1973).**

11
JEWISH BACKGROUND

Original Sources

1. **Charlesworth, James. *The Old Testament Pseudepigrapha,* 2 vols. (Doubleday, 1983–85).**
2. Coogan, Michael, ed. *The New Oxford Annotated Bible,* 3d ed. (Oxford University Press, 2001).
3. Dupont-Sommer, Andre. *The Essene Writings from Qumran* (Peter Smith, 1973).
4. García Martinez, Florentino. *The Dead Sea Scrolls Translated,* 2d ed. (Eerdmans, 1996).
5. **Maier, Paul. *The New Complete Works of Josephus: Translated by William Whiston* (Kregel, 1999). Loeb notes, commentary by Maier.**
6. **Neusner, Jacob. *The Mishnah* (Yale University, 1988).**
7. Reddish, Mitchell, ed. *Apocalyptic Literature: A Reader* (Abingdon, 1990).
8. Sparks, H., ed. *The Apocryphal Old Testament* (Oxford University Press, 1984). Twenty-five pseudepigraphical translations.
9. **Vermes, Geza. *The Complete Dead Sea Scrolls in English,* 4th ed. (Penguin, 1997).** Three introductory chapters.
10. Yonge, C. *The Works of Philo* (Hendrickson, 1993).

Concordances and Indexes

1. Borgen, Peder, Kåre Fuglseth, and Roald Skarsten. *The Philo Index* (Eerdmans, 2000).
2. Schalit, A., ed. *A Complete Concordance to Flavius Josephus,* 4 vols. (Brill, 1998).

Primary Jewish Background References

1. Davies, W. D., et al., eds. *Cambridge History of Judaism,* 3 vols. (1984, 1989, 1999).
2. Kraft, R., and George Nickelsburg, eds. *Early Judaism and its Modern Interpreters* (Scholars, 1986).
3. Neusner, Jacob, and William Green, eds. *Dictionary of Judaism in the Biblical Period* (Hendrickson, 1999).
4. **Safrai, S., and M. Stern, eds. *The Jewish People in the First Century,* 2 vols. (Van Gorcum/Fortress, 1974–1976).**
5. **Sanders, E. P. *Judaism: Practice and Belief, 63 b.c.e.–66 c.e.* (Trinity Press International, 1992).**
6. **Schürer, Emil, ed. *History of the Jewish People in the Age of Jesus Christ,* rev. ed., 3 vols. (T & T Clark, 1973–87).**
7. **Skarsaune, Oskar. *In the Shadow of the Temple* (IVP, 2002).** 200 B.C.–A.D. 300.
8. **VanderKam, James. *An Introduction to Early Judaism* (Eerdmans, 2000).**
9. Werblowsky, R. J. Zwi, and Geoffrey Wigoder, eds. *The Oxford Dictionary of the Jewish Religion* (Oxford University Press, 1997).

Other Jewish Background References

1. Argall, Randal, Beverly Bow, and Rodney Werline, eds. *For a Later Generation* (Trinity Press International, 2000).
2. Barclay, John, and J. Sweet, eds. *Early Christian Thought in Its Jewish Context* (Cambridge University Press, 1996).
3. Berlin, Andrea, and Andrew Overman, eds. *First Jewish Revolt* (Routledge, 2002).
4. **Bocaccini, Gabrielle. *Middle Jewish Thought, 200 b.c.e.–200 c.e.* (Fortress, 1991).**

5. **Fitzmyer, Joseph. *The Semitic Background of the New Testament* (Eerdmans, 1997).**
6. **Hengel, Martin. The Zealots (T & T Clark, 1989).**
7. Dunn, James. *The Parting of the Ways Between Christianity and Judaism* (Trinity Press International, 1991).
8. Elliott, Mark. *The Survivors of Israel* (Eerdmans, 2001). Sanders corrective.
9. Flusser, David. *Judaism and the Origins of Christianity* (Magnes, 1988).
10. Lesses, Rebecca. *Ritual Practices to Gain Power* (Trinity Press International, 1998). Jewish mysticism.
11. Mendels, Doron. *The Rise and Fall of Jewish Nationalism* (Doubleday, 1992; Eerdmans, 1997).
12. Moore, Carey. *Tobit,* AB (Doubleday, 1996).
13. Murphy, Frederick. *The Religious World of Jesus* (Abingdon, 1991).
14. **Saldarini, Anthony. *Pharisees, Scribes, and Sadducees in Palestinian Society* (Michael Glazier, 1988).**
15. Stemberger, Günter. *Jewish Contemporaries of Jesus* (Fortress, 1995).
16. **Talmon, Shemaryahu, ed. *Jewish Civilization in the Hellenistic-Roman Period* (Trinity Press International, 1991).**
17. Wegner, Judith. *Chattel or Person? The Status of Women in the Mishnah* (Oxford University Press, 1988).

Intertestamental

1. **Barclay, John. *Jews in the Mediterranean Diaspora from Alexander to Trajan* (T & T Clark, 1996).** Especially Egypt.
2. Bartlett, John. *1 Maccabees* (Sheffield Academic Press, 1998). Introduction.
3. Baumgarten, Albert. *The Flourishing of Jewish Sects in the Maccabean Era* (Brill, 1997).
4. **Cohen, Shaye. *From the Maccabees to the Mishnah,* LEC (Westminster, 1987).**
5. **deSilva, David. *Introducing the Apocrypha* (Baker, 2002).**
6. Doran, Robert. *1–2 Maccabees,* NIB, vol. 4 (Abingdon, 1996).

Especially valuable with its allusions to Daniel and references to Josephus and DSS.

7. **Feldman, Louis. *Jew and Gentile in the Ancient World* (Princeton University Press, 1993).**
8. Fine, Steven. *This Holy Place* (University of Notre Dame, 1997).
9. **Grabbe, Lester. *Judaism from Cyrus to Hadrian,* 2 vols. (Fortress, 1992).**
10. Gruen, Robert. *Diaspora: Jews Amidst Greeks and Romans* (Harvard University Press, 2002).
11. **Harrington, Daniel. *Invitation to the Apocrypha* (Eerdmans, 1999).**
12. **Helyer, Larry. *Exploring Jewish Literature of the Second Temple Period* (IVP, 2002).**
13. **Hengel, Martin. *Jews, Greeks, and Barbarians* (Fortress, 1980).**

    ———. *Judaism and Hellenism,* 2 vols. (Fortress, 1974).
14. **Ilan, Tal. *Integrating Women into Second Temple History* (Hendrickson, 2001).**
15. Leaney, A. *The Jewish and Christian World: 200 b.c.–a.d. 200* (Cambridge University Press, 1984).
16. **Modrzejewski, Joseph. The Jews of Egypt from Rameses II to Emperor Hadrian (T & T Clark, 1995).**
17. **Murphy, Frederick. Early Judaism (Hendrickson, 2002).** Exile-Jewish revolt.
18. Newsome, James. *Greeks, Romans, Jews* (Trinity Press International, 1992).
19. Nickelsburg, George. *Jewish Literature Between the Bible and the Mishnah* (Fortress, 1981).
20. **Richardson, Peter. *Herod* (Fortress, 1999).**
21. Sacchi, Paolo. *The History of the Second Temple Period* (Sheffield Academic Press, 2000).
22. **Scott, J. Julius. *Customs and Controversies* (Baker, 1995).**
23. **Stone, Michael, ed. *Jewish Writings of the Second Temple Period* (Fortress, 1984).**
24. Van Seters, John. *A Law Book for the Diaspora: Revision in the Study of the Covenant Code* (Oxford University Press, 2002).

Hellenistic Judaism

1. Bartlett, John. *Jews in the Hellenistic and Roman Cities* (Routledge, 2002).
2. Borgen, Peder. *Early Christianity and Hellenistic Judaism* (T & T Clark, 1996).
3. Borgen, Peder, and Søren Giversen, eds. *The New Testament and Hellenistic Judaism* (Hendrickson, 1997).
4. Collins, John. *Between Athens and Jerusalem,* 2d ed. (Eerdmans, 1999).
5. **Freyne, Sean. *Galilee from Alexander the Great to Hadrian 323 b.c.e. to 135 c.e.* (T & T Clark, 1998).**
6. **Goodman, Martin, ed. *Jews in a Greco-Roman World* (Oxford University Press, 1999).**
7. Grabbe, Lester, *An Introduction to First Century Judaism* (T & T Clark, 1996).
8. Levine, Lee. *Judaism and Hellenism in Antiquity* (University of Washington Press, 1998).
9. **Levinskaya, Irina. *The Book of Acts in Its Hellenistic Setting,* vol. 5, The Book of Acts in Its First-Century Setting (Eerdmans, 1996).**
10. *See* Barclay, Sanders, and Skarsaune above.

Josephus

1. Beall, Todd. *Josephus' Description of the Essenes Illustrated by the Dead Sea Scrolls* (Cambridge University Press, 1988).
2. Feldman, Louis. *Josephus' Interpretation of the Bible* (University of California, 1998).
3. Feldman, Louis, and Gohei Hata, eds. *Josephus, the Bible, and History* (Wayne State University Press, 1989).
4. Mason, Steve. *Josephus and the New Testament* (Hendrickson, 1992).

   ———, ed. *Understanding Josephus* (Sheffield Academic Press, 1998).
5. Rajak, T. *Josephus* (Fortress, 1983).

Dead Sea Scrolls

1. **Abegg, Martin, Peter Flint, and Eugene Ulrich, eds. *The Dead Sea Scrolls Bible* (HarperCollins, 1999; T & T Clark, 2000).**
2. Betz, Otto, and Rainier Riesner. *Jesus, Qumran, and the Vatican* (Crossroad, 1994).
3. Boccaccini, Gabrielle. *Beyond the Essene Hypothesis* (Eerdmans, 1998).
4. Cansdale, Lena. *Qumran and the Essenes* (Mohr, 1997).
5. Charlesworth, James, ed. *John and the Dead Sea Scrolls* (Crossroad, 1990).

   ———, ed. *Jesus and the Dead Sea Scrolls,* ABRL (Doubleday, 1992).

   ———. *Graphic Concordance to the Dead Sea Scrolls* (Westminster John Knox, 1991).

   ———, ed. *The Dead Sea Scrolls,* 10 vols. (Westminster John Knox, 1993–). Hebrew, Aramaic, Greek-English.

   ———. *The Pesharim and Qumran History* (Eerdmans, 2002).
6. Charlesworth, James, and Walter Weaver, eds. *Dead Sea Scrolls and the Christian Faith* (Trinity Press International, 1998).
7. Collins, John. *The Scepter and the Star,* ABRL (Doubleday, 1995). Two messiahs of the DSS.

   ———. *Apocalypticism in the Dead Sea Scrolls* (Routledge, 1997).
8. Collins, John, and Robert Kugler, eds. *Religion in the Dead Sea Scrolls* (Eerdmans, 2000).
9. Cook, Edward. *Solving the Mystery of the Dead Sea Scrolls* (Zondervan, 1994).
10. Cross, Frank. *The Ancient Library of Qumran and Modern Biblical Studies,* 3d ed. (Fortress, 1995).
11. Cross, Frank, and Shemaryahu Talmon, eds. *Qumran and the History of the Biblical Text* (Harvard University Press, 1975). DSS-MT divergence.
12. *Dead Sea Scrolls Revealed* (Logos Research Systems, 1994). Interactive CD-ROM.
13. Evans, Craig, and Peter Flint, eds. *Eschatology, Messianism and the Dead Sea Scrolls* (Eerdmans, 1997).

14. Fitzmyer, Joseph. *The Dead Sea Scrolls and Christian Origins* (Eerdmans, 2001).
   ———. *Responses to 101 Questions on the Dead Sea Scrolls* (Paulist, 1992).
   ———. *The Dead Sea Scrolls,* 2d ed. (Scholars, 1990). With bibliography.
15. Flint, Peter, ed. *The Bible at Qumran* (Eerdmans, 2001).
16. **Flint, Peter, and James VanderKam, eds. *The Dead Sea Scrolls After 50 Years,* 2 vols. (Brill, 1998).**
17. García Martinez, Florentino, and Eibert Tigchelaar, eds. *The Dead Sea Scrolls Study Edition,* 2 vols. (Eerdmans, 1999). Notes and bibliography.
18. **García Martinez, Florentino, and Julio Trebolle Barrera. *The People of the Dead Sea Scrolls* (Brill, 1995).**
19. Harrington, Daniel. *Wisdom Texts from Qumran* (Routledge, 1996).
20. Lim, Timothy, et al., eds. *The Dead Sea Scrolls in Their Historical Context* (T & T Clark, 2000).
21. Metso, S. *The Textual Development of the Qumran Community Rule* (Brill, 1997).
22. Murphy-O'Connor, Jerome, ed. *Paul and the Dead Sea Scrolls* (Crossroad, 1990).
23. Pate, Marvin. *Communities of the Last Days* (IVP, 2000). NT parallels, heavily indebted to N. T. Wright.
24. Porter, Stanley, and Craig Evans, eds. *The Scrolls and the Scriptures* (Sheffield Academic Press, 1997).
25. Ringgren, Helmer. *The Faith of Qumran* (Crossroad, 1995).
26. Scanlin, Edward. *Dead Sea Scrolls and Modern Translations of the Old Testament* (Tyndale, 1994).
27. **Schiffman, Lawrence. *Reclaiming the Dead Sea Scrolls* (Jewish Publication Society, 1994; Doubleday, 1995 pb).**
28. Schiffman, Lawrence, and James VanderKam, eds. *Encyclopedia of the Dead Sea Scrolls,* 2 vols. (Oxford University Press, 2000).

29. Shanks, Hershel, ed. *Understanding the Dead Sea Scrolls* (Random House, 1992).
30. Stegemann, Hartmut. *The Library of Qumran, on the Essenes, Qumran, John the Baptist, and Jesus* (Eerdmans, 1998).
31. Ulrich, Eugene. *The Dead Sea Scrolls and the Origins of the Bible* (Eerdmans, 1999).
32. **VanderKam, James. *The Dead Sea Scrolls Today* (Eerdmans, 1994).**
33. **Vermes, Geza. *An Introduction to the Complete Dead Sea Scrolls,* 3d ed. (Fortress, 2000).**

Rabbinics

1. **Boccaccini, Gabrielle. *Roots of Rabbinic Judaism* (Eerdmans, 2001).**
2. Maccoby, H. *Early Rabbinic Writings* (Cambridge University Press, 1988). Introduction.
3. **Neusner, Jacob. *Introduction to Rabbinic Literature,* ABRL (Doubleday, 1994).**
   ———. *Rabbinic Literature and the New Testament* (Trinity Press International, 1994).
4. Sanders, E. P. *Jewish Law from Jesus to the Mishnah* (SCM/Trinity Press International, 1990).
5. Stemberger, Günter. *Introduction to the Talmud and Midrash,* 2d ed. (T & T Clark, 1996).

12 POPULAR DICTIONARIES, ONE- AND TWO-VOLUME COMMENTARIES, AND COMMENTARY SERIES

Popular Dictionaries

1. **Elwell, Walter. ed. *Baker Encyclopedia of the Bible,* 2 vols. (Baker, 1988).**
2. **Elwell, Walter, and Philip Comfort, eds. *Tyndale Bible Dictionary* (Tyndale, 2001).**
3. Douglas, J. D., ed. *The Illustrated Bible Dictionary,* 3 vols. (Tyndale, 1980).
4. Youngblood, Ronald, et al., eds. *Nelson's New Illustrated Bible Dictionary* (Thomas Nelson, 1995).
5. Gardner, Paul, ed. *Encyclopedia of Bible Characters* (Zondervan, 1995). Formerly *The Complete Who's Who in the Bible.*

Popular One- and Two-Volume Commentaries[1]

1. **Barker, Kenneth, and John Kohlenberger, eds. *Zondervan NIV Bible Commentary,* 2 vols. (Zondervan, 1994).**
2. Elwell, Walter, ed. *Baker Commentary on the Bible* (Baker, 1989).
3. Radmacher, Earl, Ronald Allen, and Wayne House, eds. *Nelson's New Illustrated Bible Commentary* (Thomas Nelson, 1999).

1. For exposition, the *Zondervan niv Bible Commentary* (2 vols.) is packed with information. It is a condensation of the *Expositor's Bible Commentary* minus the more technical information.

4. Unger, Merrill, and Gary Larson. *The New Unger's Bible Handbook* (Moody, 1998).
5. Walvoord, John, and Roy Zuck, eds. *Bible Knowledge Commentary,* 2 vols. (Victor, 1983–85).

Popular Commentary Series[2]

1. Anders, Max, ed. *Holman Old Testament Commentary* (Broadman & Holman, 2002–).
   ———. *Holman New Testament Commentary* (Broadman & Holman, 2000–).
2. Boice, J. M. Expositions of *Genesis, Psalms, John, Romans and Ephesians* (Baker).
3. Hendriksen, William, and Simon Kistemaker. New Testament Commentary (Baker, 1954–2001).
4. Hughes, R. Kent. Preaching the Word Series (Crossway, 1989–). NT.
5. MacArthur, John. *The MacArthur New Testament Commentary* (Moody, 1983–). NT.
6. McGrath, Alister, and J. I. Packer, eds. Crossway Classic Commentaries (Crossway, 1993–).
7. Phillips, John. The John Phillips Commentary Series (Kregel, 2001–).
8. Wiersbe, Warren. *The Bible Exposition Commentary,* 6 vols. (Chariot Victor Books, 1972–).

2. Of these, Hughes and Hendriksen/Kistemaker garner some mention in the commentary survey proper (i.e., *see* Revelation: Expositional). Although the series themselves bear mention for their general utility, there are better layman-friendly options suggested per biblical book.

13
GENERAL REFERENCES

Bible Dictionaries, Encyclopedias

1. **Achtemeier, Paul, ed. *HarperCollins Bible Dictionary,* rev. ed. (HarperSanFrancisco, 1996).** Twenty-five percent new.
2. **Bromiley, Geoffrey, ed. The *International Standard Bible Encyclopedia,* 4 vols., rev. ed. (Eerdmans, 1979–1988).**[1]
3. Butler, Trent, ed. *Holman Bible Dictionary* (Broadman & Holman, 1991).[2]
4. **Freedman, David, ed. *Anchor Bible Dictionary,* 6 vols. (Doubleday, 1992).**
5. **Freedman, David, ed. *The Eerdmans Dictionary of the Bible* (Eerdmans, 2000).**[3] Includes Apocrypha.
6. **Marshall, Howard, et al., eds. *New Bible Dictionary,* 3d ed. (IVP, 1996).**
7. Metzger, Bruce, and Michael Coogan, eds. *The Oxford Companion to the Bible* (Oxford University Press, 1993).

---

1. For Bible college or seminary students planning to go into full-time ministry, obtain Geoffrey Bromiley, ed., *International Standard Bible Encyclopedia,* rev., 5 vols. (Eerdmans, 1979–1988).
2. This reference is under revision and should be a strong second choice when it reappears. It will be the most staunchly evangelical dictionary available.
3. You will also need a comprehensive, one-volume dictionary for quick reference. For advanced students, the *Eerdmans Dictionary of the Bible* (Eerdmans, 2000), though moderate in overall tone, is a potential choice, along with the *New Bible Dictionary.* Better yet, purchase both dictionaries as they complement each other well. For instance, J. Albert Harrill gives only snapshot coverage to the topic of slavery in *EDB* (giving no indication of the treatment of

———, eds. *The Oxford Guide to Ideas and Issues of the Bible* (Oxford University Press, 2001).[4]

———, eds. *The Oxford Guide to People and Places of the Bible* (Oxford University Press, 2001).

8. **Mills, Watson, ed. *Mercer Dictionary of the Bible* (Mercer University Press, 1990, 1991).**

Atlases

1. **Aharoni, Yohanan, and Michael Avi-Yonah. *The Macmillan Bible Atlas,* 3d ed. (Macmillan, 1993).** Maps of biblical events.
2. **Beitzel, Barry. *The Moody Atlas of Bible Lands* (Moody, 1985).** Detailed geographical discussion.
3. Bimson, John, and J. Kane. *New Bible Atlas* (IVP, 1985).
4. **Brisco, Thomas. *The Holman Bible Atlas* (Broadman & Holman, 1998).**
5. Dowley, Tim. *Kregel Bible Atlas* (Kregel, 2002).
6. Frank, Harry. *Hammond Atlas of the Bible Lands,* rev. ed. (Hammond, 1990). 33 maps.

---

slaves expressed in his *DNTB* entry) whereas E. A. Judge provides a more thorough, though slightly outdated, essay in *NBD3.* Conversely, *EDB* has five thousand entries as opposed to two thousand for *NBD3,* so you get a little coverage on many more subjects such as the extrabiblical topics "Akkadian," the "Genesis Apocryphon," "Ostraca," and "Zoroastrianism." Elsewhere, diverse topics such as "Lentil," "Millet," "Pomegranate," and "Tamarisk" gain individual attention whereas in *NBD3* they are subsumed under "Food," "Vegetables," and "Trees." *EDB* is also sensitive to the literary background, providing separate entries on Mishnah, midrash, and targum, for instance. Its chief deficit is its lack of cross-references. For instance, the entry "Afterlife, Afterdeath" fails to direct the reader to the entries "Death," "Sheol," and "Grave." In *NBD3,* relevant cross-references are asterisked in the body of the text. Therefore, in *EDB,* it is up to the reader to exhaust possibilities on his own.

4. These latter two volumes are based on the *Companion,* and essentially winnow and update the *Companion's* seven hundred entries down to five hundred in about the same amount of space and the same price combined. In addition to the standard fare, *Ideas and Issues* is a bit of a historical dictionary covering such issues as "Freud and the Bible" and such ideas as the "Scofield Reference Bible." *People and Places* includes only the most important people and places of the Bible. Neither claims to be encyclopedic and can be recommended only as a novelty supplement (though a very good one).

7. May, Herbert. *Oxford Bible Atlas,* 3d ed. (Oxford University Press, 1984).
8. Pritchard, James. *The Harper Atlas of the Bible* (Harper, 1987). Especially major events, battles.
   ———. *The Times Atlas of the Bible* (Crescent, 1996).
9. Rasmussen, Carl. *Zondervan NIV Atlas of the Bible* (Zondervan, 1989). Superior graphics, mostly Old Testament.
10. Rogerson, John. *The Atlas of the Bible* (Facts on File, 1985). Excellent illustrations, photos, distributed by Nelson.
11. *The Collegeville Atlas of the Bible* (Liturgical, 1998). Popular.

Specialty Atlases

1. ***Abingdon Bible Map Transparencies* (Abingdon, 1975).** Six sets: 41 transparencies (can be ordered individually); Hammond maps from Frank's *Discovering the Biblical World* (Hammond, 1975).
2. **Ben-Dov, Meir. *Historical Atlas of Jerusalem* (Continuum, 2002).** Also provides a highly readable historical and archaeological overview of the city's history.
3. Brierley, Peter, and Heather Wraight. *Atlas of World Christianity* (Thomas Nelson, 1998).
4. **Cleave, Richard. *The Holy Land Satellite Atlas,* 2 vols. (Rohr, 1999).**
5. **Gaustad, Edwin, and Philip Barlow. *New Historical Atlas of Religion in America,* 3d ed. (Oxford University Press, 2000).**
6. *Illustrated Wall Maps of the Bible* (Carta, 1999). Twelve maps, available through Kregel.
7. Littell, Franklin. *Historical Atlas of Christianity* (Continuum, 2001). *See* Dowley above, especially 1500–present. Also functions as a brief history itself.
8. Smart, Ninian, ed. *Atlas of the World's Religions* (Oxford University Press, 1999).
9. **Talbert, R., ed. *Barrington Atlas of the Greek and Roman World* (Princeton University Press, 2000).** With CD.

Charts and Reconstructions

1. **House, Wayne. *Chronological and Background Charts of the New Testament* (Zondervan, 1981).**
2. House, Wayne, and Randall Price. *Charts of Bible Prophecy* (Zondervan, 2000).
3. Smith, Marsha. *Holman Book of Biblical Charts, Maps, and Reconstructions* (Broadman & Holman, 1993).
4. *The Nelson Complete Book of Bible Maps and Charts,* rev. ed. (Thomas Nelson, 1997).
5. Thomas, Robert. *Charts of the Gospels and the Life of Christ* (Zondervan, 2000).
6. **Walton, John. *Chronological and Background Charts of the Old Testament,* rev. ed. (Zondervan, 1994).**
7. **Wilson, Neil, and Linda Taylor. *Tyndale Handbook of Bible Maps and Charts* (Tyndale, 2001).** With CD.[5]
8. Yamauchi, Edwin. *Harper's World of the New Testament* (Harper, 1981).

Cities, Geography

1. **Aharoni, Yohanan. *The Land of the Bible,* rev. ed. (Westminster, 1979).**
2. Arav, Rami, and Richard Freund, eds. *Bethsaida,* vol. 2 (Truman State University Press, 1999).
3. **Beck, John. *The Land of Milk, Honey, and Hope* (Concordia Academic Press, 2002).**
4. **Ben-Dov, Meir. *Jerusalem* (Modan, 1990).**
5. Bimson, John, ed. *Baker Encyclopedia of Bible Places* (Baker, 1995).
6. **DeVries, Lamoine. *Cities of the Biblical World* (Hendrickson, 1997).**
7. **Dorsey, David. *The Roads and Highways of Ancient Israel* (Johns Hopkins University Press, 1991).**

---

5. Contains 566 charts and 200 maps on perforated pages with topical index. CD duplicates contents with NLT text.

8. **Harris, Roberta. *The World of the Bible* (Thames and Hudson, 1995).**
9. **Hess, Richard, and Gordon Wenham, eds. *Zion, City of God* (Eerdmans, 1999).** History, religion, and theology of Jerusalem.
10. **Hill, Geva, ed. *Ancient Jerusalem Revealed* (IES, 1994).**
11. **Kallai, Zecharia. *Historical Geography of the Bible* (Magnes, 1986).**
12. **Levine, Lee. *Jerusalem* (Continuum, 1999).** Covers ancient and modern land forms.
13. **Murphy-O'Connor, Jerome. *The Holy Land,* 4th ed. (Oxford University Press, 1995).**
14. Orni, Ephraim, and Elisha Efrat. *Geography of Israel,* 4th ed. (Israel University Press, 1980).
15. **Poorthuis, M., and S. Safrai, eds. *The Centrality of Jerusalem* (Kok Pharos, 1996).**
16. Robertson, O. Palmer. *Understanding the Land of the Bible* (Presbyterian & Reformed, 1996).
17. **Scott, James. *Geography in Early Judaism and Christianity* (Cambridge University Press, 2001).**

14

BIBLICAL HEBREW RESOURCES

First Year Grammar*

1. **Garrett, Duane. *A Modern Grammar for Classical Hebrew* (Broadman & Holman, 2002).**
2. **Pratico, Gary, and Miles Van Pelt. *Basics of Biblical Hebrew* (Zondervan, 2001).**

   ———. *Basics of Biblical Hebrew: Workbook* (Zondervan, 2001).
3. Rogers, Jeffrey. *A Grammar for Biblical Hebrew Handbook* (Abingdon, 2002).
4. **Ross, Allen. *Introducing Biblical Hebrew* (Baker, 2001).**
5. Seow, C. L. *A Grammar for Biblical Hebrew,* rev. ed. (Abingdon, 1995). Updates Lambdin approach, includes excursuses on using helps, etc.

Other Grammars and Syntaxes

1. Bartelt, Andrew. *Fundamental Biblical Hebrew* (Concordia Academic Press, 2000). Brief.
2. Ben Zvi, Ehud, Maxine Hancock, and Richard Beinert. *Readings in Biblical Hebrew* (Yale University Press, 1993).
3. Kelley, Page. *Biblical Hebrew* (Eerdmans, 1993). Updates Weingreen approach.
4. Kelley, Page, Terry Burden, and Timothy Crawford. *A Handbook to Biblical Hebrew* (Eerdmans, 1994).

* Forthcoming: Mark Futato (Eisenbrauns).

5. Kittel, Bonnie, et al. *Biblical Hebrew* (Yale University Press, 1989).
6. Lambdin, Thomas. *Introduction to Biblical Hebrew* (Scribner's, 1971).
7. Martin, James. *Davidson's Introductory Hebrew Grammar,* 27th ed. (T & T Clark, 1993). *See* Johnstone, Computer Resources: interactive study complement to Davidson's revised grammar.

Reference Grammars

1. Cowley, A., and E. Kautzsch, eds. *Gesenius' Hebrew Grammar,* 2d ed. (Oxford University Press, 1910).
2. Gibson, J. *Davidson's Introductory Hebrew Grammar: Syntax,* 4th ed. (T & T Clark, 1994).
3. Horsnell, Malcolm. *A Review and Reference Grammar for Biblical Hebrew* (McMaster University Press, 1999).
4. Jouon, Paul. *A Grammar of Biblical Hebrew,* 2 vols. (Pontifical Biblical Institute, 1991).
5. **van der Merwe, Christo, et al. *Biblical Hebrew Reference Grammar* (Sheffield Academic Press, 1999).** Includes latest insights on linguistics.
6. Putnam, Frederic. *A Cumulative Index to the Grammar and Syntax of Biblical Hebrew* (Eisenbrauns, 1996). Gibson, Davidson, GKC, Waltke, O'Connor, Williams, Jouon, and Rosenthal, etc.

   ———. *Hebrew Bible Insert* (Stylus, 1997). Laminated syntax guide.

   ———. *Card Guide to Biblical Hebrew* (Stylus, 1998). Laminated.
7. **Waltke, Bruce, and Michael O'Connor. *An Introduction to Biblical Hebrew Syntax* (Eisenbrauns, 1990).** Linguistic approach.
8. Williams, R. *Hebrew Syntax,* 2d ed. (University of Toronto, 1976).

Lexicons

1. Armstrong, T., D. Busby, and C. Carr. *A Reader's Hebrew-English Lexicon of the Old Testament,* (Zondervan, 1989).
2. Brown, Francis, S. R. Driver, and Charles Briggs. *Brown-Driver-Briggs Hebrew-English Lexicon of the Old Testament* (Hendrickson, 1995). Coded to Strong's, considerably outdated.
3. Clines, David, ed. *The Dictionary Of Classical Hebrew,* 8 vols. (Sheffield Academic Press, 1993–). Includes extrabiblical sources, contextual approach.
4. Davidson, Benjamin. *The Analytical Hebrew and Chaldee Lexicon,* 2d ed. (Hendrickson, 1986).
5. **Holladay, William. *A Concise Hebrew and Aramaic Lexicon of the Old Testament* (Eerdmans, 1971).** Condensed Koehler below.
6. **Koehler, L., W. Baumgartner, and John Stamm, eds. *The Hebrew and Aramaic Lexicon of the Old Testament,* 3d ed., 5 vols. (Brill, 1994–2002).** Less expensive versions of this lexicon have been produced.

Theological Dictionaries[1]

1. **Botterweck, G. Johannes, and Helmer Ringgren, eds. *Theological Dictionary of the Old Testament,* 14 vols. (Eerdmans, 1977–).[2]**
2. **Carpenter, Eugene. *The Complete Word-Study Dictionary of the Old Testament* (AMG, 2003).**
3. **Harris, R. Laird, Gleason Archer, and Bruce Waltke, eds. *A Theological Wordbook of the Old Testament,* 2 vols. (Moody, 1980).**

---

1. A worthy companion to *NIDOTTE* (covering the three hundred most important Hebrew and Aramaic words) is Jenni and Westermann's *Theological Lexicon of the Old Testament,* 3 vols. (Hendrickson, 1997), especially for its thorough statistical data and synthetic treatment of each word's theological development. Also, Eugene Merrill is editing the *Bible Knowledge Key Word-Study* (Cook Communications, 2003), which analyzes key words in context as they appear in each Old Testament book (verse by verse).
2. The twelfth volume (P–Q) just appeared.

4. **Jenni, Ernst, and Claus Westermann, eds. *Theological Lexicon of the Old Testament,* 3 vols. (Hendrickson, 1997).**
5. **VanGemeren, Willem, ed. *New International Dictionary of Old Testament Theology and Exegesis,* 5 vols. (Zondervan, 1997).**

Concordances

1. Even-Shoshan, E. *A New Concordance of the Old Testament,* 2d ed. (Baker, 1989).
2. Katz, Eliezer, ed. *Topical Concordance of the Old Testament* (Baker, 1992). Hebrew-English.
3. **Kohlenberger, John, and James Swanson. *The Hebrew-English Concordance to the Old Testament* (Zondervan, 1998).**
4. Mandelkern, Solomon. *Veteris Testamenti Concordantiae* (Schocken, 1971; P. Shalom Publications, 1988).
5. Wigram, George. *The New Englishman's Hebrew and Chaldee Concordance of the Old Testament,* 5th ed. (Hendrickson, 1984).

Interlinears and Parallel Old Testament

1. Dotan, Aron, ed. *Parallel Bible* (Hendrickson, 2002). *BHL,* KJV.
2. JPS Hebrew-English Tanakh (JPS, 1999).
3. **Kohlenberger, John. *The NIV Hebrew-English Interlinear Old Testament* (Zondervan, 1987).**

Study Aids*

1. Beall, Todd, William Banks, and Colin Smith. *Old Testament Parsing Guide,* rev. ed. (Broadman & Holman, 2001). Parses only verbs.
2. Carpenter, Eugene, and Philip Comfort. *Holman Treasury of Key Bible Words* (Broadman & Holman, 2000). Two hundred Hebrew, two hundred Greek.

---

* Forthcoming in 2003: Peter Silzer and Thomas Finley, *How Biblical Languages Work: A Student's Guide to Understanding Hebrew and Greek* (Kregel).

3. **Chisholm, Robert. *From Exegesis to Exposition* (Baker, 1998). Sermon preparation.**
4. Davis, John. *Hebrew Language* (Stylus, 1999). Laminated verb analysis.
5. Einspahr, Bruce. *Index to the B-D-B Hebrew Lexicon* (Moody, 1976).
6. Kelley, Page, Daniel Mynatt, and Timothy Crawford. *The Masorah of the BHS* (Eerdmans, 1998).
7. Long, Gary. *Grammatical Concepts 101 for Biblical Hebrew* (Hendrickson, 2002). English grammar for Hebrew.
8. Mitchel, Larry. *A Student's Vocabulary for Biblical Hebrew and Aramaic* (Zondervan, 1984).
9. **Owens, John. *Analytical Key to the Old Testament,* 4 vols. (Baker, 1989–1992).**

Textual Criticism

1. **Brotzman, Ellis. *Old Testament Textual Criticism* (Baker, 1993).**
2. Kaiser, Walter. *The Old Testament Documents* (IVP, 2001).
3. McCarter, Kyle. *Textual Criticism* (Fortress, 1982).
4. Scott, William. *A Simplified Guide to BHS* (Bibal, 1987). Critical apparatus guide.
5. **Tov, Emmanuel. *Textual Criticism of the Hebrew Bible,* 2d ed. (Fortress, 2001).** Technical praxis and witness description.
6. Würthwein, Ernst. *The Text of the Old Testament* (Eerdmans, 1995).

Special Studies

1. Bergen, Robert, ed. *Biblical Hebrew and Discourse Linguistics* (SIL, 1994). Available through Eisenbrauns.
2. Goldfajn, Tal. *Word Order and Time in Biblical Hebrew Narrative* (Oxford University Press, 1998).
3. Young, Ian. *Diversity in Pre-Exilic Hebrew* (Mohr, 1993). Biblical Hebrew as continuation of earlier language.

15

NEW TESTAMENT GREEK RESOURCES

First-Year Grammars and Helps

1. Adam, A. K. M. *A Grammar for New Testament Greek* (Abingdon, 1999).
2. Cox, Steven. *Essentials of New Testament Greek: Workbook* (Broadman & Holman, 1995).
3. Croy, Clayton. *A Primer of Biblical Greek* (Eerdmans, 1999).
4. **Mounce, William. *Basics of Biblical Greek* (Zondervan, 1993).** Includes interactive CD-ROM.

   ———. *Basics of Biblical Greek: Workbook* (Zondervan, 1994).

   ———. *The Morphology of Biblical Greek* (Zondervan, 1994). Print-on-demand.
5. Stevens, Gerald. *New Testament Greek,* 2d ed. (University Press of America, 1997). Combined beginners, intermediate.

   ———. *New Testament Greek Workbook,* 2d ed. (University Press of America, 1997).
6. Summers, Ray, and Thomas Sawyer. *Essentials of New Testament Greek,* rev. ed. (Broadman & Holman, 1995).
7. Swetnam, James. *An Introduction to the Study of New Testament Greek,* 2d ed., 2 vols. (Pontifical Biblical Institute, 1997). Advanced beginners.
8. Vlachos, Chris, and Marvin Wilson. *A Workbook for New Testament Greek* (Hendrickson, 1998). 1 John.
9. Voelz, James. *Fundamental Greek Grammar,* 2d ed. (Concordia Academic Press, 1998).

10. Wenham, John. *The Elements of New Testament Greek* (Cambridge University Press, 1965).Wenham, John, Jonathan Pennington, and Norman Young. *The Elements of New Testament Greek* (Cambridge University Press, 2001). Book and audio CD.
11. Young, Norman. *Syntax List for Students of New Testament Greek* (Cambridge University Press, 2001).

Second Year

1. Baugh, Steven. *A First John Reader: Intermediate Greek* (Presbyterian & Reformed, 1999).
2. Black, David. *It's Still Greek to Me* (Baker, 1998).
3. Brooks, James, and Carlton Winbery. *Syntax of New Testament Greek* (University Press of America, 1979).
4. Gorman, Frank. *The Elements of Biblical Exegesis* (Hendrickson, 2001). Brief, guidelines, exegetical models.
5. **Guthrie, George, and Scott Duvall. *Biblical Greek Exegesis* (Zondervan, 1998).**
6. Mounce, William. *A Graded Reader of Biblical Greek* (Zondervan, 1996). Second and third semesters.
7. Trenchard, Warren. *The Complete Vocabulary Guide to the Greek New Testament,* rev. ed. (Zondervan, 1999).
8. **Wallace, Daniel. *The Basics of New Testament Syntax* (Zondervan, 2000).** Third semester, abridgement of *Greek Grammar Beyond the Basics.*
9. **Young, Richard. *Intermediate New Testament Greek* (Broadman & Holman, 1994).**

Reference Grammars

1. Blass, A., F. Debrunner, and Robert Funk. *A Greek Grammar of the New Testament* (The University of Chicago Press, 1962). German edition, 1990.
2. McKay, K. *A New Syntax of the Verb in New Testament Greek* (Lang, 1994).
3. Moulton, James, W. Howard, and Nigel Turner. *A Grammar of New Testament Greek,* 4 vols. (T & T Clark, 1906–76). Especially volumes 1–2.

4. Owings, Timothy. *A Cumulative Index to New Testament Greek Grammars* (Baker, 1983). Indexed to Scripture.
5. Perschbacher, Wesley. *New Testament Greek Syntax* (Moody, 1995).
6. Robertson, A. T. *A Grammar of the Greek New Testament,* 4th ed. (Broadman & Holman, 1934).
7. **Wallace, Daniel. *Greek Grammar Beyond the Basics* (Zondervan, 1996).**
8. Zerwick, Maximilian. *Biblical Greek Illustrated By Examples* (Pontifical Biblical Institute, 1963). Especially verb structure.

Developments

1. Barr, James. *The Semantics of Biblical Language* (Oxford University Press, 1961).
2. Fanning, Buist. *Verbal Aspect in New Testament Greek* (Oxford University Press, 1990).
3. Moule, C. F. D. *An Idiom Book of New Testament Greek,* 2d ed. (Cambridge University Press, 1963).
4. Porter, Stanley, and D. A. Carson, eds. *Biblical Greek Language and Linguistics* (JSOT, 1993).
   ———. *Discourse Analysis and Other Topics in Biblical Greek* (Sheffield Academic Press, 1995).
5. **Porter, Stanley. *Idioms of the Greek New Testament,* 2d ed. (Sheffield Academic Press, 1994).**
   ———. *Verbal Aspect in the Greek of the New Testament with Reference to Tense and Mood,* 2d ed. (Lang, 1993).

Lexicons

1. **Bauer, Walter, Frederick Danker, William Arndt, and F. Wilbur Gingrich. *A Greek-English Lexicon of the New Testament and Other Early Christian Literature,* 3d ed. (The University of Chicago Press, 2000).**[1]

1. The Danker-edited revision of the 1988 German lexicon (6th ed.) is a most significant improvement, especially in two respects. First, an extended definition is given for each word (e.g., the word *plasma* is defined as "that which is formed or molded" followed by the equivalents "image, figure"). Second, this

2. Fraser, P., and E. Matthews, eds. *A Lexicon of Greek Personal Names* (Oxford University Press, 1987). Ancient Greek–A.D. 600.
3. Kubo, Sakae. *A Reader's Greek-English Lexicon of the New Testament* (Zondervan, 1975).
4. Lampe, G., ed. *A Patristic Greek Lexicon* (Oxford University Press, 1961).
5. Liddell, H., and R. Scott. *A Greek-English Lexicon,* 9th ed. with rev. supplement (Oxford University Press, 1996). Pre-300 B.C.
6. **Louw, Johannes, and Eugene Nida. *Greek-English Lexicon of the New Testament: Based on Semantic Domains,* 2d ed., 2 vols. (UBS, 1989).**
   ———. *Lexical Semantics of the Greek New Testament: A Supplement* (Scholars, 1992).
7. **Moulton, James, and G. Milligan. *The Vocabulary of the Greek Testament* (Hendrickson, 1997).** Coded to Strong's; NT index.

Theological Dictionaries[2]

1. Balz, Horst, and Gerhard Schneider. *Exegetical Dictionary of the New Testament,* 3 vols. (Eerdmans, 1990–93).
2. Brown, Colin, ed. *The New International Dictionary of New Testament Theology,* 4 vols. (Zondervan, 1975–1978).
3. Kittel, Gerhard, and Gerhard Friedrich, eds. *Theological Dic-*

---

extension of meaning eliminates the need to subcategorize every equivalent with its respective examples. For instance, in the previous edition (BAGD), five equivalents and examples of usage were given for *adelphos.* In the new edition, the use of extended definitions enables Danker to implement only two subcategories. The astonishing amount of work that went into this lexicon will be repaid by the astonishing amount of labor it will save.

2. An ample abridgement of the *NIDNTT* (35 percent plus 7 percent new entries), Verlyn Verbrugge, ed., *The niv Theological Dictionary of New Testament Words* (Zondervan, 2000), excises classical references, topical articles, theological digressions, bibliographies, etc., from Colin Brown. Also, all entries are now wholly evangelical. Similarly useful as the *NIVTDNTW* is Mounce, *The niv*

tionary of the New Testament, 10 vols. (Eerdmans, 1964–76). Dated.

4. **Spicq, Ceslas. *Theological Lexicon of the New Testament,* 3 vols. (Hendrickson, 1994).** Especially papyri, extrabiblical usage.
5. **Verbrugge, Verlyn, ed. *The NIV Theological Dictionary of New Testament Words* (Zondervan, 2000).** Condensation of Colin Brown's *NIDNTT.* Use with Mounce interlinear (below).

Concordances

1. Bachmann, H., and W. A. Slaby, eds. *Computer Concordance to the Novum Testamentum Graece* (de Gruyter, 1985).
2. **Kohlenberger, John, Edward Goodrick, and James Swanson. *The Exhaustive Concordance to the Greek New Testament* (Zondervan, 1995).**

   ———. *The Greek-English Concordance of the New Testament* (Zondervan, 1997).
3. **Marshall, I. Howard, ed. *Moulton and Geden: A Concordance to the Greek New Testament,* 6th ed. (T & T Clark, 2002).** UBS[4], incorporated supplement.
4. Wigram, George. *The Englishman's Greek Concordance and Lexicon* (Hendrickson, 1997). Coded to Strong's.

Analytical Lexicons

1. **Friberg, Timothy, Barbara Friberg, and Neva Miller. *Analytical Lexicon of the Greek New Testament* (Baker, 2000).** Grammatical tags.

English-Greek New Testament (Zondervan, 2000), a reverse interlinear with cross-references to Vebrugge that doubles as an analytical GNT. A $250.00 savings can be made by purchasing Verbrugge and Mounce in favor of the *NIDNTT,* a standard interlinear and an analytical GNT. The only caveat is that you would need to have your GNT open alongside Mounce if word order is in mind. Also, Darrell Bock is editing the two-volume *Bible Knowledge Key Word-Study* (Cook Communications, 2002), which analyzes the key words in each NT book (verse by verse).

2. Mounce, William. *Analytical Lexicon to the Greek New Testament* (Zondervan, 1992).
3. Perschbacher, Wesley. *The New Analytical Greek Lexicon* (Hendrickson, 1990).

Interlinears and Parallel New Testament

1. **Aland, Kurt. *Synopsis of the Four Gospels, Nestle-Aland 27th ed.–rsv,* 10th ed. (UBS, 1994).**
2. **Aland, Kurt. *Synopsis Quattuor Evangeliorum,* 14th ed. (GBS, 1990).**
3. **Douglas, J. D. *The New Greek-English Interlinear New Testament* (Tyndale, 1990).** NA[26], UBS[4], NRSV.
4. *Greek-English New Testament: Nestle-Aland 26th ed. with rsv* (ABS, 1986).
5. **Kohlenberger, John, ed. *The Precise Parallel New Testament* (Oxford University Press, 1995).** Greek, AMPLIFIED, NASB, NRSV, NIV, etc.
6. Kohlenberger, John. *The Greek New Testament: UBS[4] with the NRSV and NIV* (Zondervan, 1994).
7. **Mounce, William, ed. *The NIV English-Greek New Testament* (Zondervan, 2000).** Reverse interlinear, morphological tags, G/K numbers, especially useful for non-Greek background, use GNT for word order, use with Verbrugge, *NIVTDNTW* (above).

Study Aids*

1. **Chapman, Benjamin, and Gary Shogren. *Greek New Testament Insert,* rev. ed. (Stylus, 1994).**
   ———. *Card Guide to New Testament Greek,* rev. ed. (Stylus, 1994).
2. **DeMoss, Matthew. *Pocket Dictionary for the Study of New Testament Greek* (IVP, 2001).** Immensely useful guide to most commonly used terms in GNT and commentaries.

---

* Forthcoming in 2003: Peter Silzer and Thomas Finley, *How Biblical Languages Work: A Student's Guide to Understanding Hebrew and Greek* (Kregel).

3. Diewert, David, and Richard Goodrich. *A Summer Greek Reader* (Zondervan, 2001). Between first and second year Greek.
4. **Friberg, Timothy, and Barbara Friberg, eds. *Analytical Greek New Testament* (Baker, 1981).** Exhaustive morphology.
5. **Han, Nathan. *A Parsing Guide to the Greek New Testament* (Herald, 1971).**
6. **Metzger, Bruce. *Lexical Aids for Students of New Testament Greek,* 3d ed. (Baker, 1998).**
7. **Pennington, Jonathan. *New Testament Greek Vocabulary* (Zondervan, 2001).** 2 CD's containing vocabulary.
8. **Rogers Jr., Cleon, and Cleon Rogers III. *The New Linguistic and Exegetical Key to the Greek New Testament* (Zondervan, 1998).**
9. Scott, Bernard, et al. *Reading New Testament Greek: Complete Word Lists* (Hendrickson, 1993).
10. Swanson. James. *That's Greek to Me* (Broadman & Holman, 1998). One hundred key words, first semester.
11. **Wilson, Mark. *Mastering New Testament Greek Vocabulary Through Semantic Domains* (Kregel, 2002).**
12. **Zerwick, Max, and Mary Grosvenor. *A Grammatical Analysis of the Greek New Testament,* 5th ed. (Biblical Institute, 1996).**

Textual Criticism Guides for Exegesis

1. Aland, Kurt, and Barbara Aland. *The Text of the New Testament,* 2d ed. (Eerdmans, 1989).
2. DeLobel, Joel. *New Testament Textual Criticism and Exegesis* (Peeters, 2002).
3. **Greenlee, J. Harold. *Introduction to New Testament Textual Criticism* (Hendrickson, 1995).**
4. Kilpatrick, George. *The Principles and Practice of New Testament Textual Criticism* (Peeters, 1990).
5. **Metzger, Bruce. *A Textual Commentary of the GNT,* 2d ed. (UBS, 1994).** Companion to UBS[4].

   ———. *The Text of the New Testament,* 3d ed. (Clarendon, 1992).

6. Vaganay, Leon. *An Introduction to New Testament Textual Criticism*, 2d ed. (Cambridge University Press, 1992).

Textual Criticism Studies

1. Black, David. *Rethinking New Testament Textual Criticism* (Baker, 2002).
2. Bruce, F. F. *The New Testament Documents: Are They Reliable?* 5th ed. (IVP, 1960).
3. Clarke, Kent. *Textual Optimism: A Critique of the UBSGNT* (Sheffield Academic Press, 1997).
4. Comfort, Philip. *Early Manuscripts and Late Translations of the New Testament* (Baker, 1996; Wipf & Stock, 2002).
5. Ehrman, Bart. *The Orthodox Corruption of Scripture* (Oxford University Press, 1993).
6. Epp, Eldon, and Gordon Fee. *Studies in the Theory and Method of New Testament Textual Criticism* (Eerdmans, 1993). Contra Aland and Kilpatrick.
7. Holmes, Michael, and Bart Ehrman, eds. *The Text of the New Testament in Contemporary Research* (Eerdmans, 1994).
8. Sharpe, John, and Kimberley Van Kampen, eds. *The Bible as Book* (British Library/Oak Knoll, 1997, 2000). Volumes 1 and 3.
9. Taylor, D., ed. *Studies in the Early Text of the Gospels and Acts* (SBL, 2001).

Introductions to the Septuagint

1. **Hengel, Martin. *The Septuagint and Christian Scripture* (T & T Clark, 2001).**
2. **Jobes, Karen, and Moisés Silva. *Invitation to the Septuagint* (Baker, 2000).**
3. Marcos, Natalios. *The Septuagint in Context* (Brill, 2001).

Septuagint Tools

1. Brooke, A. E., N. McLean, and H. Thackeray, eds. *The Old Testament in Greek According to the Text of Codex Vaticanus,* 3 vols. (Cambridge University Press, 1906–40).
2. **Hatch, Edwin, and Henry Redpath. *A Concordance to the***

***Septuagint,* 2d ed. (Baker, 1998).** With Muraoka Hebrew-Aramaic index.

3. **Lust, J., E. Eynikol, and K. Hauspie, eds. *A Greek-English Lexicon of the Septuagint,* 2 vols. (GBS, 1992, 1996).**
4. Muraoka, Takamitsu. *A Greek-English Lexicon of the Septuagint: Twelve Prophets* (Peeters, 1993).
   ———. *The Hebrew-Aramaic Index to the Septuagint: Keyed to the Hatch and Redpath Concordance* (Baker, 1998).
5. **Rahlfs, A. *Septuaginta* (GBS, 1935).**
6. Taylor, Bernard. *The Analytical Lexicon to the Septuagint* (Zondervan, 1994).

Septuagint Studies

1. Beck, John. *Translators as Storytellers* (Lang, 2000).
2. **Olofsson, Staffan. *God Is My Rock* (Almqvist and Wiksell, 1990).** Translation technique.
3. **Tov, Emmanuel. *The Text-Critical Use of the Septuagint in Biblical Research,* 2d ed. (Simor, 1997).**

16

EXEGESIS, INTERPRETATION, AND HERMENEUTICS

Handbooks for Exegesis*

1. **Black, David, and David Dockery, eds. *Interpreting the New Testament,* rev. ed. (Broadman & Holman, 2001).** Updated *New Testament Criticism and Interpretation* (Zondervan, 1991).
2. **Broyles, Craig, ed. *Interpreting the Old Testament* (Baker, 2001).**
3. Carson, D. A. *Exegetical Fallacies,* 2d ed. (Baker, 1996).
4. **Conzelmann, Hans, and A. Lindemann. *Interpreting the New Testament* (Hendrickson, 1988).**
5. **Fee, Gordon. *New Testament Exegesis,* 3d ed. (Westminster John Knox, 2002).**
6. Marshall, I. Howard, ed. *New Testament Interpretation* (Eerdmans, 1977).
7. **Porter, Stanley, ed. *Handbook to Exegesis of the New Testament* (Brill, 1997).**
8. **Silva, Moisés. *Interpreting Galatians,* 2d ed. (Baker, 2001).**

* Forthcoming: *Orientation to the Old Testament* (Zondervan) by John Walton and Andrew Hill. For a combination of how to do exegesis and introduction to issues of New Testament Interpretation, consider the newly revised Fee and Black/Dockery. The Old Testament is also well served by the Broyles-edited introduction and Stuart, whose grasp of the latest publications is impressive given his numerous commitments, including teaching at Gordon-Conwell Theological Seminary, pastoring a local church, and writing two commentaries on Exodus (Broadman & Holman) and Zechariah (Eerdmans).

Galatians 3:6–14 appendix. Uses Galatians as a model for exegesis.

9. Stenger, Werner. *Introduction to New Testament Exegesis* (Eerdmans, 1993).
10. **Stuart, Douglas. *Old Testament Exegesis,* 3d ed. (Westminster John Knox, 2001).** Outstanding bibliography.
11. VanGemeren, Willem, ed. *A Guide to Old Testament Theology and Exegesis* (Zondervan, 1999). *NIDOTTE* introduction essays.

References for Interpretation

1. **Barton, John, ed. *The Cambridge Companion to Biblical Interpretation* (Cambridge University Press, 1998).**
2. **Coggins, Richard, and Leslie Houlden, eds. *Dictionary of Biblical Interpretation* (Trinity Press International, 1990).**
3. **Dockery, David, Kenneth Mathews, and Robert Sloan, eds. *Foundations for Biblical Interpretation* (Broadman & Holman, 1994).**
4. Elwell, Walter, and J. D. Weaver, eds. *Bible Interpreters of the Twentieth Century* (Baker, 1999).
5. **Hayes, John, ed. *Dictionary of Biblical Interpretation,* 2 vols. (Abingdon, 1998).**
6. **McKim, Donald, ed. *Historical Handbook of Major Biblical Interpreters* (IVP, 1998).**
7. **Patzia, Arthur, and Anthony Petrotta. *Pocket Dictionary of Biblical Studies* (IVP, 2002).**
8. **Soulen, Richard, and R. Kendall Soulen. *Handbook of Biblical Criticism,* 3d ed. (Westminster John Knox, 2001).** Essential glossary.

Old Testament Interpretation

1. **Baker, David, and Bill Arnold, eds. *The Face of Old Testament Studies* (Baker, 1999).**
2. Barton, John. *Reading the Old Testament,* rev. ed. (Westminster John Knox, 1997).
3. Fewell, Danna, ed. *Reading Between Texts* (Westminster John Knox, 1996).

4. Goldingay, John. *Approaches to Old Testament Interpretation,* rev. ed. (IVP, 1990).
   ———. *Models for Interpretation of Scripture* (Eerdmans, 1995).

New Testament Interpretation*

1. Fitzmyer, Joseph. *To Advance the Gospel* (Eerdmans, 1998). Collected essays.
2. **Green, Joel, ed. *Hearing the New Testament* (Eerdmans, 1995).**
3. **Green, Joel, and Max Turner, eds. *Between Two Horizons* (Eerdmans, 2000).**
4. Longenecker, Richard, ed. *Life in the Face of Death* (Eerdmans, 1998). New Testament resurrection.
5. Porter, Stanley, and D. Tombs, eds. *Approaches to New Testament Study* (Sheffield Academic Press, 1995).

Old Testament in the New†

1. Baker, David L. *Two Testaments, One Bible,* 2d ed. (IVP, 1991).
2. **Beale, Gregory, ed. *The Right Doctrine from the Wrong Text?* (Baker, 1994).**
3. **Bock, Darrell. *Proclamation from Prophecy and Pattern* (Sheffield Academic Press, 1987).** Luke.
4. **Carson, D. A., and Hugh Williamson, eds. *It Is Written: Scripture Citing Scripture* (Cambridge University Press, 1988).**
5. **Ellis, E. Earle. *The Old Testament in Early Christianity* (Baker, 1992).**
   ———. *Prophecy and Hermeneutic in Earliest Christianity* (Eerdmans, 1978).
6. **Evans, Craig, and J. A. Sanders, eds. *Paul and the Scriptures of Israel* (Sheffield Academic Press, 1994).** Response to Hays.

---

* Forthcoming: Scot McKnight, ed., *The Face of New Testament Studies* (Baker).

† Forthcoming: Gregory Beale and D. A. Carson, eds., *Commentary on the Use of the Old Testament in the New* (Baker). When it appears, this work promises to be the leading study of the use of the Old Testament in the New.

7. Evans, Craig, and Werner Stegner, eds. *The Gospels and the Scripture of Israel* (Sheffield Academic Press, 1994).
8. **Feinberg, John *Continuity and Discontinuity* (Crossway, 1988).**
9. France, R. T., and David Wenham, eds. *Studies in Midrash and Historiography* (JSOT, 1983).
10. **Hays, Richard. *Echoes of Scripture in the Letters of Paul* (Yale University Press, 1989).**
11. Juel, Donald. *Messianic Exegesis* (Fortress, 1988).
12. Kaiser, Walter. *The Uses of the Old Testament in the New* (Moody, 1985).
13. Kimball, Charles. *Jesus' Exposition of the Old Testament in Luke's Gospel* (Sheffield Academic Press, 1994).
14. Lindars, Barnabas. *New Testament Apologetic* (Westminster, 1961).
15. **Longenecker, Richard. *Biblical Exegesis in the Apostolic Period,* rev. ed. (Eerdmans, 1999).**
16. Marcus, Joel. *The Way of the Lord: Christological Exegesis of the Old Testament in the Gospel of Mark* (Westminster John Knox, 1992).
17. Menken, Maarten. *Old Testament Quotations in the Fourth Gospel* (Kok Pharos, 1996).
18. Moyise, Steve, ed. *The Old Testament in the New Testament* (Continuum, 2001).
19. Stanley, C. *Paul and the Language of Scripture* (Cambridge University Press, 1992). Especially LXX.
20. Swartley, Willard. *Israel's Scripture Tradition and the Synoptic Gospels* (Hendrickson, 1994).
21. Wright, Christopher. *Knowing Jesus Through the Old Testament* (IVP, 1992).

Linguistics and Method

1. Bartholomew, Craig, et al., eds. *Renewing Biblical Interpretation* (Zondervan, 2000).

   ———. *After Pentecost* (Zondervan, 2001). Linguistics.

2. Caird, George. *The Language and Imagery of the Bible,* rev. ed. (Eerdmans, 1997).
3. **Cotterell, Peter, and Max Turner. *Linguistics and Biblical Interpretation* (IVP, 1989).**
4. **Egger, Wilhelm. *How to Read the New Testament* (Hendrickson, 1996).**
5. Porter, Stanley, ed. *DiGlossia and Other Topics in New Testament Linguistics* (Sheffield Academic Press, 2000).
6. **Silva, Moisés. *Biblical Words and Their Meaning,* rev. ed. (Zondervan, 1994).**

   ———, ed. *Foundations of Contemporary Interpretation* (Zondervan, 1996). Six volumes in one.

Problem Passages

1. **Archer, Gleason. *New International Encyclopedia of Bible Difficulties* (Zondervan, 1981).**
2. **Kaiser, Walter, et al. *Hard Sayings of the Bible* (IVP, 1996).** Five volumes in one.
3. Laney, Carl. *Answers to Tough Questions from Every Book of the Bible* (Kregel, 1997).
4. **Stein, Robert. *Interpreting Puzzling Texts in the New Testament* (Baker, 1997).**
5. Thomas, Robert, ed. *The Master's Perspective on Difficult Passages* (Kregel, 1998). Articles from *TMSTJ.*

Historical Criticism

1. **Byrskog, Samuel. *Story as Story History as Story* (Mohr, 2000).** Legitimacy of eyewitnesses.
2. Elliott, Keith, and Ian Moir. *Manuscripts and the Text of the New Testament* (T & T Clark, 1995). Introductory text criticism for English readers.
3. **Ellis, E. Earle. *The Making of the New Testament Documents* (Brill, 1999).**
4. **Gerhardsson, Birger. *The Reliability of the Gospel Tradition* (Hendrickson, 2001).**

———. *Memory and Manuscript* (Eerdmans, 1998). Posits extensive oral tradition behind gospels.

5. Levenson, Jon. *The Hebrew Bible, the Old Testament, and Historical Criticism* (Westminster John Knox, 1993).
6. Linnemann, Eta. *Biblical Criticism on Trial* (Kregel, 2001).
   ———. *Historical Criticism of the Bible* (Kregel, 2001). Noted critic of Q.
7. McKenzie, Steven, and S. Haynes, eds. *To Each Its Own Meaning,* rev. ed. (Westminster John Knox, 1999). Explains numerous criticisms.

Canon

1. Abraham, William. *Canon and Criterion in Christian Theology* (Oxford University Press, 1998).
2. Barr, James. *Holy Scripture* (Westminster, 1983).
3. Barton, John. *Oracles of God* (Longman and Todd, 1986).
   ———. *Holy Writings, Sacred Text* (Westminster John Knox, 1998).
4. **Beckwith, Roger. *The Old Testament Canon of the New Testament Church and Its Background in Early Judaism* (Eerdmans, 1985).**
5. Blenkinsopp, Joseph. *Prophecy and Canon* (University of Notre Dame, 1977). Old Testament.
6. Brenneman, James. *Canons in Conflict* (Oxford University Press, 1997).
7. **Bruce, F. F. *The Canon of Scripture* (IVP, 1988).**
8. Chapman, Stephen. *The Law and the Prophets* (Mohr, 2000).
9. Comfort, Philip, ed. *The Origin of the Bible* (Tyndale, 1996).
10. Davies, Philip. *Scribes and Schools* (Westminster John Knox, 1998).
11. Gamble, H. *The New Testament Canon* (Fortress, 1985; Wipf & Stock, 2002).
12. **Hahneman, Geoffrey. *The Muratorian Fragment and the Development of the Canon* (Clarendon, 1992).**
13. **Meade, D. *Pseudonymity and Canon* (Eerdmans, 1988).**
14. **Metzger, Bruce. *Canon of the New Testament* (Clarendon, 1987/1997).**

15. McDonald, Lee. *The Formation of the Christian Biblical Canon,* rev. ed. (Hendrickson, 1995).
16. McDonald, Lee, and James Sanders, eds. *The Canon Debate* (Hendrickson, 2002).
17. **Patzia, Arthur. *The Making of the New Testament* (IVP, 1995).**
18. Sanders, Jack. *Torah and Canon* (Fortress, 1972; Wipf & Stock 1999).
19. Steinmann, Andrew. *The Oracles of God* (Concordia Academic Press, 1999). OT.
20. **Trebolle Barrera, Julio. *The Jewish Bible and the Christian Bible* (Eerdmans, 1998).**
21. von Campenhausen, Hans. *The Formation of the Christian Bible* (Fortress, 1972).

History of Interpretation

1. **Baird, William. *History of New Testament Research,* 3 vols. (Fortress, 1992, 2002–).**
2. Blowers, Paul. *The Bible in Greek Christian Antiquity* (University of Notre Dame, 1997).
3. **Bray, Gerald. *Biblical Interpretation* (IVP, 1996).**
4. de Lubac, Henri. *Medieval Exegesis,* 2 vols. (Eerdmans, 1998–).
5. de Margerie, Bertrand. *An Introduction to the History of Interpretation,* 3 vols. (St. Bede's, 1997).
6. **Ellis, E. Earle. *History and Interpretation in New Testament Perspective* (Brill, 2001).**
7. **Epp, Eldon, and George McRae, eds. *The New Testament and Its Modern Interpreters* (Scholars, 1989).**
8. Grant, Robert, and David Tracy. *A Short History of the Interpretation of the Bible,* 2d ed. (Fortress, 1984).
9. Harrisville, Roy, and Walter Sundberg. *The Bible in Modern Culture: Baruch Spinoza to Brevard Childs,* 2d ed. (Eerdmans, 2002).
10. **Hauser, Alan, and Duane Watson, eds. *A History of Biblical Interpretation, The Ancient Period* (Eerdmans, 2002).**
11. Jeffrey, David. *People of the Book* (Eerdmans, 1996).

12. Kealy, Sean. *Matthew's Gospel and the History of Interpretation* (Mellen, 1997).
13. **Mays, James, David Petersen, and Kent Richards. *Old Testament Interpretation* (Abingdon, 1996).**
14. Montague, George. *Understanding the Bible* (Paulist, 1997). Includes comment on Catholic developments.
15. Morgan, Robert, and John Barton. *Biblical Interpretation* (Oxford University Press, 1988).
16. **Oden, Thomas, gen. ed. ACCS, 27 vols. (IVP, 1998–).**
17. Simonetti, Manlio. *Biblical Interpretation in the Early Church* (T & T Clark, 2001).

Bible Versions/History

1. **Ackroyd, Peter, and C. F. Evans, eds. *The Cambridge History of the Bible,* 3 vols. (Cambridge University Press, 1963–1970).**
2. Barker, Kenneth. *The Accuracy of the NIV* (Baker, 1996).
   ———. *The Making of the NIV* (Baker, 1997).
   ———. *The Balance of the NIV* (Baker, 1998).
3. **Beacham, Roy, and Kevin Bauder, eds. *One Bible Only?* (Kregel, 2001).** KJV controversy.
4. **Carson, D. A. *The King James Version Debate* (Baker, 1979).**
5. Comfort, Philip. *The Essential Guide to Bible Versions* (Tyndale, 2000).
   ———, ed. *The Origin of the Bible* (Tyndale, 1992).
6. **DeHamel, Christopher. *The Book: A History of the Bible* (Phaedon, 2001).**
7. Gilmore, Alec. *A Dictionary of the English Bible and Its Origins* (Sheffield Academic Press, 2000).
8. Lewis, Jack. *The English Bible from kjv to NIV,* 2d ed. (Baker, 1991).
9. Long, John. *The Bible in English: John Wycliffe and William Tyndale* (University Press of America, 1998).
10. **McGrath, Alister. *In the Beginning* (Doubleday, 2001).** Creation of KJV.
11. **Metzger, Bruce. *The Bible in Translation* (Baker, 2002).**

12. **Rogerson, John, ed. *The Oxford Illustrated History of the Bible* (Oxford University Press, 2001).**
13. Sheeley, Steven, and Robert Nash. *The Bible in English Translation* (Abingdon, 1997).
14. **Wegner, Paul. *The Journey from Texts to Translations* (Baker, 1999).** General introduction to whole Bible.
15. **White, James. *The King James Only Controversy* (Bethany House, 1995).**

Inclusive-Language Debate[1]

1. **Carson, D. A. *The Inclusive Language Debate* (Baker, 1998).**
2. **Poythress, Vern, and Wayne Grudem. *The Gender Neutral Bible Controversy* (Broadman & Holman, 2000).**
3. Storkey, Elaine. *Origins of Difference* (Baker, 2001). Gender debate.
4. **Strauss, Mark. *Distorting Scripture?* (IVP, 1998).** Gender debate.

Hermeneutics

Textbooks

1. Kaiser, Walter, and Moisés Silva. *An Introduction to Biblical Hermeneutics* (Zondervan, 1994).
2. **Klein, William, Craig Blomberg, and Robert Hubbard. *Introduction to Biblical Interpretation* (Word, 1993).**
3. Osborne, Grant. *The Hermeneutical Spiral* (IVP, 1991). General hermeneutics, genre, contextualization.
4. Tate, Randolph. *Biblical Interpretation,* rev. ed. (Hendrickson, 1997).
5. Thomas, Robert. *Evangelical Hermeneutics* (Kregel, 2002).
6. Voelz, James. *What Does This Mean?* 2d ed. (Concordia Academic Press, 1995).

---

1. I am indebted to Darrell Bock for the suggestions in "Do Gender Sensitive Translations Distort Scripture? Not Necessarily," bible.org/docs/soapbox (2002), 15.

Basic Guides

1. **Corley, Bruce, Steve Lemke, and Grant Lovejoy, eds. *Biblical Hermeneutics,* 2d ed. (Broadman & Holman, 2002).**
2. Doriani, Daniel. *Getting The Message* (Presbyterian & Reformed, 1996).
3. **Duvall, J. Scott, and J. Daniel Hays. *Grasping God's Word* (Zondervan, 2001).**
   ———. *Grasping God's Word Workbook* (Zondervan, 2001).
4. **Fee, Gordon, and Douglas Stuart. *How to Read the Bible for All It's Worth,* 2d ed. (Zondervan, 1993).**
5. Fee, Gordon, and Douglas Stuart. *How to Read the Bible Book by Book* (Zondervan, 2002).
6. Zuck, Roy. *Basic Biblical Interpretation* (Victor, 1991).

Philosophical and Theological Hermeneutics

1. Croatto, Severino. *Biblical Hermeneutics* (Orbis, 1987).
2. Erickson, Millard. *Evangelical Interpretation* (Baker, 1993).
3. Farmer, Ronald. *Beyond the Impasse* (Mercer University Press, 1997).
4. Fee, Gordon. *To What End Exegesis?* (Eerdmans, 2001).
5. **Fitzmyer, Joseph. *The Biblical Commission's Document "The Interpretation of the Bible in the Church"* (Subsidia Biblica, 1995).**
6. Fodor, James. *Christian Hermeneutics* (Oxford University Press, 1995). On Paul Ricouer.
7. **Gadamer, Hans-Georg. *Truth and Method,* 2d ed. (Continuum, 1989).**
8. **Hirsch, E. D. *Validity in Interpretation* (Yale University Press, 1967).**
   ———. *Aims in Interpretation* (The University of Chicago Press, 1976).
9. **Hoy, David. *The Critical Circle* (University of California, 1982).**
10. Lundin, Roger, Clarence Walhout, and Anthony Thiselton. *The Promise of Hermeneutics* (Eerdmans, 1999).
11. **Madison, G. B. *The Hermeneutics of Postmodernity* (Indiana University Press, 1988).**

12. **Meyer, Ben. *Reality and Illusion in New Testament Scholarship* (Liturgical, 1995).**
13. Mueller-Vollmer, Kurt, et al., eds. *The Hermeneutics Reader* (Continuum, 1989).
14. Noble, Paul. *The Canonical Approach* (Brill, 1995).
15. Patte, Daniel. *Ethics of Biblical Interpretation* (Westminster John Knox, 1995).
16. Ricoeur, Paul. *Interpretation Theory* (TCU, 1976).
17. Scalise, Charles. *Hermeneutics as Theological Prolegomena: A Canonical Approach* (Mercer University Press, 1994).
    ———. *From Scripture to Theology* (IVP, 1996).
18. Smith, James. *The Fall of Interpretation* (IVP, 2000).
19. Stiver, James. *Theology after Ricouer* (Westminster John Knox, 2001).
20. **Thiselton, Anthony. *New Horizons in Hermeneutics* (Zondervan, 1992).**
21. Vanhoozer, Kevin. *Is There a Meaning in the Text?* (Zondervan, 1998).
    ———. *First Theology* (IVP, 2002).
22. **Webb, William. *Slaves, Women, and Homosexuals* (IVP, 2001).** How to apply cultural background to interpretation.

Postmodernism

1. Adam, A. K. M. *What Is Postmodern Biblical Criticism?* (Fortress, 1995).
   ———, ed. *Handbook of Postmodern Biblical Interpretation* (Chalice, 2000).
2. **Benson, Bruce. *Graven Ideologies* (IVP, 2002).**
3. Braaten, Carl, and Robert Jenson, eds. *The Strange New World of the Gospel* (Eerdmans, 2002).
4. **Carson, D. A. *Telling the Truth: Evangelizing Postmoderns* (Zondervan, 2000).**
5. **Dockery, David. *The Challenge of Postmodernism,* 2d ed. (Baker, 2001).**
6. Erickson, Millard. *Postmodernizing the Faith* (Baker, 1998). Response to Oden, Grenz, Middleton, Walsh, etc.

———. *Truth or Consequences* (IVP, 2001).
———. *The Postmodern World* (Crossway, (2002).
7. Gay, Craig. *The Way of the (Modern) World* (Eerdmans, 1999).
8. **Gillingham, Susan. *One Bible, Many Voices* (Eerdmans, 1999).**
9. **Grenz, Stanley. *A Primer on Postmodernism* (Eerdmans, 1996).**
10. **Groothuis, Douglas. *Truth Decay* (IVP, 2000).**
11. **Horton, Michael, ed. *A Confessing Theology for Postmodern Times* (Crossway, 2000).**
12. Jobling, David, ed. *The Postmodern Bible Reader* (Blackwell, 2001).
13. **Middleton, Richard, and Brian Walsh. *Truth Is Stranger Than It Used to Be* (IVP, 1995).**
14. Murphy, Nancey. *Beyond Liberalism and Fundamentalism* (Trinity Press International, 1996).
———. *Anglo-American Postmodernism* (Westview, 1997).
15. Penchansky, David. *The Politics of Biblical Theology* (Mercer University Press, 1995).
16. **Phillips, Timothy, and Dennis Ockholm, eds. *The Nature of Confession* (IVP, 1996).**
17. **Tanner, Kenneth, and Christopher Hall, eds. *Ancient and Postmodern Christianity* (IVP, 2002).**
18. **Thiselton, Anthony. *Interpreting God and the Postmodern Self* (T & T Clark, 1995).**
19. Thornhill, John. *Modernity* (Eerdmans, 2000).
20. Ward, Graham, ed. *The Blackwell Companion to Postmodern Theology* (Blackwell, 2001).
21. **Webber, Robert. *Ancient-Future Faith* (Baker, 1999).**
———. *The Younger Evangelicals* (Baker, 2002).
22. **Wright, N. T. *The Millennial Myth* (Westminster John Knox, 1999).**

Literary and Genre Studies

1. Alter, Robert, and Frank Kermode, eds. *The Literary Guide to the Bible* (Belknap-Harvard, 1987). Especially the Old Testament.

2. Cotter, David, ed. *Berit Olam: Studies in Hebrew Narrative and Poetry,* 24 vols. (Liturgical, 1996–).
3. Dorsey, David. *The Literary Structure of the Old Testament* (Baker, 1999).
4. Exum, Cheryl, and David Clines. *The New Literary Criticism and the Hebrew Bible* (Trinity Press International, 1994).
5. House, Paul, ed. *Beyond Form Criticism* (Eisenbrauns, 1992). OT.
6. Moore, S. *Literary Criticism and the Gospels* (Yale University Press, 1989).
7. Ryken, Leland, and Tremper Longman, eds. *A Complete Literary Guide to the Bible* (Zondervan, 1993).
8. **Ryken, Leland, James Wilhoit, and Tremper Longman, eds. *Dictionary of Biblical Imagery* (IVP, 1998).**
9. Strecker, Georg. *History of New Testament Literature* (Trinity Press International, 1997).
10. Wills, Lawrence. *The Quest of the Historical Gospel* (Routledge, 1997). Gospel genre.

Introductions to the Bible as Literature

1. **Alter, Robert. *The World of Biblical Literature* (Basic, 1992).**
2. **Aune, David. *The New Testament in Its Literary Environment,* LEC (Westminster, 1987).**
3. **Bailey, James, and L. Vander Broek. *Literary Forms in the New Testament* (Westminster John Knox, 1993).**
4. **Longman, Tremper. *Literary Approaches to Biblical Interpretation* (Zondervan, 1987).**
5. **Malherbe, Abraham. *Moral Exhortation: A Greco-Roman Sourcebook,* LEC (Westminster, 1986).**
6. **Petersen, Norman. *Literary Criticism for New Testament Critics* (Fortress, 1978).**
7. **Ryken, Leland. *Words of Delight* (Baker, 1987).**
   ———. *Words of Life* (Baker, 1987). NT.
8. **Sandy, Brent, and Ronald Giese, eds. *Cracking Old Testament Codes* (Broadman & Holman, 1995).**

Apocalyptic

1. Collins, Adela Yarbro. *Cosmology and Eschatology in Jewish and Christian Apocalypticism* (Brill, 1996).
2. **Collins, John. *The Apocalyptic Imagination,* 2d ed. (Eerdmans, 1998).**
   ———, ed. *Apocalypse,* Semeia 14 (Scholars, 1979).
3. Collins, John, and James Charlesworth. *Mysteries and Revelations* (Sheffield Academic Press, 1991).
4. **Collins, John, Bernard McGinn, and Stephen Stein, eds. *The Encyclopedia of Apocalypticism,* 3 vols. (Continuum, 1998).**
5. Cook, Stephen. *Prophecy and Apocalypticism* (Fortress, 1995).
6. **Hanson, Paul. *The Dawn of Apocalyptic,* rev. ed. (Fortress, 1979).**
7. **Hellholm, David, ed. *Apocalypticism in the Mediterranean World and the Near East* (Mohr, 1983).**
8. **Himmelfarb, Martha. *Ascent to Heaven in Jewish and Christian Apocalypses* (Oxford University Press, 1993).**
9. Nickelsburg, George. *1 Enoch 1,* Hermeneia (Fortress, 2001). 1–36, 81–108.
   ———, and James VanderKam. *1 Enoch 2,* Hermeneia (Fortress, forthcoming). 37–80.
10. **Rowland, Christopher. *The Open Heaven* (Crossroad, 1982).**
    ———. *The Book of Revelation,* NIB, vol. 12 (Abingdon, 1998). Extensive bibliography on apocalyptic.
11. **Russell, D. *Prophecy and the Apocalyptic Dream* (Hendrickson, 1994).** Introduction.
12. Sandy, Brent. *Turning Plowshares into Pruning Hooks: Rethinking the Language of Biblical Prophecy and Apocalyptic* (IVP, 2002).
13. VanderKam, James, and William Adler, eds. *The Jewish Apocalyptic Heritage in Early Christianity* (Fortress, 1997).

Letter-Writing

1. **Murphy-O'Connor, Jerome. *Paul the Letter-Writer* (Liturgical, 1995).**

2. **Stowers, Stanley. *Letter Writing in Greco-Roman Antiquity*, LEC (Westminster, 1986).**
3. **White, John. *Light from Ancient Letters* (Fortress, 1986).**
   ———. *The Form and Function of the Body of the Greek Letter* (Scholars, 1972).
4. **Wilder, Terry. *Pseudonymity, the New Testament, and Deception* (University Press of America, 2002).**

Narrative

1. **Alter, Robert. *The Art of Biblical Narrative* (Basic, 1981).** Introduction.
2. Amit, Yairah. *Reading Biblical Narratives* (Fortress, 2001).
   ———. *Hidden Polemics in Biblical Narrative* (Brill, 2000).
   ———. *History and Ideology in the Bible* (Sheffield Academic Press, 1997).
3. Bar-Efrat, Shimon. *Narrative Art in the Bible* (Almond, 1989).
4. **Berlin, Adele. *Poetics and Interpretation of Biblical Narrative* (Eisenbrauns, 1994).**
5. **Burridge, Richard. *What Are The Gospels?* (Cambridge University Press, 1992).**
6. **Fokkelman, J. P. *Reading Biblical Narrative* (Westminster John Knox, 2000).** Introduction.
7. Gunn, David, and Danna Fewell. *Narrative in the Hebrew Bible* (Oxford University Press, 1993). Introduction.
8. Husser, Jean-Marie. *Dreams and Dream Narratives in the Biblical World* (Sheffield Academic Press, 2000).
9. Inch, Morris. *Scripture as Story* (University Press of America, 2000).
10. Merenlahti, Petri. *Poetics for the Gospels?* (Sheffield Academic Press, 2002).
11. Miscall, Peter. *The Workings of Old Testament Narrative* (Fortress, 1983). 1 Samuel 16–22.
12. **Powell, Mark. *What Is Narrative Criticism?* (Fortress, 1990).**
13. **Simon, Uriel. *Reading Prophetic Narrative* (Indiana University Press, 1997).**
14. **Sternberg, Meir. *The Poetics of Biblical Narrative* (Indiana University Press, 1985).**

15. Walsh, Jerome. *Style and Structure in Biblical Hebrew Narrative* (Liturgical, 2001).

Parables

1. **Blomberg, Craig. *Interpreting the Parables* (IVP, 1990).** Introduction.
2. Capon, Robert. *Kingdom, Grace, Judgment* (Eerdmans, 2002).
3. Donahue, John. *The Gospel in Parable* (Fortress, 1988).
4. **Forbes, Greg. *The God of Old* (Sheffield Academic Press, 2000).** Luke.
5. Gowler, David. *What Are They Saying About the Parables?* (Paulist, 2000).
6. Hedrick, Charles. *The Parables as Fiction* (Hendrickson, 1994).
7. Herzog, William. *The Parables as Subversive Speech* (Westminster John Knox, 1994).
8. Hultgren, Arland. *The Parables of Jesus* (Eerdmans, 2000). Commentary.
9. Jones, Ivor. *The Matthean Parables* (Brill, 1995).
10. **Kistemaker, Simon. *The Parables* (Baker, 2002).**
11. **Longenecker, Richard. *The Challenge of Jesus' Parables* (Eerdmans, 1999).**
12. Scott, Bernard. *Hear Then the Parable* (Fortress, 1989).
13. Shillington, George, ed. *Jesus and His Parables* (T & T Clark, 1998).
14. **Wright, Stephen. *The Voice of Jesus* (Paternoster, 2000).** Study of six parables.
15. Young, Brad. *The Parables* (Hendrickson, 1998).

Poetry

1. **Alter, Robert. *The Art of Biblical Poetry* (Basic, 1985).** Introduction, especially dynamics of parallels.
2. Cross, Frank, and David Freedman. *Studies in Ancient Yahwistic Poetry* (Eerdmans, 1997).
3. **Fokkelman, J. P. *Major Poems of the Hebrew Bible* (Van Gorcum, 2000).** Eighty-five psalms and Job 4–14.

   ———. *Reading Biblical Poetry* (Westminster John Knox, 2001).

4. Follis, Elaine, ed. *Directions in Biblical Hebrew Poetry* (Sheffield Academic Press, 1997).
5. **Gillingham, Susan. *The Poems and Psalms of the Hebrew Bible* (Oxford University Press, 1994).**
6. Kugel, James. *The Idea of Biblical Poetry* (Johns Hopkins University Press, 1998).
7. **Petersen, David, and Kent Richards. *Interpreting Hebrew Poetry* (Fortress, 1992).**
8. **Watson, Wilfred. *Classical Hebrew Poetry* (JSOT, 1984).**
   ———. *Traditional Techniques in Classical Hebrew Verse* (Sheffield Academic Press, 1994).
9. *See* Old Testament Resources: Introduction to Wisdom Literature.

Prophecy

1. Armerding, Carl, and Ward Gasque, eds. *A Guide to Biblical Prophecy* (Hendrickson, 1989; Wipf & Stock, 2001).
2. **Aune, David. *Prophecy in Early Christianity and the Ancient Mediterranean World* (Eerdmans, 1983).**
3. Ben Zvi, Ehud, and Michael Floyd, eds. *Writing and Speech in Israelite and Ancient Near Eastern Prophecy* (SBL, 2000).
4. Blenkinsopp, Joseph. *A History of Prophecy in Israel* (Westminster John Knox, 1996).
5. **Clements, Ronald. *Old Testament Prophecy* (Westminster John Knox, 1996).**
6. Davies, Philip, and David Clines, eds. *Among the Prophets* (Sheffield Academic Press, 1993).
7. Forbes, Christopher. *Prophecy and Inspired Speech in Early Christianity and Its Hellenistic Environment* (Hendrickson, 1997).
8. Gitay, Yehoshua, ed. *Prophecy and Prophets* (Scholars, 1997).
9. Glazov, Gregory. *The Bridling of the Tongue and the Opening of the Mouth in Biblical Prophecy* (Sheffield Academic Press, 2001).
10. House, Wayne, and Randall Price. *Charts of Bible Prophecy* (Zondervan, 2000).

11. Mayhue, Richard, and Robert Thomas, eds. *The Master's Perspective on Biblical Prophecy* (Kregel, 2002). Articles from *TMSTJ*.
12. Peckham, Brian. *History and Prophecy,* ABRL (Doubleday, 1993).
13. **Sandy, Brent. *Ploughshares and Pruning Hooks* (IVP, 2002).**
14. **Uffenheimer, Benjamin. *Early Prophecy in Israel* (Magnes, 1999).**
15. Zuck, Roy, ed. *Vital Prophetic Issues* (Kregel, 1995). The best of *BibSac* on the subject.
16. *See* Old Testament Resources: Introduction to Prophetic Literature.

Rhetoric (OT)

1. De Regt, J., et al., eds. *Literary Structure and Rhetorical Strategies in the Hebrew Bible* (Eisenbrauns, 1996).
2. **Eslinger, Lyle. *House of God or House of David* (Sheffield Academic Press, 1994).** 2 Samuel 7.
3. **Lundblom, Jack. *Jeremiah,* 2d ed. (Eisenbrauns, 1997).**
4. Patrick, Dale. *The Rhetoric of Revelation in the Hebrew Bible* (Fortress, 1999).
5. **Trible, Phyllis. *Rhetorical Criticism* (Fortress, 1994).** Jonah.
6. Watts, James. *Reading Law* (Sheffield Academic Press, 1999).

Rhetoric (NT)

1. Anderson, R. *Ancient Rhetorical Theory and Paul* (Kok Pharos, 1996).
2. **Classen, Carl. *Rhetorical Criticism of the New Testament* (Brill, 2002).**
3. **Harvey, John. *Listening to the Text: Oral Patterning in Paul's Letters* (Baker, 1998).**
4. **Kennedy, G. *New Testament Interpretation Through Rhetorical Criticism* (University of North Carolina, 1984).**
5. Mack, Burton. *Rhetoric and the New Testament* (Fortress, 1990).
6. Robbins, Vernon. *The Tapestry of Early Christian Discourse* (Routledge, 1996).

7. **Porter, Stanley, and Thomas Olbricht, eds. *Rhetoric and the New Testament* (Sheffield Academic Press, 1993).**
   ———. *Rhetoric, Scripture and Theology* (Sheffield Academic Press, 1996).
8. **Porter, Stanley, and Dennis Stamps, eds. *Rhetorical Criticism and the Bible* (Sheffield Academic Press, 2002).**
9. Wilder, Amos. *Early Christian Rhetoric* (Hendrickson, 1999).

Sociorhetorical (General)

1. Eriksson, Anders, et al., eds. *Rhetorical Argumentation in Biblical Texts* (Trinity Press International, 2002).
2. Hens-Piazza, Gina. *Of Methods, Monarchs, and Meanings* (Mercer University Press, 1996).
3. Kingsbury, Jack, ed. *Gospel Interpretation* (Trinity Press International, 1997).
4. Meynet, Roland. *Rhetorical Analysis* (Sheffield Academic Press, 1999).
5. Robbins, Vernon. *Exploring the Texts* (Trinity Press International, 1996).
6. Watson, Duane, and Alan Hauser, eds. *Rhetorical Criticism of the Bible* (Brill, 1994). Nonannotated bibliography.
7. *See* Sociorhetorical Studies and Commentaries under NT Commentaries: Acts, 1 Corinthians, Galatians, and Revelation.

Wisdom

1. Ballard, Wayne, and Dennis Tucker, eds. *Introduction to Wisdom Literature and the Psalms* (Mercer University Press, 2000).
2. Bergant, Dianne. *Israel's Wisdom Literature* (Fortress, 1997).
3. Blenkinsopp, Joseph. *Wisdom and Law in the Old Testament,* 2d ed. (Oxford University Press, 1995).
4. Brenner, Athalya, ed. *A Feminist Companion to Wisdom Literature* (Sheffield Academic Press, 1995).
5. Brown, William. *Character in Crisis* (Eerdmans, 1996).

6. Crenshaw, James. *Urgent Advice and Probing Questions* (Mercer University Press, 1995).
7. Day, John, Robert Gordon, and Hugh Williamson, eds. *Wisdom in Ancient Israel* (Cambridge University Press, 1995).
8. **Gammie, John, and Leo Perdue, eds. *The Sage in Israel and the Ancient Near East* (Eisenbrauns, 1990).**
9. Mack, Burton, and David Clines, eds. *Of Prophet's Visions and the Wisdom of the Sages* (Sheffield Academic Press, 1993).
10. Packer, J. I., and Sven Soderlund, eds. *The Way of Wisdom* (Zondervan, 2000).
11. Perdue, Leo, et al., eds. *In Search of Wisdom* (Westminster John Knox, 1993).
12. von Rad, Gerhard. *Wisdom in Israel* (Abingdon, 1972).
13. **Weeks, Stuart. *Early Israelite Wisdom* (Clarendon, 1994).** Especially Proverbs.
14. *See* Clements, Perdue (OT Theology).
15. *See* Old Testament Resources: Introduction to Wisdom Literature.

17
SYSTEMATIC THEOLOGY (ALL UNRANKED)

Classic Theologies

1. **Berkhof, Louis. *Systematic Theology* (Eerdmans, 1996). Combined *Systematic Theology,* 4th ed. (Eerdmans, 1939) and *Introduction to Systematic Theology* (Eerdmans, 1932; Baker, 1979).**
2. Berkouwer, G. *Studies in Dogmatics,* 14 vols. (Eerdmans, 1952–76).
3. Buswell, James. *A Systematic Theology of the Christian Religion,* 2 vols. (Zondervan, 1962–63).
4. Chafer, Lewis. *Systematic Theology,* 4 vols. (Kregel, 1993). Unabridged.
5. Hodge, Charles. *Systematic Theology,* 3 vols. (Hendrickson, 1997).

   ———. *Systematic Theology,* abridged 1-vol. ed. (Presbyterian & Reformed, 1997).
6. Shedd, William. *Dogmatic Theology,* 3 vols. (Klock and Klock, 1979).[1]
7. Strong, Augustus. *Systematic Theology* (Judson, 1907).
8. Thiessen, Henry. *Lectures in Systematic Theology,* rev. ed. (Eerdmans, 1977).
9. Warfield, Benjamin. *Works,* 10 vols. (Baker, 1991).

1. Currently under revision by Alan Gomes (Presbyterian & Reformed).

10. Wiley, H. Orton. *Christian Theology,* 3 vols. (Nazarene Publishing, 1940–43). Arminian perspective.

Contemporary Theologies

1. **Bloesch, Donald. *Christian Foundations,* 7 vols. (IVP, 1992–).**
2. **Enns, Paul. *Moody Handbook of Theology* (Moody, 1989).**
3. **Erickson, Millard. *Christian Theology,* 2d ed. (Baker, 1998).**
   ———. *Introducing Christian Doctrine,* 2d ed. (Baker, 2001). Abridgement of *Christian Theology.*
4. Finger, Thomas. *Christian Theology,* 2 vols. (Herald, 1985, 1989).
5. Garrett, James. *Systematic Theology,* 2 vols. (Eerdmans, 1990, 1995).
6. Geisler, Norman. *Systematic Theology,* 4 vols. (Bethany House, 2002–).
7. Grenz, Stanley. *The Matrix of Christian Theology,* 6 vols. (Westminster John Knox, 2001–).
   ———. *Theology for the Community of God* (Eerdmans, 2000).
   ———. *Renewing the Center* (Baker, 2000).
8. Grudem, Wayne. *Systematic Theology* (Zondervan, 1994). Calvinistic charismatic.
   ———. *Bible Doctrine* (Zondervan, 1999). Abridgement of *Systematic Theology.*
9. **Gunton, Colin. *The Christian Faith* (Blackwell, 2001).** Introduction.
10. **Hanson, Paul. *Introduction to Christian Theology* (Fortress, 1997).**
11. Henry, Carl. *God, Revelation, and Authority,* 6 vols. (Word, 1976–83; Crossway, 1999).
12. Horton, Stanley, ed. *Systematic Theology,* rev. ed. (Logion, 1995). Pentecostal.
13. Jenson, Robert. *Systematic Theology,* 2 vols. (Oxford University Press, 1997–99).
14. Lewis, Gordon, and Bruce Demarest. *Integrative Theology* (Zondervan, 1987–1994). Three volumes in one.

15. Livermore, Paul, Donald Bastien, and Thomas Oden. *The God of Our Salvation* (Light and Life Communications, 1995). Wesleyan.
16. McClendon, James. *Systematic Theology,* 3 vols. (Abingdon, 2002^2–, 1986–2000). Anabaptist.
17. **McGrath, Alister. *Christian Theology,* 3d ed. (Blackwell, 2001).**

    ———. ed. *The Christian Theology Reader,* 2d ed. (Blackwell, 2001).

    ———. *Studies in Doctrine* (Zondervan, 1997). Four volumes in one.
18. **McKim, Donald. *Introducing the Reformed Faith* (Westminster John Knox, 2001).**
19. Menzies, William, and Stanley Horton. *Bible Doctrines* (Logion, 1993). Pentecostal.
20. Miller, Ed, and Stanley Grenz, eds. *Fortress Introduction to Contemporary Theologies* (Fortress, 1998).
21. Oden, Thomas. *Systematic Theology,* 3 vols. (Harper, 1987–92; Prince, 2000). Methodist.
22. Pannenberg, Wolfhart. *Systematic Theology,* 3 vols. (Eerdmans, 1991, 1994, 1997).
23. Peters, Ted. *God: The World's Future,* 2d ed. (Fortress, 2000). Postmodern.
24. **Reymond, Robert. *A New Systematic Theology of the Christian Faith* (Thomas Nelson, 1998).** Reformed introduction.
25. Sawyer, James. *The Survivor's Guide to Theology* (Zondervan, 2002). Introduction.
26. Williams, Rodman. *Renewal Theology* (Zondervan, 1992). Three volumes in one, Pentecostal.

Catholic Theologies

1. Beinert, Wolfgang, and Francis Schüssler Fiorenza, eds. *Handbook of Catholic Theology* (Crossroad, 1995).
2. **Brown, Raymond E., Karl Donfried, Joseph Fitzmyer, and John Reumann. *Mary in the New Testament* (Fortress/Paulist, 1978).**

3. Chauvet, Louis-Marie. *The Sacraments* (Liturgical, 2001).
4. Collinge, William. *The A to Z of Catholicism* (Scarecrow, 2001).
5. Congar, Yves. *Diversity and Communion* (23rd Community, 1985).
6. de Lubac, Henri. *The Sources of Revelation* (Crossroad, 2000).
7. Dulles, Avery. *The Craft of Theology* (Crossroad, 1992).
   ———. *The Assurance of Things Hoped For* (Oxford University Press, 1994).
8. Fries, Heinrich. *Fundamental Theology* (Catholic University of America, 1996).
9. Kaspar, Walter. *Theology and Church II* (Herder and Herder, 2001).
   ———. *The God of Jesus Christ* (Crossroad, 1984). Idealist Christology.
10. Komanchak, Joseph, Mary Collins, and Dermot Lane, eds. *The New Dictionary of Theology* (Liturgical, 1987).
11. Küng, Hans. *Christianity* (Continuum, 1995).
    ———. *Infallible?* 2d ed. (Continuum, 1994).
12. Latourelle, Rene, and Rino Fisichella, eds. *Dictionary of Fundamental Theology* (Crossroad, 1994).
13. **O'Collins, Gerald. *Christology* (Oxford University Press, 1995).**
14. Rahner, Karl. *Foundations of Christian Faith* (Seabury, 1978). Idealist Christology.
    ———. *Theological Investigations,* 23 vols. (Helicon/Herder and Herder/Seabury/Crossroad, 1961–92).
15. Ratzinger, John. *In the Beginning* (Eerdmans, 1995).
    ———. *Principles of Catholic Theology* (Ignatius, 1987).
16. Richard, Lucien. *Christ: The Self-Emptying of God* (Paulist, 1997). Kenosis.
17. **Schillebeeckx, Edward. *Christ* (Crossroad, 1980).**
    ———. *Church* (Crossroad, 1990).
18. Schüssler Fiorenza, Francis, and John Galvin, eds. *Systematic Theology,* 2 vols. (Fortress, 1991).
19. Stuhlmueller, Carroll, ed. *The Collegeville Dictionary of Biblical Theology* (Liturgical, 1996).

20. Tracy, David. *Plurality and Ambiguity* (Harper, 1987).
21. van Beeck, Frans. *God Encountered,* 6 vols. (Liturgical, 1993–).
22. von Balthasar, Hans Urs. *Mysterium Paschale* (T & T Clark, 1990).

Theological References and Helps*

1. **Alexander, Desmond, et al., eds. *New Dictionary of Biblical Theology* (IVP, 2001).** Three parts: introduction articles, individual book theologies, 215 entries (A–Z).
2. Byrne, Peter, and Leslie Houlden, eds. *Companion Encyclopedia of Theology* (Routledge, 1995).
3. Cairns, Alan. *Dictionary of Theological Terms* (Ambassador Emerald, 1998).
4. **DeMoss, Matthew, and Edward Miller. *The Zondervan Dictionary of Bible and Theological Words* (Zondervan, 2002).**
5. **Elwell, Walter, ed. *Evangelical Dictionary of Theology,* 2d ed. (Baker, 2001).**
   ———, ed. *Baker Theological Dictionary of the Bible* (Baker, 1994). Formerly *Evangelical Dictionary of Biblical Theology.*
6. Ferguson, Sinclair, David Wright, and J. I. Packer, eds. *New Dictionary of Theology* (IVP, 1988).
7. **Grenz, Stanley, David Guretski, and Cherith Nordling. *Pocket Dictionary of Theological Terms* (IVP, 2001).**
8. Grenz, Stanley, and Roger Olson. *20th Century Theology* (IVP, 1992). Guidebook.
9. **House, H. Wayne. *Charts of Christian Theology and Doctrine* (Zondervan, 1992).**
10. Manser, Martin, et al., eds. *Zondervan Dictionary of Bible Themes* (Zondervan, 1999).
11. McKim, Donald. *Westminster Dictionary of Theological Terms* (Westminster John Knox, 1996).
    ———. *The Westminster Handbook to Reformed Theology* (Westminster John Knox, 2001).

* Forthcoming: *The Encyclopedia of Fundamentalism* (Routledge). Editors unknown.

———, ed. *Encyclopedia of the Reformed Faith* (Westminster John Knox, 1992).

12. Musser, Donald, and Joseph Price, eds. *A New Handbook of Christian Theology* (Abingdon, 1992).
13. Richardson, Alan, and John Bowden, eds. *Westminster Dictionary of Theology* (Westminster John Knox, 1983).
14. **Sawyer, James. *Taxonomic Charts of Theology and Biblical Studies* (Zondervan, 1999).**
15. **Smith, David. *A Handbook of Contemporary Theology* (Baker, 1992).**
16. *See* Church History: History of Theology.

World Religions, Sects, and Cults

1. **Bowker, John, ed. *The Oxford Dictionary of World Religions* (Oxford University Press, 1997).**

   ———, ed. *The Cambridge Illustrated History of Religions* (Cambridge University Press, 2002).
2. **Corduan, Winfried. *A Tapestry of Faiths* (IVP, 2002).**
3. **Douglas, J. D., ed. *The New 20th Century Encyclopedia of Religious Knowledge,* 2d ed. (Baker, 1991).**
4. House, Wayne. *Charts of Cults, Sects, and Religious Movements* (Zondervan, 2000).
5. Losch, Richard. *The Many Faces of Faith* (Eerdmans, 2001).
6. Marshall, Paul, Roberta Green, and Lela Gilbert. *Islam at the Crossroads* (Baker, 2002).
7. Mather, George, and Larry Nichols. *Dictionary of Cults, Sects, Religion, and the Occult* (Zondervan, 1993).
8. Moucarry, Chawkat. *The Prophet and the Messiah* (IVP, 2002). Comparison of Christianity to Islam.
9. **Partridge, Christopher, and Doug Groothius, eds. *Dictionary of Contemporary Religion in the Western World* (IVP, 2002).**
10. Smith, Jonathan, and William Green, eds. *The HarperCollins Dictionary of Religion* (HarperSanFrancisco, 1995).
11. Tennent, Timothy. *Christianity at the Religious Roundtable* (Baker, 2002).

Biblical Authority

1. **Carson, D. A. Carson, and John Woodbridge, eds. *Scripture and Truth* (Baker, 1992).**
2. **Goldingay, John. *Models for Scripture* (Eerdmans, 1994).**
3. Kistler, Don, ed. *Sola Scriptura!* (Soli Deo Gloria, 2001).
4. Mathison, Keith. *The Shape of Sola Scriptura* (Canon, 2001).
5. **Warfield, Benjamin. *The Inspiration and Authority of the Bible,* 2d ed. (Presbyterian & Reformed, 1980).**

Revelation*

1. Avis, Paul, ed. *Divine Revelation* (Eerdmans, 1997).
2. Bockmuehl, Markus. *Revelation and Mystery in Ancient Judaism and Pauline Christianity* (Mohr, 1997).
3. **Dulles, Avery. *Models of Revelation* (Doubleday, 1985; Orbis, 1991).**
4. Fackre, Gabriel. *The Doctrine of Revelation* (Eerdmans, 1997).
5. Gunton, Colin. *A Brief Theology of Revelation* (T & T Clark, 1995).
6. Tiessen, Terrance. *Revelation, Salvation, and the Religions* (IVP, 2002).

Pluralism

1. Baker, Tim. Why So Many Gods? (Thomas Nelson, 2002).
2. **Carson, D. A. *The Gagging of God* (Zondervan, 1995).**
3. Clendenin, Daniel. *Many Gods, Many Lords* (Baker, 1995).
4. Hebblethwaite, Brian. *Ethics and Religion in a Pluralistic Age* (T & T Clark, 1997).
5. Heim, Mark. *The Depth of the Riches* (Eerdmans, 2000).
6. Monsma, Stephen, and Christopher Soper, eds. *Equal Treatment of Religion in a Pluralistic Society* (Eerdmans, 1998).
   ———. *The Challenge of Pluralism* (Rowman and Littlefield, 1997).
7. **Netland, Harold. *Encountering Religious Pluralism* (IVP, 2001).**

* Forthcoming: Peter Jensen, *The Revelation of God* (IVP).

8. **Okholm, Dennis, and Timothy Phillips, eds. *Four Views on Salvation in a Pluralistic World* (Zondervan, 1996).**
9. Pandiappallil, Joseph. *Jesus the Christ and Religious Pluralism* (Herder and Herder, 2001). Rahnerian Christology.
10. Quinn, Philip, and Kevin Meeker, eds. *The Philosophical Challenge of Religious Diversity* (Oxford University Press, 1999).
11. Skillen, James, and Rockne McCarthy, eds. *Political Order and the Plural Structure of Society* (Eerdmans, 1991).
12. **Stackhouse, John, ed. *No Other Gods Before Me?* (Baker, 2001).**
    ———. *Evangelical Landscapes* (Baker, 2002).

God and His Qualities

1. Boice, J. M. *Whatever Happened to the Doctrine of Grace?* (Crossway, 2001).
2. Boice, J. M., and Philip Ryken. *The Doctrines of Grace* (Crossway, 2002).
3. **Bray, Gerald. *The Doctrine of God* (IVP, 1993).**
4. **Carson, D. A. *The Difficult Doctrine of the Love of God* (Crossway, 2000).**
5. Coppedge, Allan. *Portraits of God* (IVP, 2001). Holiness.
6. **Erickson, Millard. *God the Father Almighty* (Baker, 1998).**
7. **Feinberg, John. *No One Like Him* (Crossway, 2001).**
8. **Frame, John. *The Doctrine of God* (Presbyterian & Reformed, 2002).**
9. **Geivett, R. Douglas, and Gary Habermas. *In Defense of Miracles* (IVP, 1997).**
10. **Gunton, Colin. *The Triune Creator* (Eerdmans, 1998).**
    ———, ed. *The Doctrine of Creation* (T & T Clark, 1998).
11. **Helm, Paul, and Carl Trueman, eds. *The Trustworthiness of God* (Eerdmans, 2001).**
12. Kennard, Douglas. *The Classical Christian God* (Mellen, 2002).
13. Lewis, Peter. *The Message of the Living God,* BST (IVP, 2000).
14. Richards, Jay. *Divine Essence and Accidents* (IVP, 2002).
15. Wilkinson, David. *The Message of Creation,* BST (IVP, 2002).

16. Willis, E. David. *Notes on the Holiness of God* (Eerdmans, 2002).

Trinity

1. Davis Stephen, et al., eds. *The Trinity* (Oxford University Press, 1999).
2. Erickson, Millard. *God in Three Persons* (Baker, 1995).
   ———. *Making Sense of the Trinity* (Baker, 2000). Popular.
3. **Gunton, Colin. *The Promise of Trinitarian Theology,* rev. ed. (T & T Clark, 1997).**
4. Hunt, Anne. *What Are They Saying About the Trinity?* (Paulist, 1998).
5. Kimel, Alvin, ed. *Speaking the Christian God* (Eerdmans, 1992).
   ———, ed. *This Is My Name Forever* (IVP, 2001).
6. Olson, Roger, and Christopher Hall. *The Trinity* (Eerdmans, 2002).
7. Toon, Peter. *Our Triune God* (Victor, 1996).
8. Torrance, J. B. *Worship, Community, and the Triune God of Grace* (IVP, 1997).
9. Torrance, Thomas. *The Christian Doctrine of God* (T & T Clark, 1996).
   ———. *Trinitarian Perspectives* (T & T Clark, 2000).
10. Vanhoozer, Kevin, ed. *The Trinity in a Pluralistic Age* (Eerdmans, 1997).
11. **Witherington, Ben, and Laura Ice. *The Shadow of the Almighty* (Eerdmans, 2001).**

Divine Providence and the Will of God[2]

1. **Carson, D. A. *Divine Sovereignty and Human Responsibility,* 2d ed. (Baker, 1994; Wipf & Stock, 2000).**
2. **Beilby, James, and Paul Eddy, eds. *Four Views on Divine Foreknowledge and Divine Freedom* (IVP, 2001).**
3. Boyd, Gregory. *God at War* (IVP, 1997).

2. At the 2001 annual meeting of the Evangelical Theological Society, thirty papers were delivered on this topic, including many by authors listed here.

———. *God of the Possible* (Baker, 2000). Freewill open theistic view.

4. Feinberg, John. *The One True God* (Crossway, 2002).
5. **Frame, John. *No Other God: A Response to Open Theism* (Presbyterian & Reformed, 2001).**
6. Gannsle, Gregory, ed. *God and Time* (IVP, 2001). Four views.
7. **Geisler, Norman, and Wayne House. *The Battle for God* (Kregel, 2001).**
8. Hall, Christopher, and John Sanders. *Does God Have a Future?* (Baker, 2003).
9. **Helm, Paul. *The Providence of God* (IVP, 1994).**
10. **Huffman, Douglas, and Eric Johnson, eds. *God Under Fire* (Zondervan, 2002).**
11. Pinnock, Clark. *Most Moved Mover* (Baker, 2001). Freewill open theistic view.
12. Pinnock, Clark, et al., eds. *The Openness of God* (IVP, 1995). Freewill open theistic view.
13. Pinnock, Clark, and John Cobb, eds. *Searching for an Adequate God* (Eerdmans, 2000).
14. Sanders, John. *The God Who Risks* (IVP, 1998). Freewill view.
15. **Tiessen, Terrance. *Providence and Prayer* (IVP, 2000).**
16. Waltke, Bruce. *Finding the Will of God* (Eerdmans, 2002).
17. **Ware, Bruce. *God's Lesser Glory* (Crossway, 2000).** Rebuttal of Boyd, Sanders, Pinnock, etc.

Satan and the Powers of Darkness

1. **Arnold, Clinton. *Three Crucial Questions About Spiritual Warfare* (Baker, 1997).**

   ———. *Powers of Darkness* (IVP, 1992). In Paul's Letters.
2. Boyd, Gregory. *Satan and the Problem of Evil* (IVP, 2001).
3. **Braaten, Carl, and Robert Jenson, eds. *Sin, Death, and the Devil* (Eerdmans, 1999).**
4. Day, Peggy. *An Adversary in Heaven: Satan in the Hebrew Bible* (Scholars, 1988).
5. Ferguson, Everett. *Demonology of the Early Christian World* (Mellen, 1984).

6. **Lane, Anthony, ed. *The Unseen World* (Baker, 1997).**
7. Mayhue, Richard. *Unmasking Satan* (Kregel, 2001). Popular study.
8. **Noll, Stephen. *Angels of Light, Powers of Darkness* (IVP, 1998).**
9. **Page, Sydney. *Powers of Evil* (Baker, 1995).**
10. Pagels, Elaine. *Origin of Satan* (Random House, 1995).
11. **Russell, Jeffrey. *Mephistopheles* (Cornell University Press, 1986).** Modern.
    ———. *Satan* (Cornell University Press, 1981). NT.
    ———. *The Devil* (Cornell University Press, 1977). Antiquity.
12. **Wink, Walter. *Naming the Powers* (Fortress, 1984).**
    ———. *Unmasking the Powers* (Fortress, 1986).
    ———. *Engaging the Powers* (Fortress, 1992).

Sin and Suffering

1. Beker, Christiaan. *Suffering and Hope* (Eerdmans, 1994).
2. **Blocher, Henri. *Original Sin* (IVP, 2001).**
3. **Carson, D. A. *Love in Hard Places* (Crossway, 2002).**
   ———. *How Long, O Lord?* (Baker, 1990).
4. Gestrich, Christof. *The Return of Splendor in the World* (Eerdmans, 1997). Sin and forgiveness.
5. Goldingay, John. *Walk On: Life, Loss, Trust, and Other Realities* (Baker, 2002).
6. Kelly, Joseph. *The Problem of Evil in the Western Tradition* (Liturgical, 2002).
7. Mann, Ivan. *A Double Thirst* (Darton, Longman and Todd, 2001). Suffering.
8. McCartney, Dan. *Why Does It Have to Hurt?* (Presbyterian & Reformed, 1998). Popular study.
9. **Ortlund, Raymond. *Whoredom* (Eerdmans, 1996; IVP, 2001).** Spiritual adultery.
10. **Peters, Ted. *Sin* (Eerdmans, 1996; Wipf & Stock, 2000).**
11. **Plantinga, Cornelius. *Not the Way It's Supposed to Be: A Breviary of Sin* (Eerdmans, 1995).**

12. Smith, Barry. *Paul's Seven Explanations of the Sufferings of the Righteous* (Lang, 2002).
13. Tambasco, Anthony, ed. *The Bible on Suffering* (Paulist, 2001).
14. Wenham, John. *The Enigma of Evil* (Eagle, 1994).

Jesus Christ

1. **Bauckham, Richard. *God Crucified* (Paternoster, 1998).**
2. **Brown, Raymond E. *An Introduction to New Testament Christology* (Paulist, 1994).**
3. Dunn, James. *The Christ and the Spirit,* vol. 1: *Christology* (Eerdmans, 1998).
4. Erickson, Millard. *The Word Became Flesh* (Baker, 1991).
5. Haight, Roger. *Jesus, Symbol of God* (Orbis, 2000).
6. **Hengel, Martin. *Studies in Early Christology* (T & T Clark, 1995).**
7. **Hurtado, Larry. *One Lord, One God* (Fortress, 1988).**
8. Longman, Tremper. *Seeing Christ in Israel's Worship* (Presbyterian & Reformed, 2001).
9. MacLeod, Donald. *The Person of Christ* (IVP, 1998).
10. Marshall, Bruce, ed. *Readings in Modern Christology* (Blackwell, 2002).
11. Marshall, I. Howard. *The Origins of New Testament Christology,* rev. ed. (IVP, 1990).
12. Matera, Frank. *New Testament Christology* (Westminster John Knox, 1999).
13. McIntyre, John. *The Shape of Christology,* 2d ed. (T & T Clark, 1998).
14. Powell, Mark, and David Bauer, eds. *Who Do You Say That I Am?* (Westminster John Knox, 1999).
15. Schnackenberg, Rudolf. *Jesus in the Gospels* (Westminster John Knox, 1995).
16. Schwarz, Hans. *Christology* (Eerdmans, 1998).
17. Tuckett, Christopher. *Christology and the New Testament* (Westminster John Knox, 2001).
18. **Witherington, Ben. *The Christology of Jesus* (Fortress, 1990).**

The Cross

1. **Beasley-Murray, Paul. *The Message of Resurrection,* BST (IVP, 2000).**
2. **Demarest, Bruce. *The Cross and Salvation* (Crossway, 1997).**
3. Gorman, Michael. *Cruciformity* (Eerdmans, 2001). Paul.
4. Green, Joel, and Mark Baker. *Recovering the Scandal of the Cross* (IVP, 2000). New Testament atonement.
5. **McGrath, Alister. *The Mystery of the Cross* (Zondervan, 1998).**
6. **Morris, Leon. *The Apostolic Preaching of the Cross,* 3d ed. (Eerdmans, 1984).**
   ———. *The Atonement* (IVP, 1983).
   ———. *The Cross in the New Testament* (Eerdmans, 1965).
7. **Tidball, Derek. *The Message of the Cross,* BST (IVP, 2001).**

Salvation

1. **Bahnsen Greg, ed. *Five Views on Law and Gospel* (Zondervan, 1993).**
2. **Budziszewski, J. *Written on the Heart: The Case for Natural Law* (IVP, 1997).**
3. Geisler, Norman. *Chosen but Free,* 2d ed. (Bethany, 2001). Arminian rebuttal of Calvinism.
4. Klein, William. *The New Chosen People: A Corporate View of Election* (Zondervan, 1990; Wipf & Stock, 2000).
5. Levering, Matthew. *Christ's Fulfillment of Torah and Temple: Salvation According to Thomas Aquinas* (University of Notre Dame, 2002).
6. Oden, Thomas. *The Justification Reader* (Eerdmans, 2002). Patristic compendium.
7. **Ryken, Philip. *The Message of Salvation,* BST (IVP, 2001).**
8. Smith, Gordon. *Beginning Well* (IVP, 2001). Conversion.
9. Stackhouse, John. *What Does It Mean to Be Saved?* (Baker, 2002).
10. White, James. *The Potter's Freedom* (Calvary, 2001). Calvinist rebuttal of Geisler.

Assurance and Sanctification

1. Dieter, Melvin, et al. *Five Views on Sanctification* (Zondervan, 1987).
2. Eaton, Michael. *No Condemnation* (IVP, 1995).
3. Hafemann, Scott. *The God of Promise and the Life of Faith* (Crossway, 2001). Application of theology to life.
4. Jones, Gregory. *Embodying Forgiveness* (Eerdmans, 1996).
5. **Peterson, David. *Possessed by God* (IVP, 2001).** Sanctification as a definitive event rather than process.
6. Pinson, Matt, ed. *Four Views on Eternal Security* (Zondervan, 2002).
7. **Schreiner, Thomas, and Ardel Caneday. *The Race Set Before Us* (IVP, 2001).** Perseverance and assurance, lordship salvation.

Church and Its Mission

1. Alston, Wallace. *The Church of the Living God* (Westminster John Knox, 2002).
2. Anthony, Michael, et al., eds. *Evangelical Dictionary of Christian Education* (Baker, 2001).
3. Bock, Darrell. *Purpose-Driven Theology* (IVP, 2002). Revamped ETS address anticipating future direction of church.
4. **Clowney, Edmund. *The Church* (IVP, 1995).**
5. **Cowan, Steven, ed. *Four Views on Church Government* (Zondervan, 2002).**
6. De Arteaga, William. *Forgotten Power: The Significance of the Lord's Supper in Revivals* (Zondervan, 2002).
7. Dulles, Avery. *Models of the Church,* expanded (Random House, 2002).
8. Ferguson, Everett. *The Church of Christ* (Eerdmans, 1996).
9. Hartman, Lars. *"Into the Name of the Lord Jesus"* (T & T Clark, 1997). Baptism.
10. Köstenberger, Andreas, and Peter O'Brien. *Salvation to the Ends of the Earth* (IVP, 2001). Missions.
11. **Moreau, Scott, ed. *Evangelical Dictionary of World Missions* (Baker, 2000).**

12. **Peters, George, Keith Eitel, and Philip Roberts. *A Biblical Theology of Missions,* rev. ed. (Moody, 2003).** Developments since 1972.
13. **Saucy, Robert, *The Church in God's Program* (Moody, 1972).**
14. Snyder, Howard. *Decoding the Church: Mapping the DNA of Christ's Body* (Baker, 2002).
15. Webb, Henry. *Deacons,* updated (Broadman & Holman, 2001).

Worship

1. Bateman, Herbert, ed. *Authentic Worship* (Kregel, 2002).
2. **Carson, D. A., ed. *Worship by the Book* (Zondervan, 2002).** Free, Anglican, and Presbyterian.
3. Hart, D. G., and John Muether. *With Reverence and Awe* (Presbyterian & Reformed, 2002).
4. **Peterson, David. *Engaging with God* (IVP, 2002).**

The Holy Spirit and Spiritual Gifts
(Traditional)

1. **Badcock, Gary. *Light of Truth and Fire of Love* (Eerdmans, 1997).**
2. Bloesch, Donald. *Christian Foundations: The Holy Spirit,* vol. 5 (IVP, 2000).
3. Budgen, Victor. *The Charismatics and the Word of God* (Presbyterian & Reformed, 2001).
4. Dunn, James. *Baptism in the Spirit* (Westminster, 1970).
5. Edgar, Thomas. *Satisfied by the Power of the Spirit* (Kregel, 1996).
6. **Ewert, David. *The Holy Spirit in the New Testament* (Herald, 1983).**
7. Ferguson, Sinclair. *The Holy Spirit* (IVP, 1997).
8. Gaffin, Richard. *Perspectives on Pentecost* (Presbyterian & Reformed, 1979).
9. McIntyre, John. *The Shape of Pneumatology* (T & T Clark, 1997). History of doctrine.
10. **Packer, J. I. *Keep in Step with the Spirit* (Revell, 1984).**

11. Schandorff, Esther. *The Doctrine of the Holy Spirit,* 2 vols. (Scarecrow, 1995). Exhaustive bibliography.
12. Thomas, Robert, ed. *The Master's Perspective on Contemporary Issues* (Kregel, 1998). Farnell on Prophecy; Mayhue on Holy Spirit.
———. *Understanding Spiritual Gifts,* rev. ed. (Kregel, 1999). 1 Corinthians 12–14.
13. Welker, Michael. *God the Spirit* (Fortress, 1994).
14. *See* New Testament Commentaries: Luke: The Holy Spirit in Luke–Acts.

The Holy Spirit and Spiritual Gifts
(Pentecostal and Charismatic)

1. Albrecht, Daniel. *Rites in the Spirit* (Sheffield Academic Press, 1999). Spirit baptism always postconversion.
2. Burgess, Stanley. *The Holy Spirit,* 3 vols. (Hendrickson, 1984–1997).
3. **Fee, Gordon. *God's Empowering Presence* (Hendrickson, 1994).**
———. *Gospel and Spirit* (Hendrickson, 1991).
———. *Paul, the Spirit, and the People of God* (Hendrickson, 1996).
4. Grieg, Gary, and Kevin Springer, eds. *The Kingdom and the Power,* rev. ed. (Regal, 1993).
5. **Grudem, Wayne. *The Gift of Prophecy in 1 Corinthians* (University Press of America, 1982; Wipf & Stock, 1999).**
———. *The Gift of Prophecy in the New Testament and Today,* rev. ed. (Crossway, 2000).
———, ed. *Are Miraculous Gifts for Today? Four Views* (Zondervan, 1996).
6. Hill, Clifford. *Prophecy, Past and Present,* 1st American ed. (Vine, 1991).
7. Houston, Graham. *Prophecy* (IVP, 1989).
8. Hovenden, Gerald. *Speaking in Tongues* (Sheffield Academic Press, 2002).
9. **Hunter, Harold. *Spirit-Baptism* (University Press of America, 1983).**

10. **Keener, Craig. *Gift and Giver* (Baker, 2001).**
11. **McDonnell, Kilian, and George Montague. *Christian Initiation and Baptism in the Holy Spirit* (Liturgical, 1994).**
12. McGee, Gary, ed. *Initial Evidence* (Hendrickson, 1991).
13. **Menzies, William, and Robert Menzies. *Spirit and Power* (Zondervan, 2000).**
14. Montague, George. *The Holy Spirit* (Hendrickson, 1976).
15. Palma, Anthony. *The Holy Spirit* (Logion, 2001).
16. **Ruthven, Jon. *On the Cessation of the Charismata* (Sheffield Academic Press, 1993).**
17. **Schatzmann, Siegfried. *A Pauline Theology of Charismata* (Hendrickson, 1987).**
18. Stronstad, Roger. *The Prophethood of All Believers* (Sheffield Academic Press, 1999).
19. **Turner, Max. *The Holy Spirit and Spiritual Gifts* (Eerdmans, 1998).** OT, intertestamental background.
20. Yong, Amos. *Discerning the Spirits* (Sheffield Academic Press, 2001).
21. *See* New Testament Commentaries: Luke; The Holy Spirit in Luke–Acts.

The Last Days

1. Baker, David, ed. *Looking Into the Future* (Baker, 2001).
2. Bauckham, Richard, and Trevor Hart. *Hope Against Hope* (Eerdmans, 1999).
3. Benware, Paul. *Understanding Endtime Prophecy* (Moody, 1995). Introduction.
4. **Bock, Darrell, ed. *Three Views on the Millennium and Beyond* (Zondervan, 1999).** Premillennial, amillennial, and postmillennial.
5. Brower, Keith, and Mark Elliott, eds. *Eschatology in the Bible and Theology* (IVP, 1997).
6. Bull, Malcolm, ed. *Apocalypse Theory and the Ends of the World* (Blackwell, 1995).
7. **Clouse, Robert, ed. *The Meaning of the Millennium: Four Views* (IVP, 1977).**

8. Clouse, Robert, Robert Hosack, and Richard Pierard. *The New Millennium Manual* (Baker, 1999).
9. Doyle, Robert. *Eschatology and the Shape of Christian Belief* (Paternoster, 1999).
10. Dumbrell, William. *The Search for Order* (Baker, 1995; Wipf & Stock, 2001).
11. Erickson, Millard. *A Basic Guide to Eschatology* (Baker, 1998).
12. Fergusson, John, and Marcel Sarot, eds. *The Future as God's Gift* (T & T Clark, 2000).
13. **Grenz, Stanley. *The Millennial Maze* (IVP, 1992).**
14. Gundry, Robert. *First the Antichrist* (Baker, 1997). Posttribulational.
15. Hill, Charles. *Regnum Caelorum,* 2d ed. (Eerdmans, 2001). Early church views.
16. Holman, Charles. *Till Jesus Comes* (Hendrickson, 1996).
17. **Horton, Michael. *Covenant and Eschatology* (Westminster, 2002).**
18. Ice, Thomas, and Timothy Demy, eds. *The Return* (Kregel, 1999).
19. Ice Thomas, and Kenneth Gentry. *The Great Tribulation: Past or Future?* (Kregel, 1999).
20. Kyle, Richard. *The Last Days Are Here Again: A History of the End Times* (Baker, 1998).
21. Lewis, Daniel. *Three Crucial Questions about the Last Days* (Baker, 1998).
22. Mathison, Keith. *Postmillennialism* (Presbyterian & Reformed, 1999).
23. Mealy, Webb. *After the Thousand Years* (Sheffield Academic Press, 1992). Revelation 20.
24. Moltmann, Jürgen. *The Coming of God* (Fortress, 1996).
25. **O'Leary, Stephen. *Arguing the Apocalypse* (Oxford University Press, 1994).**
26. Otto, Randall. *Coming in the Clouds* (University Press of America, 1994).
27. Plevnik, Joseph. *Paul and the Parousia* (Hendrickson, 1996).
28. Polkinghorne, John. *The God of Hope and the End of the World* (Yale University Press, 2002).

29. Polkinghorne, John, and Michael Welker, eds. *The End of the World and the End of God* (Trinity Press International, 2000).
30. Robertson, O. Palmer. *The Israel of God* (Presbyterian & Reformed, 2000).
31. Russell, J. Stuart. *The Parousia* (Baker, 1999).
32. Schmidt, Thomas, and Moisés Silva, eds. *To Tell the Mystery* (Sheffield Academic Press, 1994).
33. Stackhouse, Reginald. *The End of the World* (Paulist, 1997).
34. Stone, Jon. *A Guide to the End of the World* (Garland, 1993).
35. Walvoord, John. *Prophecy in the New Millennium* (Kregel, 2001).
36. **Witherington, Ben. *Jesus, Paul, and the End of the World* (IVP, 1992).**

The Last Days
(Issues in Dispensationalism)*

1. Bahnsen, Greg, and Kenneth Gentry. *House Divided,* 2d ed. (Institute for Christian Economics, 1997).
2. **Bateman, Herbert, ed. *Three Central Issues in Contemporary Dispensationalism* (Kregel, 1999).** Hermeneutics, covenant, Israel, and the church.
3. **Blaising, Craig, and Darrell Bock. *Progressive Dispensationalism* (Baker, 1993).**
4. Blaising, Craig, and Darrell Bock, eds. *Dispensationalism, Israel, and the Church* (Zondervan, 1992).
5. Doukhan, Jacques. *Israel and the Church* (Hendrickson, 2002).
6. Fuller, Robert. *Naming the Antichrist* (Oxford University Press, 1995).
7. Holwerda, David. *Jesus and Israel: One Covenant or Two?* (Eerdmans, 1995).
8. House, Wayne, ed. *Israel, the Land, and the People* (Kregel, 1998).
9. Mathison, Keith. *Dispensationalism* (Presbyterian & Reformed, 1995).

---

* Forthcoming: Mike Stallard, *The History of Dispensationalism* (Kregel).

10. **Pate, C. Marvin, ed. *Four Views on the Book of Revelation* (Zondervan, 1998).** Preterist, idealist, dispensationalist, progressive dispensationalist.
11. Pate, Marvin, and Calvin Haines. *Doomsday Delusions* (IVP, 1995).
12. Poythress, Vern. *Understanding Dispensationalism,* 2d ed. (Presbyterian & Reformed, 1993).
13. Ryrie, Charles. *Dispensationalism,* rev. ed. (Moody, 1995).
14. **Saucy, Robert. *The Case for Progressive Dispensationalism* (Zondervan, 1993).**
15. Thomas, Robert, ed. *The Master's Perspective on Contemporary Issues* (Kregel, 1998). Mayhue on dispensationalism, Thomas on progressive dispensationalism.
16. **Walton, John. *Covenant* (Zondervan, 1994).** Mediating view with dispensationalism.
17. Willis, Wesley, and John Master, eds. *Issues in Dispensationalism* (Moody, 1994).

Heaven and Hell*

1. Blanchard, John. *Whatever Happened to Hell?* (Crossway, 1995).
2. Bonda, Jan. *The One Purpose of God* (Eerdmans, 1998). Universalist denial of eternal punishment.
3. **Connelly, Douglas. *After Life: What the Bible Really Says* (IVP, 1995).**
4. **Crockett, William, ed. *Four Views on Hell* (Zondervan, 1992).** Including doctrine of purgatory.
5. Erickson, Millard. *How Shall They Be Saved?* (Baker, 1996).
6. **Fackre, Gabriel, Ronald Nash, and John Sanders. *What About Those Who Have Never Heard?* (IVP, 1995).**
7. Fernando, Ajith. *Crucial Questions About Hell* (Crossway, 1994).
8. **Fudge, Edward, and Robert Peterson. *Two Views of Hell* (IVP, 2000).**

---

* Forthcoming: Christopher Morgan and Robert Peterson, eds., *Hell Under Fire* (Zondervan).

9. **Habermas, Gary, and James Moreland. *Beyond Death* (Crossway, 1998).**
   ———. *Immortality* (Thomas Nelson, 1992).
10. Hilborn, David. *The Nature of Hell* (Acute, 2000). Drafted by five British theologians.
11. **House, Paul, and Greg Thornbury, eds. *Who Will Be Saved?* (Crossway, 2000).**
12. **Johnston, Philip. *Shades of Sheol* (IVP, 2002).**
13. Kvanvig, Jonathan. *The Problem of Hell* (Oxford University Press, 1993).
14. Llassen, Randy. *What Does the Bible Really Say About Hell?* (Pandora, 2001).
15. Ludlow, Morwenna. *Universal Salvation* (Oxford University Press, 2001).
16. **Moore, David. *The Battle for Hell* (University Press of America, 1996).**
17. **Peterson, Robert. *Hell on Trial* (Presbyterian & Reformed, 1995).**
18. Powys, David. *Hell* (Paternoster, 1998).
19. **Russell, Jeffrey. *A History of Heaven* (Princeton University Press, 1997).** Brilliant evaluation of Christian expectations from Christ-Dante.
20. **Sanders, John. *No Other Name* (Eerdmans, 1992; Wipf & Stock, 2001).**
21. **Walls, Jerry. *Heaven* (Oxford University Press, 2002).**

18

CHURCH HISTORY RESOURCES

General Church History

1. **Armstrong, Karen. *A History of God* (A. A. Knopf, 1993).** Covers 2,000 B.C.–present.
   ———. *The Battle for God* (Knopf, 2000). Covers 1492–present. Modernity versus Fundamentalism.
2. Atwood, Craig. *Always Reforming* (Mercer University Press, 2000). Covers 1300–present, use with Hinson.
3. Baker, Robert, and Jon Landers. *A Summary of Christian History,* rev. ed. (Broadman & Holman, 1999).
4. Bauman, Michael, and Martin Klauber, eds. *Historians of the Christian Tradition* (Broadman & Holman, 1995).
5. Bingham, D. Jeffrey. *Pocket History of the Church* (IVP, 2002).
6. Cairns, Earle. *Christianity Through the Centuries,* 3d ed., rev. ed. (Zondervan, 1996).
7. **Clouse, Robert, Richard Pierard, and Edwin Yamauchi. *Two Kingdoms* (Moody, 1994).**
8. **Dowley, Timothy, ed. *Introduction to the History of Christianity* (Fortress, 1995).**
9. Edwards, David. *Christianity* (Orbis, 1999).
10. Ellingsen, Mark. *Reclaiming Our Roots,* 2 vols. (Trinity Press International, 1999). Introduction.
11. **González, Justo. *The Story of Christianity* (Prince, 2000).**
    ———. *Church History: An Essential Guide* (Abingdon, 1996). Basic introduction.

12. Irvin, Dale, and Scott Sunquist. *History of the World Christian Movement,* 2 vols. (Orbis, 2002–03).
13. **Hastings, Adrian, ed. *A World History of Christianity* (Eerdmans, 1999).**
14. Hinson, E. Glenn. *The Church Triumphant* (Mercer University Press, 1995). NT–A.D. 1300, use with Atwood.
15. Miller, Glenn. *The Modern Church* (Abingdon, 1996). Reformation–present.
16. McGonigle, Thomas, and James Quigley. *A History of the Christian Tradition,* 2 vols. (Paulist, 1988, 1996).
17. **McGrath, Alister. *An Introduction to Christianity* (Blackwell, 1997).**
18. **McManners, John, ed. *The Oxford Illustrated History of Christianity* (Oxford University Press, 1993).**
19. Moynihan, Brian. *Faith* (Doubleday, 2001).
20. **Noll, Mark. *Turning Points: Decisive Moments in the History of Christianity,* rev. ed. (Baker, 2000).**
21. Shelley, Bruce. *Church History in Plain Language* (Word, 1982).
22. **Walker, Williston, et al. *A History of the Christian Church,* 4th ed. (Scribner's, 1985).**
23. **Woodbridge, John. *Great Leaders of the Christian Church* (Moody, 1988).**

Church History References and Helps

1. Anderson, Gerald, ed. *Biographical Dictionary of Christian Missions* (Macmillan Reference US, 1998).
2. **Barrett, David, et al., eds. *World Christian Encyclopedia,* 2 vols., rev. ed. (Oxford University Press, 2001).**
3. Bradley, James, and Richard Muller. *Church History* (Eerdmans, 1995). Research and bibliographical guide.
4. Cohn-Sherbok, Lavinia. *Who's Who in Christianity* (Routledge, 1998).
5. **Cross, Frank, and E. Livingstone, eds. *Oxford Dictionary of the Christian Church,* 3d ed. (Oxford University Press, 1996).**

6. ***Dictionary of Late Antiquity* (Harvard University Press, 1999).**
7. Douglas, J. D., ed. *Twentieth-Century Dictionary of Christian Biography* (Baker, 1995).
8. Douglas, J. D., and Earle Cairns, eds. *The New International Dictionary of the Christian Church,* rev. ed. (Zondervan, 1978).
9. Douglas, J. D., and Philip Comfort, eds. *Who's Who in Christian History* (Tyndale, 1992).
10. Dwyer, John. *Church History,* rev. ed. (Paulist, 1998).
11. **Fahlbusch, Erwin, et al., eds. *The Encyclopedia of Christianity,* 5 vols. (Eerdmans/Brill, 1998, 1999–).** All-purpose, including statistics, ethics, church history, theology, world religions, and Scripture.
12. **Hannah, John. *Charts of Ancient and Medieval History* (Zondervan, 2001).** Companion CD replicating contents for audio-visual use and printouts.
13. Littell, Franklin, ed. *Historical Atlas of Christianity* (Continuum, 2001). Especially 1500–present.
14. McKim, Donald, ed. *Historical Handbook of Major Biblical Interpreters* (IVP, 1998).
15. **Noll, Mark, ed. *Biographical Dictionary of Evangelicals* (IVP-UK, 2002).**
16. O'Brien, Patrick, gen. ed. *Oxford Atlas of World History* (Oxford University Press, 1999).
17. Parrinder, Geoffrey. *A Concise Encyclopedia of Christianity* (Oneworld, 1998).
18. Sundquist, Scott, ed. *Dictionary of Asian Christianity* (Eerdmans, 2001).
19. Walsh, Michael, ed. *Dictionary of Christian Biography* (Liturgical, 2001).
20. **Walton, Robert. *Chronological And Background Charts of Church History* (Zondervan, 1986).**

History of Theology

1. Anderson, William, ed. *A Journey Through Christian Theology* (Fortress, 2000). Anthology and commentary.

2. Cunliffe-Jones, Hubert, ed. *A History of Christian Doctrine* (T & T Clark, 1990).
3. **Di Berardino, Angelo, et al., eds. *History of Theology,* 4 vols. (Liturgical, 1997–).**
4. Elwell, Walter. *A Handbook of Evangelical Theologians* (Baker, 1993). 20th century.
5. **Ford, David, ed. *The Modern Theologians,* 2d ed. (Blackwell, 1997).**
6. González, Justo. *A History of Christian Thought,* 3 vols., rev. ed. (Abingdon, 1987).
7. **Hannah, John. *Our Legacy* (NavPress, 2001).**
8. **Hart, Trevor, ed. *Dictionary of Historical Theology* (Eerdmans, 2000).**
9. Kerr, Hugh, ed. *Readings in Christian Thought,* 2d ed. (Abingdon, 1990). Anthology.
10. Loshe, Berhard. *A Short History of Christian Doctrine* (Fortress, 1983).
11. McGrath, Alister, ed. *The Blackwell Encyclopedia of Modern Christian Thought* (Blackwell, 1993).
    ———. *Historical Theology* (Blackwell, 1998). Companion to *Christian Theology.*
12. Muller, Richard. *Post-Reformation Reformed Dogmatics,* 4 vols. (Baker, 1987–2002).
13. Oberman, Heiko. *The Harvest of Medieval Theology* (Baker, 2000).
14. **Olson, Roger. *The Story of Christian Theology* (IVP, 1999).**
15. Peterson, Susan. *Timeline Charts of the Western Church* (Zondervan, 1999).
16. Placher, William. *A History of Christian Theology* (Westminster John Knox, 1983).
17. *See* Catholic Church History below.

Early Church

1. Anatolios, Khaled. *Athanasius* (Routledge, 1998).
2. **Carroll, John, et al. *The Return of Jesus Christ in Early Christianity* (Hendrickson, 2000).**

3. **Carroll, John, and Joel Green, et al. *The Death of Jesus in Early Christianity* (Hendrickson, 1995).**
4. Cruse, C. *Eusebius' Ecclesiastical History,* updated ed. (Hendrickson, 1998).
5. **Hinson, Glenn. *The Early Church* (Abingdon, 1996).**
6. **Kelly, J. N. D. (Hendrickson, 1999).**
   ———. *Golden Mouth: the Story of John Chrysostom* (Baker, 1999).
7. Lieu, Samuel, and Dominic Montserrat. *Constantine* (Routledge, 1998).
8. **Maier, Paul. *Eusebius—The Church History* (Kregel, 1999).**
9. Pettersen, Alvyn. *Athanasius* (Morehouse, 1995). Introduction.
10. **Robinson, Thomas, and Brent Shaw. *The Early Church* (Scarecrow, 1993).** Abstracts of a thousand books covering the second to sixth centuries.
11. Seitz, Christopher, ed. *Nicene Christianity* (Brazos, 2001). Focus on Creed.
12. **Stemberger, Günter. *Jews and Christians in the Holy Land* (T & T Clark, 1999).** Fourth century.
13. Tilley, Maureen. *The Bible in Christian North Africa: The Donatist World* (Fortress, 1997).
14. Trigg, Joseph. *Origen* (Routledge, 1999).
15. **Williams, Rowan. *Arius,* rev. ed. (Eerdmans, 2001).**

Augustine

1. **Brown, Peter. *Augustine of Hippo* (University of California, 1999).**
2. Clark, Mary. *Augustine* (Continuum, 2001).
3. **Fitzgerald, Allan, ed. *Augustine Through the Ages: An Encyclopedia* (Eerdmans, 1999).**
4. Harrison, Carol. *Augustine* (Oxford University Press, 2000).
5. **Stump, Eleanore, and Norman Kretzmann, eds. *The Cambridge Companion to Augustine* (Cambridge University Press, 2001).**
6. Wills, Garry. *Saint Augustine* (Viking, 1999).

Eastern Orthodoxy

1. Hussey, J. *The Orthodox Church in the Byzantine Empire* (Oxford University Press, 1986).
2. Kazhdan, Alexander, ed. *The Oxford Dictionary of Byzantium,* 3 vols. (Oxford University Press, 1991).
3. Nichols, Aidan. *Rome and the Eastern Churches: A Study in Schism* (T & T Clark, 1992).
4. Norwich, John. *A Short History of Byzantium* (Knopf, 1999).
5. **Parry, Ken, et al., eds. *The Blackwell Dictionary of Eastern Christianity* (Blackwell, 2001).**
6. Prokurat, Michael, Michael Peterson, and Alexander Golitzin. *Historical Dictionary of the Orthodox Church* (Scarecrow, 1996).
7. Rosser, John. *Historical Dictionary of Byzantium* (Scarecrow, 2001).
8. Treadgold, Warren. *A Concise History of Byzantium* (St Martin's, 2001).
9. **Ware, Timothy. *The Orthodox Church,* rev. ed. (Penguin, 1993).**

Medieval

1. Brown, Harold. *Heresies* (Hendrickson, 2000).
2. **Cavill, Paul. *Vikings* (Zondervan, 2002).** Conversion by Anglo-Saxons.
3. **Evans, G. *The Medieval Theologians* (Blackwell, 2001).**
4. Hamilton, Bernard. *Christian World of the Middle Ages* (Sutton, 2002).
5. Hicks, Michael. *Who's Who in Late Medieval England* (Shepheard-Walwyn, 1991).
6. Loyn, H. R., ed. *The Middle Ages: A Concise Encyclopaedia* (Thames and Hudson, 1989).
7. Madden, Thomas. *A Concise History of the Crusades* (Rowman and Littlefield, 1999).
8. **Markus, R. A. *Gregory the Great and His World* (Cambridge University Press, 1998).**
9. **Riley-Smith, Jonathan. *The Atlas of the Crusades* (Facts on File, 1991).**

———. *The Oxford History of the Crusades* (Oxford University Press, 2000).

10. Tyerman, Christopher. *Who's Who in Early Medieval England* (Shepheard-Walwyn, 1996).
11. **Vauchez, Andre, ed. *Encyclopedia of the Middle Ages,* 2 vols. (James Clarke, 2000).**
12. Volz, Carl. *The Medieval Church* (Abingdon, 1997).
13. Ward, Benedicta. *The Venerable Bede* (Morehouse, 1990).
14. *See* Catholic Church History.

Aquinas

1. Davies, Brian. *Aquinas* (Continuum, 2000).
2. Kretzmann, Norman, and Eleanore Stump, eds. *The Cambridge Companion to Aquinas* (Cambridge University Press, 1993).
3. Nichols, Aidan. *Discovering Aquinas* (Darton, Longman and Todd, 2002).
4. Renick, Timothy. *Aquinas for Armchair Theologians* (Westminster John Knox, 2002).
5. Torrell, Jean-Pierre. *Saint Thomas Aquinas,* vol. 1 (Catholic University of America Press, 1996–).

Catholic Church History

1. Berry, Jason. *Lead Us Not into Temptation: Catholic Priests and the Sexual Abuse of Children* (Doubleday, 1992).
2. **Chadwick, Owen. *A History of the Popes, 1830–1914* (Oxford, 1998).**
3. Cozzens, Donald. *The Changing Face of the Priesthood* (Liturgical, 2000). Homosexual trends.
4. Descouvement, Pierre. *Therese and Liseaux* (1962; Eerdmans, 2001).
5. DeVries, Kelly. *Joan of Arc: A Military Leader* (Sutton, 1999).
6. **Duffy, Eamon. *Saints and Sinners: A History of the Popes* (Yale University Press, 1997).**
7. **Farmer, David. *The Oxford Dictionary of Saints,* 4th ed. (Oxford, 1998).**

8. Johnson, Luke, and William Kurz. *The Future of Catholic Biblical Scholarship* (Eerdmans, 2002).
9. Jordan, Mark. *The Silence of Sodom* (The University of Chicago Press, 2000). Priesthood up to 50 percent gay.
10. Kelly, J. N. D. *The Oxford Dictionary of Popes* (Oxford, 1986).
11. **LaCouture, Jean. *The Jesuits* (Counterpoint, 1997).**
12. Maxwell-Stuart, P. *Chronicles of the Popes* (Thames and Hudson, 1997).
13. McBrien, Richard, ed. *The HarperCollins Encyclopedia of Catholicism* (HarperCollins, 1994).
14. McNamara, Jo Ann. *Sisters in Arms* (Harvard University Press, 1996). History of nuns.
15. Medwick, Cathleen. *Teresa of Avila* (Knopf, 1999). Especially on her relationship with St. John of the Cross and their dealings with both the Spanish and Vatican hierarchies.
16. Nash-Marshall, Siobhan. *Joan of Arc* (Crossroad, 1999).
17. **O'Malley, William. *The First Jesuits* (Harvard University Press, 1993).**
18. Pelikan, Jaroslav. *Mary Through the Centuries* (Yale University Press, 1996).
19. Plante, Thomas, ed. *Perspectives on Sexual Abuse Committed by Roman Catholic Priests* (Praeger, 1999).
20. **Steimer, Bruno, ed. *Dictionary of Popes and the Papacy* (Crossroad, 2001).**
21. **Woodrow, Alain. *The Jesuits* (Geoffrey Chapman, 1996).**

Renaissance and Reformation

1. **Barzun, Jacques. *From Dawn to Decadence: 1500 to the Present* (HarperCollins, 2000).**
2. Bireley, Robert. *The Refashioning of Catholicism* (Catholic University of America, 1999). Counter-Reformation.
3. **Brady, Thomas, Heiko Oberman, and James Tracy, eds. *Handbook of European History, 1400–1600,* 2 vols. (Eerdmans, 1996).**
4. **Cameron, Euan. *The European Reformation* (Oxford University Press, 1991).**

5. **Chadwick, Owen. *The Early Reformation on the Continent* (Oxford University Press, 2002).**
6. **d'Aubigne, Jean. *For God and His People* (Bob Jones University Press, 2000).** Ulrich Zwingli.
7. D'Onofrio, Giulio, ed. *History of Theology,* vol. 3: *The Renaissance* (Liturgical, 1998).
8. Estep, William. *Renaissance and Reformation* (Eerdmans, 1983).

   ———. *The Anabaptist Story,* 3d ed. (Eerdmans, 1996).
9. **Friesen, Abraham. *Erasmus, the Anabaptists, and the Great Commission* (Eerdmans, 1998).**
10. **George, Timothy. *Theology of the Reformers,* rev. ed. (Broadman & Holman, 1999).**
11. **Hall, Basil. *Humanists and Reformers, 1500–1900* (T & T Clark, 1996).** Especially Erasmus.
12. **Hillerbrand, Hans. *Historical Dictionary of the Reformation and Counter-Reformation* (Scarecrow, 2000).**

    ———, ed. *The Oxford Encyclopedia of the Reformation,* 4 vols. (Oxford University Press, 1996).
13. Janz, Denis, ed. *A Reformation Reader* (Fortress, 1999). With CD-ROM.
14. **Lindberg, Carter. *The European Reformations* (Blackwell, 1995).**
15. Lindsay, Thomas. *A History of the Reformation,* 2 vols. (T & T Clark, 1964; Wipf & Stock, 1999).
16. Lovegrove, Deryck, ed. *The Rise of the Laity in Evangelical Protestantism* (Routledge, 2002).
17. **McGrath, Alister. *Reformation Thought,* 3d ed. (Blackwell, 1999).**
18. Monod, Paul. *The Power of Kings: Monarchy and Religion in Europe, 1589–1715* (Yale University Press, 1999).
19. Oberman, Heiko. *The Dawn of the Reformation* (Eerdmans, 1992).

    ———. *The Reformation* (Eerdmans/T & T Clark, 1994).
20. **Ozment, Steven. *Protestants: The Birth of a Revolution* (Doubleday, 1992).**

21. **Pearse, Meic. *The Great Restoration* (Paternoster, 1998).**
22. Saari, Peggy, and Aaron Saari, eds. *Renaissance and Reformation: Almanac* (UXL, 2002).
23. **Spitz, Lewis. *The Renaissance and Reformation,* 2 vols. (Concordia Academic Press, 1980).**
24. **Thompson, Bard. *Humanists and Reformers* (Eerdmans, 1996).**
25. Tracy, James. *Europe's Reformations, 1450–1650* (Rowman and Littlefield, 1999).
26. Ward, W. *Protestant Evangelical Awakening* (Cambridge University Press, 1992).
27. Yarnell, Malcolm. *Royal Priesthood in the English Reformation* (Oxford University Press, 2002).

Martin Luther and Lutheranism

1. **Brecht, Martin. *Martin Luther,* 3d ed., 3 vols. (Fortress, 1983).**
2. **Gritsch, Eric. *A History of Lutheranism* (Fortress, 2002).** Reformation–present.
3. Gassman, Günther, Duane Larson, and Mark Oldenburg. *Historical Dictionary of Lutheranism* (Scarecrow, 2001).
4. Kolb, Robert. *Martin Luther as Prophet, Teacher, and Hero* (Baker, 1999).
5. **Oberman, Heiko. *Luther* (Yale, 1989).**
6. **Steinmetz, David. *Luther in Context,* 2d ed. (Baker, 1995).**

John Calvin and Reformed Churches

1. **Benedetto, Robert, Darrell Guder, and Donald McKim. *Historical Dictionary of the Reformed Churches* (Scarecrow, 1999).**
2. Bouwsma, William. *John Calvin* (Oxford University Press, 1987).
3. **Cottret, Bernard. *John Calvin* (Eerdmans, 2000).**
4. Elwood, Christopher. *Calvin for Armchair Theologians* (Westminster John Knox, 2002).
5. Jones, Serene. *Calvin and the Rhetoric of Piety* (Westminster John Knox, 1995).
6. **Lane, Anthony. *John Calvin* (Baker/T & T Clark, 1999).**

7. McGrath, Alister. *A Life of John Calvin* (Blackwell, 1990).
8. **McKim, Donald, ed. *The Cambridge Companion to John Calvin* (Cambridge University Press, 2002).**
9. **Muller, Richard *The Unaccommodated Calvin* (Oxford University Press, 2000).**
10. **Parker, T. H. L. *Calvin* (Westminster John Knox, 1975; Continuum, 2002).**
11. **Steinmetz, David. *Calvin in Context* (Oxford University Press, 1995).**

North American

1. Baker, William, ed. *Evangelicalism and the Stone-Campbell Movement* (IVP, 2002).
2. **Bobrick, Benson. *Wide as the Waters: The Story of the English Bible and the Revolution It Inspired* (Simon and Schuster, 2001).**
3. Brock, David. *Blinded by the Right: The Conscience of an Ex-Conservative* (Crown, 2002).
4. **Byrd, James. *The Challenges of Roger Williams* (Mercer University Press, 2002).**
5. **Carpenter, Joel. *Revive Us Again* (Oxford University Press, 1997).**
6. Delbanco, Andrew. *The Puritan Ordeal* (Harvard University Press, 1989).
7. **Gaustad, Edwin. *Sworn on the Altar of God* (Eerdmans, 1996).** Jefferson.
8. **Gutjahr, Paul. *An American Bible* (Stanford University Press, 1999).** Cultural meaning of the Scriptures in American history.
9. Harding, Susan. *The Book of Jerry Falwell* (Princeton University Press, 2000). Illuminating Fundamentalist critique.
10. **Hart, D. J. *Defending the Faith* (Baker, 1995).** Places into historical context J. Gresham Machen's involvement in the Modernist-Fundamentalist debate.
11. **Hatch, Nathan. *The Democratization of American Christianity* (Yale University Press, 1989).**

12. Hutson, James, ed. *Religion and the New Republic* (Rowman and Littlefield, 1999).
13. Jacobsen, Douglas, and William Trollinger, eds. *Re-Forming the Center* (Eerdmans, 1998). Covers 1900 to the present.
14. **Keillor, Steven. *This Rebellious House* (IVP, 1996).** Apologetic.
15. Longfield, Bradley. *The Presbyterian Controversy* (Oxford University Press, 1991). Modernism controversy 1922–36.
16. Marsden, George. *Fundamentalism and American Culture* (Oxford University Press, 1980).

    ———. *Reforming Fundamentalism: Fuller Seminary and the New Evangelicalism* (Eerdmans, 1987).

    ———. *Understanding Fundamentalism and Evangelicalism* (Eerdmans, 1991).
17. Marty, Martin. *Protestantism in the United States* (Scribners, 1986).
18. McClymond, Michael. *Encounters with God* (Oxford University Press, 1998). Jonathan Edwards.
19. **Mullin, Robert. *The Puritan as Yankee* (Eerdmans, 2002).** Critique of popular conception of Horace Bushnell as father of American liberalism.
20. **Noll, Mark. *American Evangelical Christianity* (Blackwell, 2001).**

    ———. *A History of Christianity in the United States and Canada* (Eerdmans, 1992).
21. Noll, Mark, et al. *Evangelicalism: Comparative Studies of Popular Protestantism in North America, the British Isles and Beyond 1700–1990* (Oxford University Press, 1994).
22. **Smith, Christian. *American Evangelicalism* (The University of Chicago Press, 1998).** Sociology.
23. **Stewart, John, and James Moorhead, eds. *Charles Hodge Revisited* (Eerdmans, 2002).**
24. **Thuessen, Peter. *In Discordance with the Scriptures* (Oxford University Press, 1999).** Battle of translations in American history.
25. Wells, Ronald, ed. *The Wars of America: Christian Views* (Mercer University Press, 1991).

26. Williams, D. H., ed. *The Free Church and the Early Church* (Eerdmans, 2002).

American Evangelists

1. Bailey, Faith. *D. L. Moody* (Moody, 1959). Popular.
2. Bruns, Roger. *Billy Sunday and Big Time* (University of Illinois, 2000).
3. Collins, Kenneth. *A Real Christian: The Life of John Wesley* (Abingdon, 1999).
4. **Dorsett, Lyle. *Billy Sunday and the Redemption of Urban America* (Eerdmans, 1991).**
   ———. *A Passion for Souls: The Life of D. L. Moody* (Moody, 1997).
5. **Hambrick-Stowe, Charles. *Charles G. Finney and the Spirit of American Evangelicalism* (Eerdmans, 1996).**
6. **Hardman, Keith. *Charles Grandison Finney, 1792–1875* (Syracuse University Press, 1987; Baker, 1990).**
7. Martin, Robert. *Hero of the Heartland* (Indiana University Press, 2002). Billy Sunday.
8. **Mouw, Richard. *The Smell of Sawdust* (Zondervan, 2000).** Brief history of evangelicalism's pietist, revivalist, fundamentalist roots.
9. **Rack, Henry. *Reasonable Enthusiast,* 2d ed. (Abingdon, 1993).** John Wesley.
10. **Stout, Harry. *The Divine Dramatist* (Eerdmans, 1991).** George Whitefield.

North American References and Helps

1. **Balmer, Randall. *Encyclopedia of Evangelicalism* (Westminster John Knox, 2002).** Handy for subjects hard to find in church history dictionaries.
2. Bowden, John. *Dictionary of American Religious Biography,* 2d ed. (Greenwood, 1993).
3. **Gaustad, Edwin, and Philip Barlow. *New Historical Atlas of Religion in America,* 3d ed. (Oxford University Press, 2001).**

4. **Hart, D. J., and Mark Noll, eds. *Dictionary of Reformed and Presbyterian Tradition in America* (IVP, 1999).**
5. **Lippy, Charles, and Peter Williams, eds. *The Encyclopedia of American Religious Experience,* 3 vols. (Scribners, 1988).**
6. **Melton, J. Gordon. *Encyclopedia of American Religions,* 3d ed., 3 vols. (Gale Publishers, 1993).**
7. Murphy Terrence, and Roberto Perin, eds. *A Concise History of Christianity in Canada* (Oxford University Press, 1996).
8. Newman, William, and Peter Halvorson. *Atlas of American Religion* (AltaMira, 2000).
9. **Noll, Mark. *The Old Religion in a New World* (Eerdmans, 2001).**
10. Prothero, Stephen, et al., eds. *The Encyclopedia of American Religious History,* 2 vols. (Facts on File, 1996).
11. **Reid, Daniel, et al., eds. *Dictionary of Christianity in America* (IVP, 1991).**
12. Toulouse, Mark, and James Duke, eds. *Makers of Christian Theology in America* (Abingdon, 1997).
    ———, eds. *Sources of Christian Theology in America* (Abingdon, 1999).

African-American

1. Angell, Stephen. *Bishop Henry McNeal Turner and African-American Religion in the South* (University of Tennessee, 1992).
2. Campbell, James. *Songs of Zion: The African Methodist Episcopal Church in the United States and South Africa* (Oxford University Press, 1995).
3. **Frey, Sylvia, and Betty Wood. *Come Shouting to Zion* (University of North Carolina, 1999).** Until 1830.
4. Johnson, Alonso, and Paul Jersild, eds. *"Ain't Gonna Lay My 'Ligion Down"* (University of South Carolina, 1996).
5. **Lincoln, C. Eric, and Lawrence Mamiya. *The Black Church in the African American Experience* (Duke University Press, 1990).**

6. **Pinn, Anthony. *Varieties of African-American Religious Experiences* (Fortress, 1998).**
7. Raboteau, Albert. *Slave Religion* (Oxford University Press, 1978).
8. **Sanders, Cheryl. *Saints in Exile* (Oxford University Press, 1996).** Holiness-Pentecostal background.
9. Young, Jeffrey. *Domesticating Slavery* (University of North Carolina, 1999). Georgia and South Carolina, 1670–1837.

The Civil War and Reconstruction

1. **Aamodt, Terrie. *Righteous Armies, Holy Cause: Apocalyptic Imagery and the Civil War* (Mercer University Press, 2002).**
2. Daly, John. *When Slavery Was Called Freedom* (University Press of Kentucky, 2002).
3. **Donald, David. *Lincoln* (Simon and Schuster, 1995).**
4. Fuller, James. *Chaplain to the Confederacy* (Louisiana State University Press, 2000). Basil Manly.
5. Gardner, Robert. *A Decade of Debate and Division: Georgia Baptists and the Formation of the Southern Baptist Convention* (Mercer University Press, 1995).
6. **Genovese, Eugene. *A Consuming Fire: The Fall of the Confederacy in the Mind of the White Christian South* (University of Georgia, 1998).**
7. **Goodman, Paul. *Of One Blood* (University of California, 1998).** Abolitionism.
8. **Guelzo, Allen. *Abraham Lincoln* (Eerdmans, 1999).** Lincoln's spirituality.
9. **Haynes, Stephen. *Noah's Curse* (Oxford University Press, 2001).** Slavery justification.
10. Kaufman, Paul. *"Logical" Luther Lee and the Methodist War Against Slavery* (Scarecrow, 2000).
11. **Klein, Martin. *A Historical Dictionary of Slavery and Abolition* (Scarecrow, 2002).**
12. **Long, Kathryn. *The Revival of 1857–58* (Oxford University Press, 1998).**

13. **Miller, Randall, Harry Stout, and Charles Wilson, eds. *Religion and the American Civil War* (Oxford University Press, 1998).**
14. **Stowell, Daniel. *Rebuilding Zion* (Oxford University Press, 1998).** Reconstruction, 1863–77.
15. **Trulock, Alice. *In the Hand of Providence* (University of North Carolina, 1992).** Joshua L. Chamberlain, Gettysburg hero.
16. **Wilson, Charles. *Baptized in Blood: The Religion of the Lost Cause, 1865–1920* (University of Georgia, 1980).**
17. *See* Religion in the South below.

Religion in the South

1. Aldridge, Marion, and Kevin Lewis, eds. *The Changing Shape of Protestantism in the South* (Mercer University Press, 1996).
2. Boles, John. *The Great Revival* (University Press of Kentucky, 1996). Bible Belt 1787–1805.
3. **Calhoon, Robert. *Evangelicals and Conservatives in the Early South, 1740–1861* (University of South Carolina, 1989).**
4. **Harvey, Paul. *Redeeming the South* (University of North Carolina, 1996).** Southern Baptists, 1865–1925.
5. Heyrman, Christine. *Southern Cross* (Knopf, 1997).
6. **Hill, Samuel. *On Jordan's Stormy Banks* (Mercer University Press, 1983).**

   ———, ed. *Encyclopedia of Religion in the South* (Mercer University Press, 1984, 1997).

   ———. *One Name but Several Faces* (University of Georgia, 1997).

   ———. *Southern Churches in Crisis Revisited* (University of Alabama, 1999). Racism and churches.
7. **Mulder, Philip, *A Controversial Spirit* (Oxford University Press, 2002).** Rivalry of Churches 1740–1820.
8. **Sheldon, Garrett, and Daniel Dreisbach. *Religion and Political Culture in Jefferson's Virginia* (Rowman and Littlefield, 2000).**

9. **Startup, Kenneth. *The Root of All Evil: The Protestant Clergy and the Economic Mind of the Old South* (University of Georgia, 2001).**
10. Wilson, Charles. *What's Judgment and Grace in Dixie* (University of Georgia, 1997).

General Baptist History

1. **Brackney, William. *Historical Dictionary of the Baptists* (Scarecrow, 1999).**
2. Brackney, William, Paul Fiddes, and John Briggs, eds. *Pilgrim Pathways* (Mercer University Press, 1999).
3. Bush, Russ, and Thomas Nettles. *Baptists and the Bible,* rev. ed. (Broadman & Holman, 1999).
4. **George, Timothy, and David Dockery, eds. *Theologians of the Baptist Tradition,* rev. ed. (Broadman & Holman, 2001).**
5. George, Timothy, and Denise George, eds. *Library of Baptist Classics,* 12 vols. (Broadman & Holman, 1997).
6. **Glass, William. *Strangers in Zion: Fundamentalists in the South, 1900–1950* (Mercer University Press, 2001).** Baptists versus Presbyterians presaging the current conflict.
7. **McBeth, H. Leon. *The Baptist Heritage* (Broadman, 1987).**
8. McGoldrick, James. *Baptist Successionism* (Scarecrow, 1994).
9. Norman, Stan. *Preserving Our Baptist Identity* (Broadman & Holman, 2001).
10. Tull, James (edited by Morris Ashcroft). *High-Church Baptists in the South,* ed. Morris Ashcroft, rev. ed. (Mercer University Press, 2001). Landmarkism.

Southern Baptist Convention and Controversy

1. DeWeese, Charles. *Defining Baptist Convictions* (Providence House, 1996).
2. **Dockery, David. *Southern Baptists and American Evangelicals* (Broadman & Holman, 1993).**
3. Draper, James, and Kenneth Keathley. *Biblical Authority* (Broadman & Holman, 2001).
4. **Fletcher, James. *The SBC* (Broadman & Holman, 1995).**

5. Flynt, Wayne. *Alabama Baptists* (University of Alabama, 1998).
6. Goodwin, Everett. *Baptists in the Balance* (Judson, 1997). Defense of moderate-liberals.
7. Harper, Keith. *Send the Light: Lottie Moon's Letters and Other Writings* (Mercer University Press, 2002).
8. Hefley, James, and Mark Coppenger. *The Truth in Crisis: The Winning Edge,* vol. 5 (Hannibal Books, 1991).
9. Hobbs, Herschel. *My Faith and Message* (Broadman & Holman, 1990).
10. Leonard, William. *God's Last and Only Hope: The Fragmentation of the Southern Baptist Convention* (Eerdmans, 1990).
11. Nettles, Thomas, and Russell Moore. *Why I Am a Baptist* (Broadman & Holman, 2001).
12. Pool, Jeff. *Against Returning to Egypt* (Mercer University Press, 1998). Moderate.
13. Pressler, Paul. *A Hill on Which to Die* (Broadman & Holman, 1998).
14. Rogers, James. *Richard Furman* (Mercer University Press, 2001).
15. Shurden, Walter, ed. *The Struggle for the Soul of the SBC* (Mercer University Press, 1993).
16. Shurden, Walter, and Randy Shepley, eds. *Going for the Jugular* (Mercer University Press, 1996). Moderate documentary.
17. Stricklin, David. *A Genealogy of Dissent* (University Press of Kentucky, 1999). Ascendancy of fundamentalism in the SBC and feminist issues.
18. Sutton, Jerry. *The Baptist Reformation* (Broadman & Holman, 2000).
19. Wills, Gregory. *Democratic Religion* (Oxford University Press, 1996). 1785–1900.

Holiness and Methodism

1. **Andrews, Dee. *The Methodists and Revolutionary America, 1760–1800* (Princeton University Press, 2000).**
2. **Dieter, Melvin. *The Holiness Movement in the Nineteenth Century,* 2d ed. (Scarecrow, 1996).**

3. **Heitzenrater, Richard. *Wesley and the People Called Methodists* (Abingdon, 1995).**
4. Kostevly, William. *Historical Dictionary of the Holiness Movement* (Scarecrow, 2001).
5. Lyerly, Cynthia. *Methodism and the Southern Mind, 1770–1810* (Oxford University Press, 1998).
6. **Wigger, John. *Taking Heaven By Storm* (Oxford University Press, 1998).**
7. **Wigger, John, and Nathan Hatch, eds. *Methodism and the Shaping of American Culture* (Abingdon, 2001).**
8. Yrigoyen, Charles, and Susan Warrick, eds. *Historical Dictionary of Methodism* (Scarecrow, 1996).

Pentecostal and Charismatic History

1. Anderson, Robert. *Vision of the Disinherited* (Hendrickson, 1993).
2. **Burgess, Stanley, and Eduard van der Maas, eds. *The New International Dictionary of Pentecostal and Charismatic Movements,* rev. ed. (Zondervan, 2002).**
3. Cox, Harvey. *The Rise of Pentecostal Christianity and the Reshaping of Religion in the 21st Century* (DaCapo/Addison-Wesley, 1994).
4. Dayton, Donald. *The Theological Roots of Pentecostalism* (Hendrickson/Scarecrow, 1987).
5. Dayton, Donald, and Robert Johnston, eds. *The Variety of American Evangelicalism* (IVP, 1991).
6. Faupel, William. *The Everlasting Gospel* (Sheffield Academic Press, 1996).
7. **Gillespie, Thomas. *The First Theologians: A Study in Early Christian Prophecy* (Eerdmans, 1994).**
8. Hollenwegger, Walter. *The Pentecostals* (Hendrickson, 1972).
   ———. *Pentecostalism* (Hendrickson, 1997).
9. **Jones, Charles. *A Guide to the Study of the Pentecostal Movement,* 2 vols. (Scarecrow, 1983).**
   ———. *The Charismatic Movement,* 2 vols. (Scarecrow, 1995). Bibliography with focus on Anglo-American sources.

10. **Kydd, Ronald. *Healing Through the Centuries* (Hendrickson, 1998).**
11. **Land, Steven. *Pentecostal Spirituality* (Sheffield Academic Press, 1993).**
12. **Ma, Wonsuk, and Robert Menzies, eds. *Pentecostalism in Context* (Sheffield Academic Press, 1997).**
13. **Martin, David. *Pentecostalism* (Blackwell, 2001).**
14. Shaull, Richard, and Waldo Cesar. *Pentecostalism and the Future of the Christian Churches* (Eerdmans, 2000).
15. **Synan, Vinson. *The Holiness-Pentecostal Tradition* (Eerdmans, 1997).**

    ———. *The Century of the Holy Spirit* (Thomas Nelson, 2001).
16. **Wacker, Grant. *Glory Below* (Harvard University Press, 2001).** Early Pentecostalism.

19 COMPUTER RESOURCES

Optimal Package

1. ***BibleWorks for Windows 5.0*** **(Hermeneutika).** Operational improvements include a greatly simplified interface for beginners, a detailed statistics window with graphical display, a Word List Manager that generates word frequencies for arbitrary verse ranges, a synopsis window that parallels gospel accounts, and a new Copy Center that lets you format the output of reference lists. *HALOT* and *BDAG* available as add-on modules. 800-74-BIBLE.
2. **Clendenen, Ray, gen. ed. The New American Commentary Series, 46 vols. (Broadman & Holman).** Libronix and Logos-Compatible, available from Logos Research Systems. 800-87-BIBLE.
3. **Metzger, Bruce, gen. ed. Word Biblical Commentary Series (Thomas Nelson).** Includes NA^{26}, *BHS, BDB,* Louw-Nida, and seven translations. Libronix and Logos compatible. 800-251-4000.
4. ***Scholar's Library: Logos Bible Software Series X*** **(Logos Research Systems).** More than a 230-volume combination exegetical, pastoral, Bible study program. About forty of these are exegetical works, sixty-five are pastoral studies from the *Leadership Journal,* about thirty-five would fall under the rubric of a *Christian Home Library* (home schooling texts, discipleship, etc.), while the remaining ninety or more would

constitute an extensive biblical study base. In addition to the new software platform, herein lies the principal advantage of *Scholar's Library.* Exegetical references in *Scholar's Library* include *Nestle-Aland with McReynolds English Interlinear,* Louw-Nida, *BAGD,* Liddell-Scott, the unabridged *TDNT, BDB, TWOT,* and *Biblical Hebrew Reference Grammar.*

Study references include *Harper's Bible Dictionary,* Gower's *New Manners and Customs,* Archer's *A Survey of Old Testament Introduction,* Guthrie's *New Testament Introduction,* the *Moody Handbook of Theology,* the *Biblical Theology of the Old Testament,* the *Biblical Theology of the New Testament,* Josephus, Philo, Douglas's *Who's Who in Christian History,* the *Archaeological Encyclopedia of the Holy Land* (3d ed.), the *Logos Deluxe Map Set,* the *Bible Knowledge Commentary,* the *NBC*[4] and *NBD*[3], the *IVP Bible Background Commentary: New Testament,* and the *Hard Sayings of the Bible* (these last four are also on the Essential IVP Reference Collection below).

Pastoral references include the *Leadership Library Series, Mastering Ministry Series,* and the *Pressure Points Series.* The Christian home library references include eleven creationism texts.

The advantage of operating under its single, brand new software platform is that the *Libronix Digital Library System* enables the user to do rapid passage, word, or exegetical studies in which all research is paralleled on the desktop by the passage and related references. Although this new feature is not a replacement for more complex original language constructions, it brings up a host of links for more simple searches. Furthermore, *Scholar's Library* is expandable with the other options mentioned below. See *Libronix Integrated Digital Library System* under Computer Resources: References for add-ons. Libronix and Logos compatible. 800-875-6467.

5. ***The Essential IVP Reference Collection* (IVP, 2001).** Includes the four-volume *DJG, DPL, DLNTD,* and *DNTB;* the *New Dictionary of Biblical Theology* (2001); the *NBD*[3], *NBC*[4], and

Atlas; the *New Dictionary of Theology;* the *Dictionary of Biblical Imagery; Hard Sayings of the Bible;* and the *IVP Bible Background Commentaries: Old Testament* and *New Testament.* Libronix and Logos compatible. 630-734-4321.

6. **VanGemeren, Willem, and Colin Brown, gen. eds. *Zondervan Theological Dictionaries* (Zondervan, 2002).** *NIDOTTE* and *NIDNTT* bundled together. STEP compatible. 800-727-1309.

Comprehensive Packages[1]
(Windows compatible)

1. *Bible Windows 6.01* (Silver Mountain Software). Interlinear display, read-aloud Hebrew and Greek, *AGNT*[2] morphology, ANLEX database, Liddell-Scott, Louw-Nida, LXX, *BDB, Church Fathers, Josephus, Silver Classical,* etc. 800-214-2144.
2. ***Gramcord for Windows (GNT 5.3, HMT 3.1e, LXX) Ultimate Bundle* (Gramcord Institute).** Fast searches, updated *BHS* and LXX morphology, excellent online Greek syntax, Princeton Edition Expanded *BDB* lexicon *NAS Exhaustive Concordance,* Lust, et al., eds. *A Greek-English Lexicon of the Septuagint,* highlighting accessory available. 360-576-3000.
3. ***Lightning Study Bible* (Hendrickson, 2002).** UBS, *BHL,* nine translations, fourteen language references, fifteen general references, and atlas. *Lightning Study Bible* compatible (Gramcord) with compendium of digital publishers. 800-358-3111.
4. ***Zondervan Bible Study Library: Scholar's Edition* (Zondervan, 2002).** *TNIV*[2] and fourteen other translations, NIV

---

1. Gramcord has just released its new package featuring the *Lightning Study Bible* platform. It will be joining a host of publishers who will use the same format (only HeavenWord and Hendrickson can be mentioned now). Also, it will have the world's most powerful Bible note system (undergirded by *Nota Bene*), making Gramcord the first choice for authors of multiple publications since it allows for easy interchange between formats. Initially, *HALOT* and *BDAG* will be offered with many more modules to follow.
2. *TNIV* differs from the original by 7 percent; mostly on points of clarity and gender.

text with extensive study notes, *NIV Nave's Topical Bible, NIV Compact Dictionary, NIV Exhaustive Concordance, Zondervan NIV Bible Commentary* (2 vols.), *Asbury Bible Commentary, New International Bible Commentary, New International Encyclopedia of Bible Words, Zondervan Pictorial Encyclopedia* (5 vols.), *Encyclopedia of Bible Difficulties,* Grudem's *Systematic Theology,* Dillard and Longman's *Introduction to the OT,* Carson, et al. *Introduction to the NT* UBS[4], ten language grammars, lexicons and helps with superior, interlinear concordance and word statistic function. Book value $2,500 (approx. one hundred volumes) at $300 retail. Also available in three other editions. STEP compatible. 800-727-1309.

Laymen

1. *Baker Digital Reference Library* (BakerBytes). Logos/Libronix compatible.
2. ***eBible: Discover Edition* (Thomas Nelson).** For those with minimal study needs, this astonishingly low-priced ($50.00 retail) Logos and Libronix-Compatible program contains Gower's *Manners and Customs, Unger's Bible Handbook,* Dowley's *Atlas of the Bible,* and N. Hillyer's *Dictionary of the Bible.* 800-251-4000.
3. *PC Study Bible 3.0 for Windows: New Reference Library* (BIBLESOFT). Basic Bible study program with simple, inductive interface. 800-995-9058.
4. *Quickverse Multimedia Life Application Bible* (Tyndale). NLT, *Life Application* notes, 360 photos, child friendly.

References

1. **Barton, John, and John Muddiman, eds. *The Oxford Bible Commentary* (Oxford University Press, 2001).** Unlockable Logos CD with book. 800-334-4249.
2. *Biblical Studies Library 4* (Biblical Studies). *NET Bible* (see above) and five thousand documents, including many unpublished Bible studies. Logos and Libronix compatible. 800-GALAXIE.

3. *Catalogue of the French Biblical and Archaeological School of Jerusalem* (Brill, 2000). Bibliographical research of École Biblique, French-English, Logos.
4. *Early Church Fathers on CD-ROM,* 38 vols. (BIBLESOFT). Logos and Libronix compatible.
5. ***English Standard Version Bible Reference Library* (Crossway/iExalt 2001).** 800-888-9898. ESV with multiple, unlockable resources. STEP compatible.
6. **Freedman, David, ed. *The Anchor Bible Dictionary on CD-ROM* (Doubleday).** Logos and Libronix compatible.
7. Gaebelein, Frank, ed. The Expositor's Bible Commentary on CD-ROM, 12 vols. (Zondervan, 1998). STEP compatible. Be aware that the NEBC commences in 2003.
8. **Hannah, John. *Charts of Ancient and Medieval History* (Zondervan, 2001).** Companion CD replicating contents for audio-visual use and printouts.
9. Hanson, K., and Douglas Oakman. *Palestine in the Time of Jesus* (Fortress, 1996/2002). With multiple-link CD.
10. Kaiser, Walter, et al. *Hard Sayings of the Bible* (Parsons Technology). In *Quickverse Library* collection and Libronix.
11. **Keathley, Hampton, ed. *Theological Library Journal CD5* (Galaxie Software).** In both Logos (Libronix) and Folio format. Contains *Bib Sac* (1930–2001), *Chafer Theological Seminary Journal* (1998–2001), *Conservative Theological Journal, GTJ* (1960–91), *Emmaeus Journal* (1991–2001), *Journal of Biblical Manhood and Womanhood* (1995–2001), *JETS* (1978–2001), *Journal of the Grace Evangelical Society* (1988–2000), *TMSTJ* (1990–99), *TJ* (1980–2000), and *WTJ* (1960–2001). Also includes Calvin's *Institutes, Josephus,* Schaff's *History, Church Fathers,* etc. Available through CBD (800-CHRISTIAN). Upgrades (800-GALAXIE). Represents 245 years of journal articles.
12. Keck, Leander, gen. ed. *The New Interpreter's Bible: A Commentary in 12 Volumes, Electronic Edition* (Abingdon). 800-251-3320.
13. ***Libronix Integrated Digital Library System*** (*see*

www.logos.com). Hundreds of top-rated resources from several publishers, including the IVPNTC commentary series, Bright's *History of Israel,* Motyer's *Prophecy of Isaiah,* Howard's *Introduction to the Old Testament Historical Books, the Anchor Bible Dictionary,* etc.

14. ***Logos Bible Atlas* (Logos Research Systems).** Satellite data base, 3-D custom maps, plus standard maps from the *Lion Bible Map Book* (Lion, 1985); notations from *New Bible Dictionary* (IVP, 1982).

15. Musser, Donald, and Joseph Price, eds. *The Abingdon Dictionary of Theology: Electronic Edition* (Abingdon, 1997).

16. ***NET Bible* (Biblical Studies, 2001).** *New English Translation.* Features 60,000 footnotes excellent for identifying key Hebrew, Greek words and phrases. Logos and Libronix compatible. 800-GALAXIE.

17. *PC Bible Atlas* (Parsons Technology). Includes a hundred color maps with accompanying articles.

18. ***Thesaurus Linguae Graecae* on CD-ROM (University of California).** Data only. Needs helping program.

19. **Wilson, Neil, and Linda Taylor. *Tyndale Handbook of Bible Maps and Charts* (Tyndale, 2002).** CD replicating book with links to NLT. Also Mac compatible.

Language Helps

1. **Archer, Gleason. *HeavenWord GreekMaster on CD-ROM* (HeavenWord).** Archer recitation of all Greek words, links to NASB and UBS[4] dictionary.

2. *Bible Reader* (Olive Tree). NA[27] for Palm OS.

3. ***GRAMCORD Lite* (Olive Tree).** Morphology-tagged NA[27] for Palm OS.

4. *GreekFlash Pro 2* (Paradigm Software Development). Vocabulary drilling.

5. **Hildebrandt, Ted. *Greek Tutor and Hebrew Tutor Multimedia CD-ROMS* (Parsons Technology, 1995).** Reviews grammar, parsing, translation skills, quizzes. 800-644-6344.

6. Johnstone, William, et al. *A Computerized Introductory Hebrew*

Grammar (T & T Clark, 2000). Interactive, cross-referenced complement to Davidson; also Mac.

7. **Koehler, L., W. Baumgartner, and J. Stamm, eds. *The Hebrew-Aramaic Lexicon of the Old Testament CD-ROM* (Brill, 2000).**
8. **Louw, J., and E. Nida. *A Greek-English Lexicon of the New Testament on CD-ROM* (iExalt).**
9. **McLean, John. Handbook of Grammatical Diagramming (Gramcord Institute).** 360-576-3000.
10. *MemCards* (Greek and Hebrew). Parsing, forms, vocabulary review (cf. to Seow, Kelley, Waltke, O'Connor, Lambdin, and Weingreen).
11. *NET Bible for Handhelds* (Biblical Studies). Palm Pilot, WinCE version to help get started on sermon preparation while on the run. 800-GALAXIE.
12. **Pennington, Jonathan. *New Testament Greek Vocabulary* (Zondervan, 2001).** Two CDs.
13. Swanson, James. *A Dictionary of Biblical Languages with Semantic Domains* (Logos). Available in Hebrew, Greek, and Aramaic.
14. ***The New Greek-English Interlinear New Testament on CD-ROM* (iExalt).** UBS[4], Friberg's *AGNT,* STEP compatible, vocalizes pronunciation and definition.
15. **Van der Merwe, H., et al. *A Biblical Hebrew Reference Grammar* (Sheffield).** Logos and Libronix compatible.
16. **Wallace, Daniel. *Greek Grammar Beyond the Basics* (Galaxie Software).** 800-GALAXIE.

Pastoral Helps

1. *Bible Illustrator 3.0 Deluxe* (Parsons Technology, 2000). CD with 6,000 illustrations from *Christianity Today* and others, 12,000 historical quotes, 1,700 humorous stories, etc.
2. Koessler, John, and Steven Albrecht, eds. *How to Preach a Sermon* (BakerBytes, 2000). CD based on Robinson's and Chapell's volumes.
3. Morgan, Robert, ed. *Nelson's Complete Electronic Library of*

Stories, Sermons, Outlines, and Quotes on CD-ROM (Thomas Nelson, 1999).

4. **Severance, Murray. *That's Easy for You to Say* (Broadman & Holman, 1997).** Pronunciation guide with audio CD; seven thousand entries.

Miscellaneous Resources

1. *Christian History Interactive* (Logos, 1997). Fifty-issue CD-ROM, Logos and Libronix compatible.
2. *Church Bytes Magazine* (919-490-8927).
3. Dead Sea Scrolls Revealed (Logos Research Systems, 1994). Interactive CD-ROM.
4. *Great Electronic Books for Christians* (Woodlawn Electronic Publishing). 215-657-9935.
5. **Hildebrandt, Ted. *Get Lost in Jerusalem CD-ROM* (Zondervan, 2001).** Virtual tour.
6. *Logos Lesson Builder* (Logos Research Systems, 1997). Five hundred prepared Bible study lessons from IVP.
7. Vander Laan, Ray. Jesus CD-ROM: An Interactive Journey (Zondervan, 1998).
8. *Walk in the Footsteps of Jesus* (Parsons Technology, 1997). Interactive travel guide.

Macintosh

1. *Accordance Bible Atlas* (Oaktree Software). See *Scholar's Collection* below.
2. Blum, Ed, ed. *Holman Christian Standard Bible* (Broadman & Holman, 2002). Accordance-Compatible. 800-251-3225.
3. Brown, Colin, ed. *NIDNTT* (*see* Windows above). Accordance-Compatible.
4. Clines, David, ed. *The Dictionary of Classical Hebrew,* 8 vols. (Sheffield Academic Press, 1993–).
5. Freedman, David, gen. ed. *The Anchor Bible Dictionary* (Oaktree Software).
6. Gaebelein, Frank, ed. *The Expositor's Bible Commentary for Macintosh* (Zondervan). Accordance compatible.

7. ***Scholar's Collection with Accordance 5.3* (Oaktree Software).** Best overall exegetical program, excellent morphological data base and statistics, Spicq's *Theological Lexicon,* Louw-Nida, Jenni-Westermann *TLOT,* Abridged *BDB,* Wallace's *An Exegetical Syntax of the GNT* and Parallel Texts (OT, Gospels, Old Testament in NT). Expandable by two hundred modules (including Keathley's *Theological Library Journal, Oxford Bible Companion, HALOT,* and *BDAG*) on up to thirteen CDs. 360-576-3000.
8. *The Online Bible* (Yeshua's Ministry). Also Windows compatible. 888-224-2537.

20 INTERNET WEB SITES

Internet Guidebooks

1. **Baker, Jason. *Christian Cyberspace Companion,* 2d ed. (Baker, 1997).**
2. **Careaga, Andrew. *eMinistry* (Kregel, 2001).** Especially teens.
   ———. *Hooked on the Net* (Kregel, 2002).
3. **Durusau, Patrick. *High Places in Cyberspace,* 2d ed. (Scholars, 1998).**
4. **Groothuis, Douglas. *The Soul in Cyberspace* (Baker, 1997).**
5. **Lawrence, Bruce. *The Complete Idiot's Guide to Religions Online* (Alpha, 2000).**
6. **Schultze, Quentin. *Internet for Christians* (Gospel Films, 1995).** Logos and Libronix compatible.
7. **Stover, Mark, ed. *Theological Librarians and the Internet* (Haworth, 2001).**
8. **Swisher, Steven. *aol.com* (Times Business, 1999).**
9. **Veith, Gene, and Christopher Stamper. *Christians in a .com World* (Crossway, 2000).**
10. **Wendland, Mike. *The Complete "No Geek-Speak" Guide to the Internet* (Zondervan, 1998).**
11. **Zaleski, Jeffrey. *The Soul of Cyberspace* (HarperEdge, 1997).**

Publishing Houses and Software

abingdonpress.com (800-251-3320). *The New Interpreter's Bible on CD-ROM.*

academicbooks.com (Wipf & Stock). Windows Booksellers imprint specializing in reprints (800-779-1701)

ageslibrary.com (AGES Software Master Christian Library). Over 600 titles.

augsburgfortress.org

bakerbooks.com (800-877-2665). Baker Digital Reference Library.

biblecd.com (Online Bible USA). 800-243-7124.

Biblecompanion.org (Loizeaux Bros.). 800-257-0775.

bible.org (Galaxie Software, Biblical Studies Press). 800-GALAXIE, 800-575-2425. *The Theological Journal Library CD5, Biblical Studies Library, 10,000 Sermon Illustrations CD, NET Bible, NET Bible for Handhelds.*

biblesoft.com (800-995-9058). *PC Study Bible.*

bibleworks.com (Hermeneutika). 800-74BIBLE, *BibleWorks 5.0, HALOT,* and *BDAG.*

blackwellpublishers.co.uk

brill.nl

broadmanholman.com

continuumbooks.com (Continuum/T & T Clark USA/Sheffield Academic Press).

crosswaybooks.com

doubleday.com

eerdmans.com

fortresspress.com

gospelcom.net/navsoft (NavPress). 800-888-9898.

GRAMCORD.org (360-576-3000). *GRAMCORD for Windows.*

heavenword.com (888-726-4715). *GreekMaster.*

hendrickson.com (800-358-3111). *Lightning Study Bible.*

ivpress.com (800-841-3225). *The Essential IVP Reference Collection.*

kregel.com

litpress.org (Liturgical).

logos.com (Logos Research Systems). *Libronix Integrated Digital Library System* (800-87LOGOS). *Scholar's Library, Anchor Bible Dictionary,* New American Commentary.

moodypress.org

morehousegroup.org (Trinity Press International).

mupress.org (Mercer University Press).

oaksoft.com (Oaktree Software ACCORDANCE). 360-576-3000, *Accordance for Macintosh, Anchor Bible Dictionary, HALOT,* and *BDAG.*

OliveTree.com *(Bible Reader, GRAMCORD Lite).*

oup-usa.org (Oxford University Press). 800-334-4249, *The New Oxford Annotated Biblical Reference Library, The Oxford Bible Commentary.*

paulistpress.com

prpbooks.com (Presbyterian & Reformed).

quickverse.com (Parsons Technology). 800-644-6344, *Greek Tutor, Hebrew Tutor.*

scarecrowpress.com (800-462-6420).

silvermnt.com (Silver Mountain Software). 800-214-2144, *Bible Windows.*

tandtclark.co.uk

thomasnelson.com (Thomas Nelson Publishers). 800-251-4000, Word Biblical Commentary on CD-ROM, *eBible.*

trinitypressintl.com

tyndale.com (630-784-5275). *Tyndale Handbook of Bible Maps and Charts.*

uci.edu/~tlg *(Thesaurus Linguae Graecae).* 714-824-7031.

wjkbooks.com (Westminster John Knox).

zondervan.com (800-727-1309). *NIDOTTE, NIDNTT, Zondervan Dictionary of Theological Words, Zondervan Bible Study Library, New Testament Vocabulary.*

Books

amazon.com.

bn.com (Barnes and Noble).

Christianbook.com (Christian Book Distributors). Twenty-four hours a day, more than 75,000 products, 800-CHRISTIAN (online books, music, movies, specialty products).

Used Books[1]

abebooks.com (Advanced Book Exchange). Search engine, finds location of both new and used books.

academicbooks.com (Windows Booksellers). Average 43 percent off second-hand books. 800-779-1701.

archivesbookshop.com (used books).

bakerbooks.com (616-957-3110, [fax] 616-957-0965). More than 70,000 used and slightly damaged Baker books (including those missing a dust jacket).

bookfinder.com (search engine). New and used books.

booktown.com (Loome Theo.Booksellers). Offers 250,000 used books.

eerdmans.com (800-253-7521). Ask for bookstore, where many discontinued, slightly damaged, and overstocked books can be purchased at a significant discount.

kregel.com (Kregel Used Books). More than 250,000 used religious and theological books. 616-459-9444; fax: 888-USD-BOOK.

TheologyBooks.com.

UsedTheologyBooks.com.

Academic Sites

best.com/~dolphin/asstbib.shtml (The Lambert Dolphin Library). Multiple links.

bhum.ac.uk/theology/goodacre/links.htm (The New Testament Gateway). All New Testament studies links, references.

1. I would first check the Baker, Eerdmans, and Kregel sites, where slightly damaged books can often be found at 40–50 percent off, then I would turn to Windows Booksellers, which regularly purchases entire libraries for resale. Another good source is eBay. If a book is particularly difficult to locate, consult abebooks.com. It is conceivable that you could construct a library of completely second-hand titles, and generally these are as good as new. Look out for CBD closeouts also, although it is less likely that you will find frontline references there.

bible.org (Biblical Studies Foundation). Extensive Bible studies, commentaries, pastoral helps, *NET* translation.
biblestudytools.com (fourteen translations, links to commentaries and other references).
ccel.org (Worldwide Study Bible).
earlygospels.net (Jesus of Nazareth in the Early Christian Gospels).
hivolda.no/asf/kkf/rel-stud.html (Resource Pages for Biblical studies).
leaderu.com (Leadership University). Articles on dozens of topics by pastors, scholars, etc.
library.yale.edu/div/xtiangde.htm (Yale University Library Research Guide for Christianity).
perseus.tufts.edu (ancient texts, maps, archaeology).
princeton.edu/~jwm/synopsis/met-syni.htm (A Synopsis of the Gospels).
soc.religion.christian.com (Bible Study Software FAQ). Usenet.
theologywebsite.com (Trinity Evangelical Divinity School, Int'l University). Historical Theology department list of resources.
tms.edu/other.htm (The Master's Seminary Online). Research/information links.
tren.com (Theological Research Exchange Network). Offers 7,800 unpublished theses, dissertations from seventy institutions plus society meeting papers.

Theological Journals and Christian Magazines

atla.com (ATLA Religion Database). Listing of all journals.
booksandculture.net (numerous book reviews).
brill.nl *(Novum Testamentum, Vetus Testamentum).*
calvin.edu *(Calvin Theological Journal).*
cba.cua.edu *(Catholic Biblical Quarterly).*
ccmag.com *(Christian Computing magazine).* 800-456-1868.
christianity.net *(Christianity Today, Books and Culture, Leadership Journal).*
churchsociety.org *(Churchman).*
cssr.org *(Religious Studies Review).* Numerous brief reviews in several categories.
denver-journal.densem.edu *(Denver Journal).* Online review of cur-

rent biblical and theological studies principally by Denver professors Blomberg, Carroll, Hess, and Klein.

dts.edu/bib_sac *(Bibliotheca Sacra).*

interp.org *(Interpretation).*

rtabst.org *(Religious and Theological Abstracts).* Covers 1959–2001 editions, updated annually.

scholar.cc.emory.edu *(Journal of Biblical Literature).* 877-725-3334.

tandtclark.co.uk *(Expository Times).*

tiu.edu *(Trinity Journal).*

tms.edu/journal.asp *(The Master's Seminary Theological Journal).* Full text of articles and book reviews available (tms.edu/links.asp for thorough listing of online journals).

wts.edu *(Westminster Theological Journal).*

Christian Site Search[2]

botcw.com (Best of the Christian Web). Directory.

cadvision.com/Home_Pages/accounts/haynese/sites.htm (Christian Sites to Be Seen).

cforc.com/home.html (Computers for Christ).

christianity.net (church locator, etc.).

churchsurf.com (all online churches).

crosssearch.com (Christian CrossSearch). By topic.

cs.odu.edu,/eisen_j/ccn/list.html (Christian White Pages).

goshen.net (directory, links to software, etc.).

gospelcom.net/ifc/newsletter.html (Internet for Christians). Also electronic mailing lists, 9 translations in twelve languages, etc.

ibelieve.com

iclnet.org/pub/resources/christian-resources.html *(Not Just Bibles: A Guide to Christian Resources on the Internet).*

interlog.com/-mkoehler/allinone/allinone.html (All-in-One Christian Search).

iugm.org/links (Christian Resources).

omnilist.crosswalk.com.

---

2. Mike Wendland, *The Complete "No Geek-Speak" Guide to the Internet* (Zondervan, 1998).

saturn.colorado.edu:8080/Christian/list.html (Christian Resource List).
xir.com (Christian Internet Resources).
yahoo.com/Society_and_Culture/Religion (Church locators).

21 THE ULTIMATE COMMENTARY COLLECTION

Genesis
Gordon Wenham (2 vols.)
Bruce Waltke
John Walton

Exodus
Cornelius Houtman
John Currid
Peter Enns

Leviticus
Jacob Milgrom (3 vols.)
John Hartley
Allen Ross
Mark Rooker

Numbers
Timothy Ashley
Gordon Wenham
Dennis Cole

Deuteronomy
Duane Christensen (2 vols.)
Gordon McConville
Eugene Merrill

Joshua
David Howard
Richard Hess
Marten Woudstra

Judges
Daniel Block
Barry Webb
Lawson Younger

Ruth
Robert Hubbard
Frederic Bush
David Atkinson

1–2 Samuel
Ralph Klein (1 Sam.)
Kyle McCarter (2 Sam.)
Robert Bergen

1–2 Kings
Michael Cogan (1 Kings)
T. R. Hobbs (2 Kings)
Donald Wiseman

1–2 Chronicles
Sara Japhet
Roddy Braun (1 Chron.)
Raymond Dillard (2 Chron.)
Martin Selman (2 vols.)
Leslie Allen

Ezra/Nehemiah
Hugh Williamson
Derek Kidner
Ralph Klein

Esther
Michael Fox
Frederic Bush
Karen Jobes

Job
David Clines (2 vols.)
John Hartley
Robert Alden

Psalms
Peter Craigie, Martin Tate, and Leslie Allen (3 vols.)
Michael Wilcock
Gerald Wilson (2 vols.)

Proverbs
Richard Clifford
Michael Fox (2 vols.)
David Hubbard

Ecclesiastes
Choon-Leong Seow
Tremper Longman
Iain Provan

Song of Songs
Roland Murphy
Tremper Longman
Thomas Gledhill

Isaiah
John Oswalt (2 vols.)
Hans Wildberger
Alec Motyer

Jeremiah
William Holladay
Jack Lundblom (2 vols.)
Andrew Dearman

Lamentations
Adele Berlin
Iain Provan
F. Dobbs-Allsopp

Ezekiel
Daniel Block (2 vols.)
Leslie Allen (2 vols.)
Iain Duguid

Daniel
John Goldingay
Ernest Lucas
Stephen Miller

Hosea–Amos
Duane Garrett
Shalom Paul
Gary Smith

Obadiah–Micah
Leslie Allen
Thomas Finley

Nahum–Zephaniah
Richard Patterson
Kenneth Barker
D. Waylon Bailey

Haggai–Malachi
Eric and Carol Meyers
Pieter Verhoef
Andrew Hill
Joyce Baldwin

Matthew
Donald Hagner (2 vols.)
Craig Keener
Craig Blomberg

Mark
Robert Gundry
Richard France
David Garland

Luke
Darrell Bock (2 vols.)
François Bovon (2 vols.)
Robert Stein

John
Craig Keener (2 vols.)
D. A. Carson
Craig Blomberg

Acts
C. K. Barrett (short)
Ben Witherington
John Stott
William Larkin

Romans
C. E. B. Cranfield (2 vols.)
Douglas Moo
Thomas Schreiner
John Stott

1 Corinthians
Anthony Thiselton
Gordon Fee
Richard Hays

2 Corinthians
Margaret Thrall
David Garland
Scott Hafemann

Galatians
Richard Longenecker
F. F. Bruce
Walter Hansen

Ephesians
Ernest Best
Harold Hoehner
Peter O'Brien

Klyne Snodgrass

Philippians

Peter O'Brien
Gordon Fee
Markus Bockmuehl
Frank Thielman

Colossians & Philemon

Peter O'Brien
James Dunn
David Garland

1–2 Thessalonians

F. F. Bruce
Gene Green
Michael Holmes

1–2 Timothy–Titus

I. Howard Marshall
William Mounce
Luke Johnson

Hebrews

William Lane (2 vols.)
David deSilva
George Guthrie

James

Luke Johnson
Peter Davids
Douglas Moo

1 Peter

Paul Achtemeier
Ramsey Michaels
I. Howard Marshall

2 Peter & Jude

Richard Bauckham
Douglas Moo
Dick Lucas and Christopher Green

1–3 John

Stephen Smalley
I. Howard Marshall
Colin Kruse
John Stott

Revelation

Grant Osborne
Gregory Beale
Dennis Johnson

BIBLIOGRAPHY

Barber, Cyril, and Robert Krauss. *An Introduction to Theological Research: A Guide for College and Seminary Students.* University Press of America, 2000.

Barton, John, and John Muddiman, eds. *Oxford Bible Commentary* (Oxford University Press, 2001). Bibliographical guide and extensive individual bibliographies.

Bauer, David. *Biblical Resources for Ministry.* Rev. ed. Evangel, 1995.

Birch, Bruce, et al. *A Theological Introduction to the Old Testament.* Abingdon, 1999.

Bock, Darrell. *Studying the Historical Jesus.* Baker, 2002.

Brown, Raymond E. *An Introduction to the New Testament.* Doubleday, 1997.

Carroll R., M. Daniel. *Writing on Amos.* Westminster John Knox, 2002. Annotated bibliography.

Carson, D. A. *New Testament Commentary Survey.* 5th ed. Baker, 2001.

Childs, Brevard. *The New Testament as Canon.* Trinity Press International, 1994.

Corley, Bruce, Steve Lemke, and Grant Lovejoy. *Biblical Hermeneutics.* 2d ed. Broadman & Holman, 2002.

Danker, Frederick. *Multipurpose Tools for Bible Study.* Rev. ed. Fortress, 1993.

Douglas, Stacey, ed. *An Annotated Bibliography for the Bible and the Church.* 3d ed. Alumni Publications, 2002. Trinity Evangelical Divinity School.

Ehrman, Bart. *The New Testament.* Oxford University Press, 1997. Annotated bibliographies.

Enns, Peter. *Poetry and Wisdom.* IBR. Baker, 1998.

Evans, Craig. *Life of Jesus Research: An Annotated Bibliography.* Rev. ed. Brill, 1996.

Fee, Gordon. *New Testament Exegesis.* 3d ed. Westminster John Knox, 2002.

Fitzmyer, Joseph. *An Introductory Bibliography for the Study of Scripture.* 3d ed. Pontifical Biblical Institute, 1990.

Goldingay, John. *OT Commentary Survey.* Rev. ed. Religious and Theological Studies Fellowship, 1994.

Green, Joel, and Michael McKeever. *Luke–Acts and New Testament Historiography.* IBR. Baker, 1994.

Grudem, Wayne. *Bible Doctrine.* Zondervan, 1999. "Annotated Bibliography of Theologies."

Gundry, Robert. *A Survey of the New Testament.* 3d ed. Zondervan, 1994.

Guthrie, George, and Scott Duvall. *Biblical Greek Exegesis.* Zondervan, 1998. Extensive bibliographical suggestions.

Hagner, Donald. *New Testament Exegesis and Research.* 4th ed. Fuller Seminary, 1999.

Harrington, Daniel. *The New Testament.* Michael Glazier, 1985.

Hill, Andrew, and John Walton. *A Survey to the Old Testament.* 2d ed. Zondervan, 2000. Annotated bibliographies.

Hostetter, Edwin. *Old Testament Introduction.* IBR. Baker, 1995.

Johnston, William. *Recent Reference Books in Religion.* IVP, 1996.

Keener, Craig. *The IVP Bible Background Commentary: New Testament.* IVP, 1993.

Klein, William, Craig Blomberg, and Robert Hubbard. *Introduction to Biblical Interpretation.* Word, 1993. Annotated bibliography.

Longman, Tremper. *Old Testament Commentary Survey.* 2d ed. Baker, 1994.

Martens, Elmer. *Old Testament Theology.* IBR. Baker, 1997.

McDonald, Lee, and Stanley Porter. *Early Christianity and Its Sacred Literature.* Hendrickson, 2000.

McKnight, Scot, and Matthew Williams. *The Synoptic Gospels.* IBR. Baker, 2000.

Mills, Watson, ed. *Bibliographies for Biblical Research: The New Testament in 21 Volumes.* Mellen, 1997–.

Moo, Douglas, ed. *An Annotated Bibliography on the Bible and the Church.* 2d ed. Alumni Publications, 1987. Trinity Evangelical Divinity School.

Porter, Stanley, and Lee McDonald. *New Testament Introduction.* IBR. Baker, 1995.

Rosscup, James. *Commentaries for Biblical Expositors.* Grace Book Shack, 1993.

Seifrid, Mark, and Randall Tan. *The Pauline Writings.* IBR. Baker, 2002.

Sparks, Kenton. *The Pentateuch.* IBR. Baker, 2002.

Stuart, Douglas. *A Guide to Selecting and Using Bible Commentaries.* Word, 1990.

———. *Old Testament Exegesis.* 3d ed. Westminster John Knox, 2001. Excellent suggestions.

Vos, Howard. *Nelson's New Illustrated Bible Manners and Customs.* Thomas Nelson, 1999. Excellent bibliography.

Walton, John, Victor Matthews, and Mark Chavalas. *The IVP Bible Background Commentary: Old Testament.* IVP, 2000.

Wenham, Gordon, et al., eds. *New Bible Commentary: 21st Century Edition.* IVP, 1994.

Zannoni, Arthur. *The Old Testament: A Bibliography.* Liturgical, 1992.

Annotated Commentary Series

Furnish, Victor, gen. ed. Abingdon New Testament Commentaries (Abingdon).

Keck, Leander, et al., eds. *The New Interpreter's Bible: A Commentary in 12 Volumes* (Abingdon).

Muck, Terry, gen. ed. The NIV Application Commentary Series (Zondervan).

Unpublished, Self-Published, Journal, and Internet Sources

Annotated Bibliographies (various departments) in the *Ashland Theological Journal.* Ashland Theological Seminary, 1996–2001.

Association of Theological Booksellers. *Theological Best Books.* Consortium catalog, 2002.

Blomberg, Craig, and William Klein. "New Testament Exegesis Bibliography." *Denver Journal* 5, no. 20 (2002). Denver Seminary (denverseminary.edu/dj).

Building a Basic Ministerial Library. Reformed Theological Seminary, 1993.

Carroll R, M. Daniel, and Richard Hess. "Old Testament Annotated Bibliography." *Denver Journal* 5, no. 20 (2002).

Christian, Mark. *Hebrew Bible Bibliography.* Vanderbilt Divinity School Library, 2001 (divinity.lib.vanderbilt.edu).

The Division of Biblical Studies, *Biblical Resources for Ministry.* Asbury Theological Seminary, 1990.

Evans, John. *A Guide to Biblical Commentaries and Reference Works.* Rev. ed. Covenant Theological Seminary, 1993.

Knight, George W. *New Testament Commentaries for a Minister's Library.* Dallas Theological Seminary, 1995. OT, NT Faculty Annotated Bibliographies, 1985–1986.

Pope, Anthony, and Vernon Ritter. *A Directory of Exegetical Aids for Bible Translators.* 2d ed. (SIL, 1989/1993 supp.). Summer Institute of Linguistics.

Silva, Moisés. *Commentaries on the Greek New Testament.* Rev. ed. 1993.

Stitzinger, James. *Books for Biblical Expositors.* The Master's Seminary (tms.edu/750books.asp).

Suggs, Martha, and John Trotti. *Building a Pastor's Library.* Union Theological Seminary, Va., 1991.

Swanson, Dennis. *How to Do Library Research.* The Master's Seminary (tms.edu/research.asp).

VanderHill, Steve. *Top Picks from the Westminster Campus Bookstore,* 1994, 1996.

Weatherly, Jon. *An Annotated Bibliography of Commentaries and Reference Works on the Greek New Testament.* Cincinnati Bible College and Seminary, 2000 (cincybible.edu).

LATE ADDITIONS*

Old Testament Commentaries

Technical, Semitechnical

E	**1.**	**Finley, Thomas J. *Joel, Amos, Obadiah* (Biblical Studies Press, 2003).**[1]
L/Cr	2.	Fritz, Volkmar. *1 and 2 Kings*. Continental (Fortress, 2003).
E	3.	Merrill, Eugene H. *Haggai, Zechariah, Malachi* (Biblical Studies Press, 2003).
L/Cr	4.	Nelson, Richard. *Deuteronomy*. OTL (Westminster John Knox, 2002).
E	5.	Patterson, Richard D. *Nahum, Habakkuk, Zephaniah* (Biblical Studies Press, 2000).
L/Cr	**6.**	**Terrien, Samuel. *The Psalms: Strophic Structure and Theological Commentary*. ECC (Eerdmans, 2003).** Majors on theology, minors on strophic structure.[2]

---

* These commentaries appeared too late to be included in the body of the text. Because of this, I've emended my specific recommendations for certain books in the footnotes below.

1. Thankfully, Biblical Studies Press has resurrected volumes by Finley, Patterson, and Merrill from the shortlived Wycliffe Exegetical Commentary series (Moody). Available in either paperback or as a *Logos/Libronix* download, they can be obtained on-line at galaxie.com/store. Until now, these commentaries were virtually impossible to find; fortunately, I had obtained them before they went out of print.

2. With the choice of the evangelical, three-volume commentary on Psalms in the WBC series or the two-volume offering in the NIVAC series, one could afford the luxury (if, indeed, one could afford $95.00) of the recently-deceased, Union Theological Seminary professor Terrien's take on the psalter. However, a less expensive option might be Richard Clifford's forthcoming, two-volume exposition in the AOTC series (Abingdon).

Expositional

E 1. Arnold, Bill T. *1 & 2 Samuel*. NIVAC (Zondervan, 2003).[3]

C/M 2. Balentine, Samuel E. *Leviticus*. IBC (Westminster John Knox, 2003).[4]

E 3. Hawk, Daniel. *Joshua*. NIVAC (Zondervan, forthcoming). Reassigned from Robert Hubbard to Ashland Theological Seminary professor Hawk.

E 4. Hill, Andrew. *1 & 2 Chronicles*. NIVAC (Zondervan, 2003).[5]

E 5. Nixon, Rosemary. *The Message of Jonah*. BST (IVP, 2003).

E 6. Oswalt, John N. *Isaiah*. NIVAC (Zondervan, 2003).

E 7. Roop, Eugene F. *Ruth, Jonah, Esther*. BCBC (Herald, 2002).

L/Cr 8. Seow, Choon-Leong. *Daniel*. WBComp (Westminster John Knox, 2003).

Old Testament Introduction

E 1. Kitchen, Kenneth A. *On the Reliability of the Old Testament* (Eerdmans, 2003). Vigorous defense of OT historicity.

E/Cr 2. Wenham, Gordon. *Exploring the Old Testament: A Guide to the Pentateuch* (IVP, 2003).

Old Testament Theology

E 1. Cowles, C. S., Eugene Merrill, Daniel Gard, and Tremper Longman. *Show Them No Mercy: 4 Views on God and Canaanite Genocide* (Zondervan, 2003).

---

3. Substitute Arnold for Klein and Anderson (a savings of $50.00 for the same number of pages). Keep Bergen and look forward to Tsumura. Scholars may wish to retain Klein and Anderson and should consider Jesuit Antony Campbell's *1 Samuel*. FOTL (Eerdmans, 2003).
4. Forthcoming: Roy Ganes, *Leviticus, Numbers*. NIVAC (Zondervan).
5. To supplement Knoppers and Japhet, choose Martin Selman's *2 Chronicles* (IVP, 1994)—a great value at $14.00 for 550 pp.—and Andrew Hill in the NIVAC (Zondervan, 2003).

E/Cr 2. Goldingay, John. *Old Testament Theology, Vol. 1: Israel's Gospel.* (IVP, 2003).

E 3. Pate, C. Marvin, ed. *The Story of Israel: A Biblical Theology* (IVP, forthcoming).

New Testament Commentaries

Technical, Semitechnical

L/Cr 1. Collins, Raymond F. *I and II Timothy and Titus*. NTL (Westminster John Knox, 2002).

E/Cr 2. Green, Joel. *James*. NTL (Westminster John Knox, forthcoming).

C/M 3. Johnson, Luke. *Hebrews*. NTL (Westminster John Knox, forthcoming).

E/Cr 4. Meye Thompson, Marianne. *John*. NTL (Westminster John Knox, forthcoming).

E 5. Schreiner, Thomas P. *1, 2 Peter, Jude*. NAC (Broadman, 2003).[6]

Expositional

E 1. Geddert, Timothy J. *Mark*. BCBC (Herald, 2002).

L/Cr 2. Moloney, Francis J. *The Gospel of Mark* (Hendrickson, 2002). Good on narrative analysis.

E 3. Thomas, John C. *1 John, 2 John, 3 John*. Pentecostal (Continuum, 2003). An emerging series, 312 pp.[7]

---

6. The beauty of Schreiner's ambidextrous commentary on 1–2 Peter/Jude (much like his commentary on Romans in the BECNT series) is that it could equally function as an expositional as well as a semi-technical choice. For 1 Peter, I would wait for Martin and Jobes with Schreiner and Hafemann as expositional choices. For 2 Peter/Jude, Schreiner would fill a much-needed, evangelical, semi-technical gap until Gene Green's BECNT entry appears. Together with Douglas Moo (NIVAC), these three would provide formidable coverage, even though Bauckham is hard to beat as a conservative/moderate choice.

7. In 1–3 John I would now recommend the commentaries of Daniel Akin, Colin Kruse, and W. Hall Harris III. Harris' commentary, *1, 2, 3 John: Comfort and Counsel for a Church in Crisis* (Biblical Studies, 2003) is an exegetical gem and is available from the Biblical Studies Foundation (bible.org) as a paperback or *Logos/Libronix* download. Harris is also known for his well-regarded monograph on Eph. 4:7–11, *The Descent of Christ* (Baker, 1998).